THE
BOLIVIA HILL
FOUNDLING

PIET VALLEI

Ordering Information:

Prime Seven Media
518 Landmann St.
Tomah City, WI 54660

Printed in the United States of America

Table of Contents

Some Notes

Note 1: Inspired by George Eliot's 1861 novel *Silas Marner*,[1] this story is about a lonely twenty-first century man in his seventies who takes on parenting and protection of an abandoned newborn baby. Partly through his influence as a retired teacher, this baby turns out to be intelligent, switched on, and articulate. However, her early childhood is sometimes a rocky road for both of them.

While this story is fiction, much of it is based on real events. As Alan Paton said of his seminal novel about South Africa, it is a 'compound of truth an fiction … but considered as a social record it is the plain and simple truth'.[2]

Note 2: The main characters are fictitious as are locations and towns central to this story.

Note 3: Internet references cited were functional at date of writing, although some have a 'paywall' and require a subscription or free membership for access.

Note 4: Photographs without acknowledgement were taken by the author. The main front cover photo is by the author. The inset photo on the front cover is by *iStockphoto* and posed by a model seen many times in photos throughout the book.

Note 5: At times, it may seem that the heroine, Eppie, is portrayed as too advanced for her age. Actually, she is not so unusual. For example, a five-year-old British girl, Brooke Blair, has a strong opinion about then British Prime Minister Theresa May: 'Five-year-old gives Theresa May a telling-off about the homeless'. *ITV News*, London, 05 October 2016. https://www.youtube.com/watch?v=xncfOR1X9n4 Later, her mother explains that the girl was not coached or indoctrinated, has a social conscience, and has always been interested in current affairs: https://www.youtube.com/watch?v=IyX9MWF3Bd0 The way five-year-old Brooke has become interested in current affairs and social issues is similar to how Eppie has been growing in her life with the old man. (From the age of six, the author used to regularly listen to BBC World Service news on shortwave radio.)

Note 6: Court proceedings in the telling of this story have been simplified.

Note 7: There has been a plethora of commissions of inquiry, reviews, and investigations into child welfare in Australia. Often, these have been stimulated by deaths of children "in care" and the resulting public outcry. A wide range of people, institutions, stakeholders, and frontline staff are usually consulted but almost invariably the one most important stakeholder in a child's life is ignored: the parents or parent. (Perhaps, there was one review in Queensland which did consult parents: the 2013 Carmody *Child Protection Commission Inquiry*. However, when some were able to air grievances, nothing came of parents' input. The chairman dutifully nodded his head and that

---

[1] George Eliot (1861), *Silas Marner: The Weaver of Raveloe*, William Blackwood: London. George Eliot is the pseudonym or pen name for Mary Ann Evans. Her novel is set in early nineteenth century England.
[2] Alan Paton (1948), *Cry the Beloved Country*, Johnathan Cape, London. Page 5.

was it for a very token consultation.) A typical disregard for the child's most significant stakeholder can be seen in the 2017 Queensland Family & Child Commission's *Keeping Queensland's children more than safe: Review of the foster care system,* a review brought about by the murder of foster child Tiahleigh Palmer. Her parent is not even mentioned in the review. Not one of the Review's 42 recommendations involves parents of children in foster care. Therefore, this novel makes no apology for highlighting failures in an entrenched fundamentally flawed system.

Note 8: Footnotes are an integral part of this story.

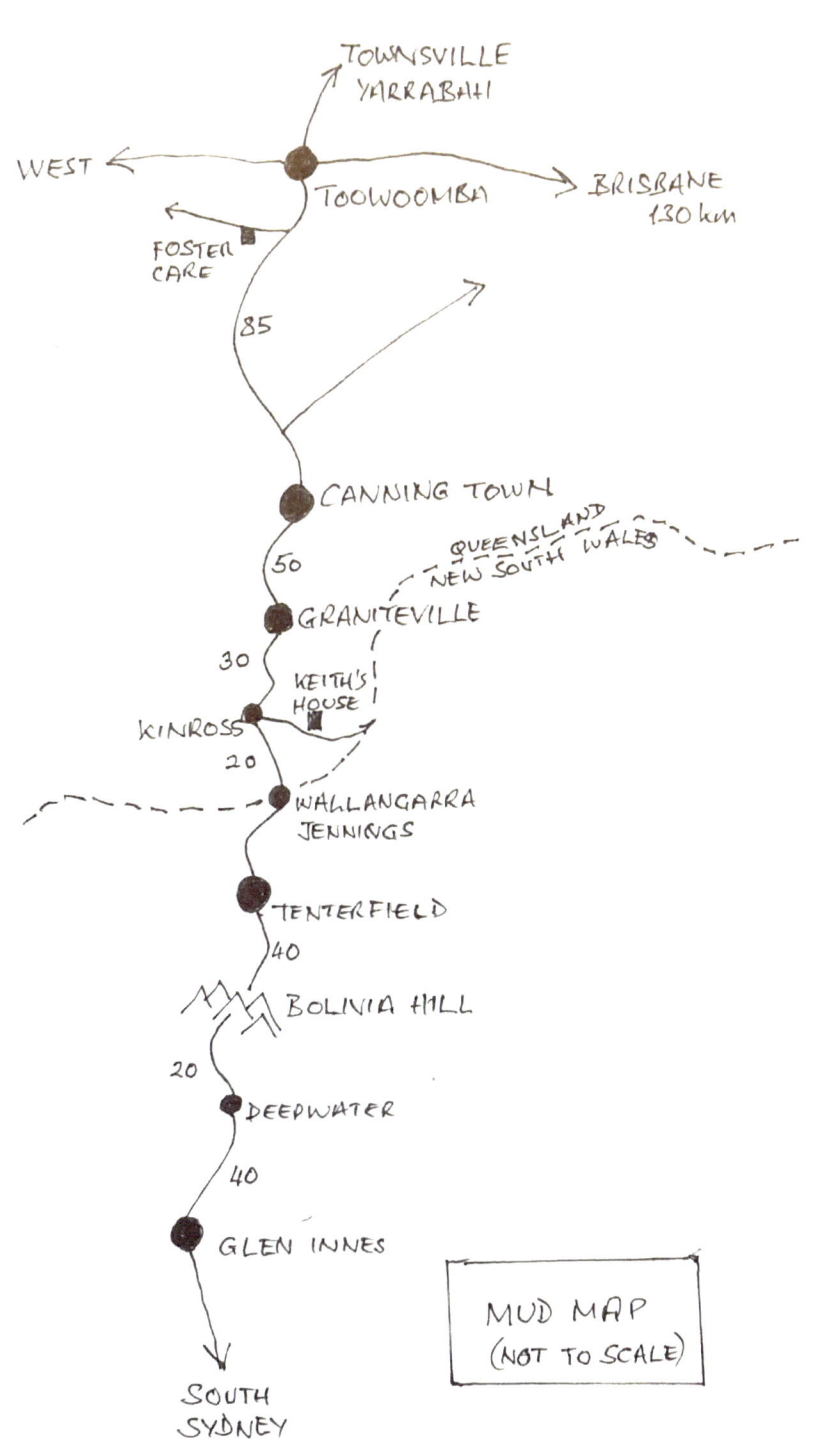

TOWNSVILLE
YARRABAH

WEST ←

→ BRISBANE
130 km

TOOWOOMBA

FOSTER
CARE

85

CANNING TOWN

QUEENSLAND
NEW SOUTH WALES

50

GRANITEVILLE

30

KEITH'S
HOUSE

KINROSS

20

WALLANGARRA
JENNINGS

TENTERFIELD

40

BOLIVIA HILL

20

DEEPWATER

40

GLEN INNES

MUD MAP
(NOT TO SCALE)

SOUTH
SYDNEY

CHAPTER 1

Keith's Origin

In 1960 Keith emigrated to Australia from Northern Rhodesia (now Zambia) as a sixteen-year-old and lived in Sydney with his parents and two older sisters.

He ended up going to the University of Armidale in northern New South Wales where he majored in Geography. He then completed a Graduate Diploma of Teaching. Nevertheless, he still has feelings for the land of his birth, Northern Rhodesia. Born in Lusaka, his first few years of school were at the Lusaka Boys School where life was rough. There were never any teachers on playground duty during the two breaks. The result was a continual gang war by the Afrikaans boys (the '*boeties*') against the English speaking boys (the '*soeties*') who they regarded as soft weaklings. Afrikaans boys would grab one of the 'Engels', put him up on the raised playground boxing ring, and get a bigger '*boetie*' to taunt and bash him. Thus, most '*soeties*' would try to hide during lunch break.

For two years, his best friend was George, a Chewa. Both boys used to spend hours playing together with their Dinky toy cars in the sand. One day, Keith's mother paid for the two boys to go to the circus. But, seating was segregated. She made a fuss. A compromise was reached. The two boys could sit next to each other but separated only by a single token length of rope between them.

At nine-years-old his parents sent him to a boarding school in Natal in South Africa. It was austere. The headmaster was an ex-army colonel. Cold showers were the *de rigueur* early morning ritual even in freezing conditions. It snows regularly in July. In his first year, he was anally raped by the boarding master. Other boys suffered the same fate. In those days you didn't complain. You would be caned for telling lies and having a dirty mind. You might also be branded a 'homo', something totally abhorrent in the homophobic 1950s. Like the other boys, you just got on with life. There was no alternative.[3]

While at school in Australia, he was picked on for his accent. Because of his African origin, some kids accused him of keeping slaves in Africa. And others, including teachers, assumed he was a racist supporter of *Apartheid*, something he was very upset about because he was a Quaker and he did not come form South Africa but Northern Rhodesia.[4]

He met and married his wife while they studied at University. They both completed BA degrees and postgraduate teaching diplomas. They had two daughters but got divorced years ago.

Keith was a very involved father and loved parenting. He spent a lot of time with his girls. He was a little unusual in those days for not mixing with blokes at pubs, football matches, and barbecues. If baby needed a nappy change he would do it while other men would tend to pass baby to Mum because that was mother's work.

Their second daughter arrived when the first was two.

By the time they divorced, the youngest was seven. Probably because Keith had been a close involved father with the girls, it was a bitter divorce, and Gwen must have felt threatened. In those days the Family Court rarely made shared parenting decisions. Instead, the Court would decide in favour of one parent, usually the mother because mothers were

_____

[3] Sexual assault of the author is described in "The dorm master and his pets". *Survivor Voices*. http://survivorvoices.co.za/the-dorm-master-and-his-pets/. That was seventy years ago. Times were different then. Typically, in stiff upper lip style, you would move on and get on with life. There was no alternative. The author never told his parents. Most boys didn't. (In that description, the photo mentioned of the author as a little boy on his way to boarding school was deleted.)

 See also a typical example: Corner, N., "Shocking scale of sexual abuse at UK boarding schools revealed by ITV documentary". *Daily Mail*, London, 20 February 2018. http://www.dailymail.co.uk/femail/article-5408899/ITV-Exposure-programme-investigates-boarding-school-abuse.html#ixzz57cFhUaW0

 Williams, G. (2004), *Nightmare at Neerkol*, Toowoomba: Cranbrook Press. As a little boy raped by a priest many times at the Sisters of Mercy orphanage at Neerkol at Rockhampton in Queensland, Gary was injured internally and had to have an operation years later to cure the anal incontinence. Whether the priest used Vaseline or not, it is likely that Gary would still have been injured. And, after being raped by a priest, some boys in the Neerkol orphanage were also molested by Sisters of Mercy nuns: "At the time, Dan didn't know men and women were different - until the day he was taken to bed by a nun. She wanted a completely different set of things to be done to her." (pages 48-49) [Quoted with permission of the late Gary Williams].

[4] This is something the author experienced.

regarded as the 'primary carer'. Granting custody to the father was rare. It also meant that men ended up as the vast majority of parents having to pay child support to the mother for many years. With most custody decisions in favour of the mother, the post-divorce bitterness was exacerbated. For some, it became a men's rights issue. In rare cases, the mother ended up bitter and having to pay. There has been a recent case where a mother was so bitter that one day she murdered her ex-husband very publicly in the street and in front of their ten-year-old son. She even told Police she resented having to pay child support to the father.[5]

In Keith's case his wife feared the Court's decision might go against her because of Keith's very close parenting of the girls. She feared losing her kids, especially because of what her female friends might think of her as a mother. She was prominent in the local Nursing Mothers Association. It would not look good for her if she lost. In those days, women's primary rôle in society was still seen by many as mothers. Involved fathers and single fathers were relatively rare.[6] Worried about the impending divorce, Gwen tended to bad mouth him in front of the girls.

Leading up to the divorce, they were having an argument. Gwen punched him in the face. As a pacifist Quaker, he did not respond in kind but retreated to the study and locked himself in. Eventually, things calmed down. In the Family Court she made an accusation

---

[5] A mother who the Family Court did NOT give child custody to, was extremely bitter and objected to having to pay child support to the father. She killed the father in the street in public by stabbing him many times in front of their 10-year-old son. Ross, J., "Woman charged with murder of estranged husband in Newmarket street", *ABC News*, Brisbane, 17 June 2021. abc.net.au/news/qld-murder-court-man-stabbed-newmarket/100223016

Ransley, E., "'I heard the screaming': Brisbane woman charged with murder", *NCA News Wire*, Brisbane, 17 June 2021. https://www.news.com.au/national/queensland/crime/brisbane-woman-charged-with-murder-after-allegedly-stabbing-man-to-death/news-story/e0086944df6717d3debd4ea25a17ba73 "Ms Coue told Police she had killed her ex-husband because she no longer wished to pay child support." There are many other reports of this killing.

[6] It was not until 1978 that the "supporting mother's benefit" or pension became available for men and it became known as the "single parent's pension" or 'SPP'. In 1979 only 2.07% of SPP recipients were male and male SPP recipients with a child under 4 amounted to less than 0.1 per 1000. (Source: "Sole Parent Pensions 1979-1989", Statistical Services Section, *Department of Social Security*, Canberra, December 1989.) Women were still seen as the carers and nurturers and men the workers and providers. Even as single parents, men were reluctant to take up the newly available benefit and relied on grandparents or other relatives to care for their children. They felt they needed to be employed in the workforce or be branded socially as a 'bludger'.

of domestic violence. When asked to elaborate by Keith's lawyer, she said: "I feared the violence in his voice." Later, while in the witness box, Keith's lawyer asked him to tell the Court his own experience of domestic violence but he wouldn't because he believed "men aren't domestic violence victims". Yet, at the behest of his lawyer, he had previously written an affidavit describing what had happened.

When his first daughter, Sarah, was nearly two, the three of them went on a camping trip to the Gibraltar Range National Park in northern NSW. Gwen was eight months pregnant with their second child, Denise. While he was cooking breakfast on a portable kerosene stove, toddler Sarah needed a nappy change. Gwen verbally abused her, picked up a knife, and went for the toddler. Keith grabbed little Sarah in the nick of time. He tried to reason with Gwen, but she went for him. She slashed at him causing a small cut on his arm. Carrying Sarah, he fled into the forest with her. Gwen had the knife and the car keys. He had to wash Sarah's bum in a cold stream in the bush. They weren't able to emerge from the forest until the afternoon when Gwen seemed to have calmed down. Sarah would not go near her mother until the next day.[7]

After the divorce proceedings, Keith's lawyer asked why he didn't tell the Court about this domestic violence when asked. He had actually mentioned it in his affidavit. He told his lawyer he believed Gwen's behaviour in threatening him and toddler Sarah was hormonal because of the pregnancy (which was likely true) and stress. "Anyway, men aren't DV victims. If I had reported it to the Police, they would have just smirked. Our society sees men who are beaten by their wives as weak." His lawyer told him: "Domestic violence is domestic violence regardless of gender. There are no excuses. Hormones, alcohol, infidelity accusations, stress, and drugs, the consequences are the same. It must not happen. You just blew it! That was your chance to retain custody."

That was typical of Keith as a Quaker, making excuses for others' failings and being 'decent'. That decency allowed him to be walked over many times in his life. Added to this, he was also very much a loner. He didn't like socialising, sport, and parties. That was one

---

[7]   This happened to the author while camping in Fiordland in New Zealand.

of the problems in the marriage. Gwen was a 'party girl'. While she liked social gatherings, he preferred camping and going for bush walks with the girls.

In the end, the Judge gave Gwen custody basically because even though she was also teaching, she was a woman and the children were girls. In his summing up, he said: "Both parents love their children and are equally able to care for them on their own." But, he gave custody to Gwen and condescendingly told Keith: "A father has a rôle in our society which values men pursuing careers in support of the family. The mother is prepared to parent the children full-time." Yet, Keith had said in his affidavit that he was prepared to leave his job to parent the girls. This seems to have been ignored by the Judge. Since then, Keith has felt the Judge's decision was classic unconscious bias or 'implicit stereotyping'.[8] His difference from usual fathers was ignored.

His daughters are now grown-up, married, and live in Victoria. After the Court decision, his ex-wife made it her business to continually denigrate him in front of the children.[9] Yet, he had been a loving, caring, and involved father changing nappies, cuddling the kids to bed every night with a story he made up. The children loved his stories and loved their time with him. The divorce came at a time when the mother, because of her gender, was almost invariably seen by Family Court judges as the 'primary carer'.[10] This was despite the 1979 High Court ruling that fathers were just as capable of parenting.[11] His grown-up children have not overcome the badmouthing of Keith. These days, he has only sporadic, detached, and aloof contact with them. The divorce was not particularly traumatic for him. The marriage had been on the rocks. However, the loss of his children affected him deeply.

---

[8] "Implicit stereotype", *Wikipedia*, https://en.wikipedia.org/wiki/Implicit_stereotype.

[9] This happens a lot in divorce cases where custody of children is contested. Subconsciously, the parent who gains custody frequently tends to see the children as the spoils of war. This is not good for the children and it adversely affects their relationship with the losing parent well into the children's adulthood. These days, the Family Court tries to set up a shared parenting arrangement but often this still doesn't work.

[10] The assumption was and so often still is that a mother is the more appropriate carer of the children. It is ingrained in our society's psyche.

[11] See: *Gronow v Gronow* (1980 27 FLR 427). http://en.wikipedia.org/wiki/Gronow_v_Gronow This landmark High Court appeal case confirmed that the 'preferred role of the mother' is not a principle, a presumption, a preference, or even a norm. It is a factor to be taken into consideration only where relevant. (These days, the Family Court emphasises shared parenting in its decision making and also factors in domestic violence.)

CHAPTER 2

Keith the Teacher

Keith has been teaching for twelve years at Fulham State High School in Townsville, a city of some 230,000 people in northern Queensland. It is an important port from where agricultural, pastoral and mining products are exported. Its climate is distinctly tropical but the headland to the south-east at Cape Cleveland tends to reduce the amount of rainfall it receives from the South East trade winds. Inland to the north-west the rainfall is higher in rainforest around the Paluma Ranges. As a Geography teacher at Fulham High, Keith sees this as important. He is a diligent, committed teacher and his students appreciate him. However, things are soon to go terribly wrong for him.

He has had three limited relationships with women but nothing came of them. One woman had a daughter and they visited National Parks together twice at Paluma and Alligator Creek. He liked the little girl but he and her Mum had little in common. She was more interested in pubs and parties and tended to use Keith as a babysitter. He did not like her discipline of the little girl. She would smack her on her legs with a wooden spoon. When she didn't wipe her bum properly and this soiled her pants, she would berate her and rub the soiled part of the pants under the girl's nose.

The second woman was a divorcée who had her two little girls removed from her by the Child Safety Department. Her ex-husband was in prison serving a long sentence for an armed robbery. Her house was always a chaotic shambles and she frequently went out partying at night leaving the kids, 2 and 6, alone at home. On two occasions on Sunday mornings the older girl telephoned Keith to tell him that Mum had not come home. By 10:00 a.m. he would drive around to the house and take the two little girls in his car driving from place to place looking for Mum. Usually, she was found but would berate him for interfering. Eventually, while Keith was away on a school excursion, the Child Safety Department was involved and the girls were removed into foster care. Essentially, she was told by Child Safety Officers and the Court Magistrate to stop partying and get her act together. She was devastated and, with Keith's moral support, she battled unsuccessfully in the Children's Court to get the girls back. Typically, she could not obtain top legal support and was dependent on successive ineffectual Legal Aid solicitors. After just over two years since the children were taken 'into care', the Department argued that the girls needed 'permanency' in their lives and were now well-settled with a loving foster family. This won over the Court. Yet, the Department had done nothing to try and improve the woman's parenting. Sometimes, her previously arranged contact with her daughters was cancelled by the Department because the children had supposedly preferred to attend a function organised by the foster carer. It had been especially galling for the mother to hear during Court proceedings that the children now called the female foster carer "Mum". Then, to hear the Court's decision that their removal from her was permanent on long term foster care orders with her contact to be phased out was the last straw. Shortly after that, she took her car and a bottle of wine into the Mount Spec National Park north of Townsville. She parked in a secluded spot in the forest and committed suicide using a hose attached to her car's exhaust.[12] This tragedy had a profound effect on Keith. He had seen how the Department operated and seen the effect on the little girls as they were systematically and subtly estranged and alienated from their mother by the Department and its officers.

Keith becomes friends with another teacher at the school, Fiona. They are never 'an item' as such but they talk a lot in the staff lounge and even at his or her house sometimes. Although she is in her early forties, she had only recently started teaching when they met. She had just completed a Graduate Diploma in Education. Prior to that she was a social worker with the Department of Child Safety working as a Child Safety Officer or CSO. She left the Department in disgust. She had seen the stress and trauma caused to children when

---

[12]   The author had a daughter who took her own life in a similar way after one of her children was removed into foster care but the circumstances which prompted the removal were very different.

they are removed from their parents and families and was convinced that generally the short and long term effects of removal were bad for children. She reminded Keith about the large roadside billboard on the edge of the city which promoted foster care and sought to recruit

The billboard just out of town along the highway showing happy little vegemites in foster care.

foster carers. It showed sweet happy kids. "That imagery is totally false. Foster care is traumatic for so many kids. It's not sugary-sweet. To be truthful, they should show a billboard of sad, frightened kids desperately trying to cling to Mum or Dad as they are removed by officious women accompanied by Police officers."

Keith: "Do Police attend when a child is removed?"

Fiona: "Not always but frequently. It's very intimidating for children. And, also for parents who understandably regard it as child theft by the state. Sometimes parents resist and put up a physical fight. Basically, they are defending their children. It's instinctive. But, the Department and Police come down hard on parents when they resist either physically or in the Childrens Court. Sometimes the children resist physically, especially older children. It really worries me. There is a classic scene in the film version of Doris Garimara's novel *The Rabbit Proof Fence* as two little girls and their Mum desperately try to resist removal by the authorities. It was set in the 1930s and depicted part Aboriginal kids being removed from their mother merely because they had some 'white blood' in them. It was the racism of the day.[13] But, even now the same scenario of child uprooting is played out every day with children of all colours and origins being peremptorily removed to a so-called 'place of safety'."

---

[13] Pilkington Garimara, D. (1995), *Follow the Rabbit Proof Fence.* Brisbane: University of Queensland Press. Lovely but sad story. The traumatic and devastating removal of the three girls in the beginning still happens daily all over Australia today and to children of all colours and creeds. Made into a sensitive film released in 2002 by the Australian Film Commission. See: https://en.wikipedia.org/wiki/Rabbit-Proof_Fence

She explained: "It's a knee-jerk reaction to simply walk in and remove a child. Sometimes the harm to children in 'care' is worse than if they remained with their parent(s).[14] If they work with parents, not against them, the outcomes for children are usually far better. A bad parent is better than no parent - and parents are never perfect. A foster carer with several kids to look after all with different trauma histories is not a good recipe for a child's new life. These children are invariably traumatised either by what happened to them at home or by the very act of being forcibly removed from their parents or both scenarios. As such, they are vulnerable to further abuse and exploitation by the people who are supposedly charged with protecting them and providing a secure and safe environment."[15, 16]

Fiona: "Sometimes, the Department deliberately frustrates moves towards re-unification. They try to alienate the kid from her or his parents by showering the kid with presents which some parents can't afford or taking the kid to theme parks on the Gold Coast like 'Dream World' or 'Movie World', very expensive places. They will often do that when a contact day with the parents is scheduled. The kid is faced with a choice of a one hour contact time with parents in an artificial supervised contact venue or a trip to the Gold

---

[14]   This is the argument of Prof. Ros Thorpe: "The system could do better in promoting children's interests in supporting their own family." Galloway, A., "Kids at risk of abuse in care." *Townsville Bulletin*, 12 November 2012.

[15]   A recent excellent critique: Newcombe, M., "Our child protection system is clearly broken. Is it time to abolish it for a better model?" *The Conversation*, Sydney, 23 March 2023. She concludes: "Isn't it time we ditch an ineffective child protection system and instead invest in keeping children with their families and communities?" https://theconversation.com/our-child-protection-system-is-clearly-broken-is-it-time-to-abolish-it-for-a-better-model-200716?

[16]   In an *ABC News* article on the 2014 *Children's Rights Report* the Australian National Children's Commissioner Megan Mitchell says: "several hundred children in foster care were abused in the last year. … The 41,000 Australian children in care have suffered enough. … The number needed to be brought down." *ABC News*, Sydney, 28 January 2015. http://www.abc.net.au/news/2015-01-28/hundreds-of-children-in-foster-care-abused-last-year-report-find/6052006

   As of 30 June 2022, 45,400 children in Australia were in 'out of home care'. *Child Protection Australia*, Australian Institute of Health and Welfare, Canberra, 07 May 2024. https://www.aihw.gov.au/reports/child-protection/child-protection-australia-2021-22/contents/insights/supporting-children

   Although it is now dated but still relevant, the 2003 Gwenn Murray *Audit Report on Foster Carers in Queensland* said: "Despite an underlying expectation that once children and young people are removed from their parents they are safe from further harm or risk of harm, children and young people entering the alternative care system are vulnerable to a number of risks. One of these risks relates to the risk of further harm to them by the people entrusted to care for them." (page 18).

Coast theme parks with the foster carer and other foster care kids. So, contact is put off for another fortnight. They do things like that saying the welfare of the child is their paramount duty. In other words, a trip to 'Dream World' is more important than time with parents. They will even tell the parents that their kid preferred a Gold Coast trip to contact time. Their values are skewed towards removing kids from their families, keeping them in foster care, and parental alienation. They won't listen to any argument that kids need parents and that having a parent is in the best interests of the child. It's too hard for them to work with troubled parents."

Keith is quite shocked.

Fiona: "It's true. They set up delaying tactics and excuses in order to reduce contact. That's par for the course. I've seen it too often and I've been compelled to work within that system. Of course, there are some parents who are no good for their children but not the 72,300 that are in out of home care across Australia.[17] You can't tell me that seventy-two thousand parents in this country are beyond redemption. That number is a disgrace and a shame on our society for allowing so many to be removed into what they call 'out of home care'. It's really quite Orwellian."

Keith: "Yes."

Fiona: "Sometimes, there isn't a problem with the family and the kids. That's a 'false positive' when the child is taken. You see, the Department is risk averse. There could be a notification from the public because of suspicion or even vindictiveness. Without proper investigation or talking to parents, officers just move in and take a child. The hapless parents have to go through the awful and expensive process of court procedures to get the kid back. And, if the case proved to be a 'false positive' it can take at least 28 days. And, magistrates usually tend to accept the word of child safety officers because they are supposed to have the expertise. That is, unless the parents have been able to engage a good and usually expensive lawyer who can effectively contest the Department's case. And, there is no recompense to the parents if they win."

---

[17] "Out-of-Home Care", *Child Protection*. Australian Institute of Health and Welfare, Canberra, 15 June 2022. https://www.aihw.gov.au/reports/australias-welfare/child-protection

Keith: "That must be terrible to have your child wrongly removed and have to go to Court and deal with lawyers and so on."

Fiona: "Yes, it is. I saw a case, not mine, where a mother went to a service station to put petrol in her car. Sensibly, when she went to the console to pay she took her three-month-old baby out of the car and with her. On returning to the car and struggling to unlock the door, she accidentally dropped the baby. Later in the afternoon, she was worried about her baby's bruise on the head. So, she took her to the doctor who said she was okay. But, the next morning, Child Safety Officers appeared at the front door and took the baby into foster care. With mandated reporting rules, the doctor had to report even the slightest suspicion of abuse. The parents were absolutely distraught. Fortunately, they were well-off and went to a top lawyer. He went to the petrol station and got a copy of the closed circuit television (CCTV) footage which showed clearly that the baby had been accidentally dropped. The parents still had to wait the prescribed 28 days of Childrens Court proceedings to get their baby back. And, the baby had been breastfed."[18]

Keith: "That's rotten!"

Fiona: "Of course, but the Department likes to remove children. It's their business. And, believe me, they are experts. Look, I'm not just being cynical. Now, in New South Wales, they have implemented a policy where if a kid is in foster care for two years, he or she may be adopted out permanently. And, the kid will be given a new birth certificate with the adopted family's name on it. And, what's worse, the child's links to its biological family are erased.[19] This is a new 'Stolen Generations' all over again.[20] Only, it isn't only indigenous kids."

Keith is shocked.

---

[18] A case related in confidence to the author by a respected solicitor during 2005.

[19] Allam, L., "Fears of another stolen generation after New South Wales move on foster care". *The Guardian*, Sydney. 26 October 2018. https://www.theguardian.com/australia-news/2018/oct/27/fears-of-another-stolen-generation-after-new-south-wales-move-on-foster-care?

[20] The "Stolen Generations", *Wikipedia*, https://en.wikipedia.org/wiki/Stolen_Generations#Northern_Territory Indigenous children, especially those perceived as 'half-caste' were forcibly removed from their biological families and placed with 'white' families. Many were physically and sexually abused.

The same loss of family and heritage as well as abuse occurred with the 'Oranges and Sunshine' children removed from their families in Britain at the end of World War II and sent to Australia, Canada and Southern Rhodesia. See: *Wikipedia* at https://en.wikipedia.org/wiki/Oranges_and_Sunshine.

Fiona told him: "There is a culture promoted by state governments which sees foster carers as long suffering devoted angels. This is reflected in press releases and in the way foster carers's misdemeanours are usually ignored, covered up, or even defended by the Department.[21] Moreover, the secrecy provisions of the child protection legislation in each state allow these crimes not to get publicity. The public is only aware of rather bland annual statistics."

Continuing: "Occasionally, some details come out and the public is outraged. There was the scandalous case of the murder of a 12-year-old girl by one of her foster carers. The foster carers' 19-year-old son was also convicted for having had sex with her and she was alleged to be pregnant to him at the time of her death.[22] Of course, you know about Tiahleigh Palmer. But, nobody focuses on foster care as the fatal flaw in that girl's life. And, nobody asks why she could not have been left with her mother but with pro-active Departmental support. They actually encouraged her to prefer to spend time with the foster care family instead of with her mother. She had a crush on one of the foster carer's sons (who raped her) and she liked the horses on their property. I believe this sort of double standard is a major factor causing stresses for Departmental staff and why so many do not stay with the Department. The staff retention rate is low especially in rural areas."[23]

---

21 Godde, C., "Over a thousand Aussie kids abused in care." *The West Australian*, Perth, 09 December 2021. https://thewest.com.au/lifestyle/parenting/over-a-thousand-aussie-kids-abused-in-care-c-4887709 20% of abuse was sexual.

22 See: "Murder of Tiahleigh Palmer" in *Wikipedia* at https://en.wikipedia.org/wiki/Murder_of_Tiahleigh_Palmer
    Was Tiahleigh Palmer pregnant when she died?" *News.com.au* 21 September 2016, https://www.news.com.au/national/queensland/crime/murdered-schoolgirl-tiahleigh-palmers-mother-says-car-seized-by-Police-belonged-to-foster-family/news-story/e9fb1d6b9a7cc316e23685294918b867
    See also: Wenham, M., "Foster care abuse victim gets taxpayer-funded settlement". *Courier Mail*, Brisbane, 16 June 2009. A woman who was savagely beaten and raped as a child while in state foster care is one of nine people in the past five years to have received secret taxpayer-funded settlements totalling nearly $1.2 million.
    Asher, N., "Melbourne woman placed in abusive foster home receives record $2.6m payout". *ABC News*, Melbourne, 05 April 2023. https://www.abc.net.au/news/2023-04-05/foster-care-abuse-survivor-receives-record-court-payout/102174764

23 McKay, J., "Child safety falls short." *Courier Mail*, Brisbane, 04 April 2022, page 7. In Far North Queensland the average tenure is only 3.1 years and in the South West it is 4.6 years and even in the South East it is only 5.1 years.

There was something else which had really disturbed Fiona about foster care. That was the drugging for children taken into foster care. One lunch hour in the staff room she told him about this and showed him some news reports on her computer. She said: "It is illegal to give psychotropic medication to control the behaviour of a child in out of home care, 'unless it is part of the child's approved behaviour management plan'. That last phrase is what allows them to do it. You see, if a child is upset about being taken and resists or becomes difficult for a foster carer to manage, then a doctor will prescribe medication to calm the child.[24] We in Australia have taken the lead from what happens in some American states like Texas where this is done almost routinely."[25]

Keith is shocked.

She added: "Sometimes foster carers sedate a difficult child in their own amateur way. You know, a foster carer dosed up a 22-month-old toddler on Valium[26] and other opiates. He became dopey, was not watched, fell into the family swimming pool, and died.[27] Then there was a case of a five-year-old boy who died from a drug overdose. Not only were traces of drugs found in his system, but there were marks on his arm where he was likely injected

[24] Branley, A. & Scott, S. "Seven-year-old boy prescribed anti-psychotic medication while in foster care, lost vibrancy". *ABC News*, Sydney, 16 November 2014. https://www.abc.net.au/news/2014-11-14/seven-year-old-boy-lost-vibrancy-while-on-anti-psychotics/5892612
  Also: Branley, A. & Scott, S. "Anti-psychotic medication overprescribed to Australian children, experts say." *ABC News*, Sydney, 16 November 2014. https://www.abc.net.au/news/2014-11-16/anti-psychotics-over-prescribed-australian-children-experts-say/5892822 Scroll down to where this article discusses "Chemical restraint in foster care" and "Children in foster care are being inappropriately overmedicated".
[25] "4-year-old Texas girl taken from parents and heavily drugged by Child Protective Services". *HomeUSA News*, 18 May 2012. https://psychrights.org/2012/120518Texas4yearoldDruggedByState.htm The Texas Child Protective Services Department routinely gets a doctor to prescribe psychotropic drugs to foster care children, even children not especially upset or difficult. In this case, the parents of a drugged child were able to make a big fuss. They eventually got their daughter returned to them. Other states in the USA do it, too. https://www.acf.hhs.gov/sites/default/files/documents/opre/psych_med.pdf
[26] Valium is also known as Diazepam. https://en.wikipedia.org/wiki/Diazepam A doctor's prescription isneeded.
[27] Chettle, N., "Toddler Braxton Slager's drowning death 'preventable accident', coroner finds." *ABC News*, Sydney, 27 March 2018. https://www.abc.net.au/news/2018-03-27/inquiry-into-braxton-slagers-death/9589326 The Coroner found he had been given Valium and other drugs; clearly illegal. They must have been trying to calm a distressed little 22-month-old toddler. Yet, they were not blamed. The Coroner even called for more support for foster carers. Nobody asked whether the parents could have been given more support before he was removed from them.

with heroin. Had they given these to him to calm him? His foster care was not managed by the NSW Family and Community Services Department but by a contractor, the Wesley Mission's Uniting Care. The same organisation had in their care a fourteen-year-old girl known as "Girl X". She was raped repeatedly while in their so-called 'care' and then died of a drug overdose." That little boy and the teenage girl are buried next to each other.[28]

Fiona's influence had a profound affect on Keith, compounding his views derived from what had happened to his friend who took her own life.

Fiona eventually left Fulham State High to teach at the Yarrabah Aboriginal community south of Cairns. This former Anglican Mission is quite idyllic with a sandy beach, coconut palms, a wrecked ship within metres of the beach, and a church almost on the beach. It is only an hour's drive from Cairns and yet still relatively secluded from the rest of the mainland.

Keith was sad to see her go. He had taken on board a lot of what she said. They also shared a deep scepticism of psychology[29] which she said was dominating the Department and impeding common sense. As a farewell present she gave him a copy of a classic work on the effects of removing children from their families by British academic Spencer Milham.[30] He was subsequently further influenced by this book which backed up much of what Fiona described. Thus, he learned of the disaster for children when they are removed from their families and taken into 'care'.

With Fiona gone, he feels lonely. This is partly related to the fact he does not drink or smoke and is not gregarious. He does not party with mates and is not interested in football and cricket. His interests lie more in travel, current affairs, and the environment.

---

[28] "Five-year-old foster boy had 'toxic drug cocktail' in system at death, reports." *Yahoo News Australia*, 18November 2016. https://au.news.yahoo.com/five-old-foster-boy-had-025455364.html This report is not in the mainstream press.

[29] Even some world renowned psychiatrists reflect some scepticism: "psychology is a very soft science". Judith Herman interviewed in http://globetrotter.berkeley.edu/people/Herman/herman-con2.html,page 2, 21 September 2000.

[30] Millham, S.(1986), *Lost in Care: Problems of Maintaining Links Between Children in Care and Their Families*. Avebury: London.

See also: Little, M. "Spencer Millham obituary", *The Guardian*, London, 22 June 2015. https://www.theguardian.com/society/2015/jun/21/spencer-millham

As a result of his loneliness, he tends to devote himself to his teaching job and spends a lot of time at the school either in lesson preparation and marking or helping out with extra-curricular activities. His involvement with the school is beginning to dominate his life - not necessarily a good thing, especially for a lonely man. Yet, he increases his rôle in organising outdoor activities for the students, particularly co-ordinating study-related excursions and camps to places like the Paluma rainforest, Hinchinbrook Island, Magnetic Island, and even to the Great Barrier Reef. With all this activity and involvement with school life, he doesn't have much time to himself.

Then, one day just a month from retirement, to his surprise and shock, plain clothes Police arrive at the school late one afternoon after school and take him in for questioning. At first, he is bewildered and cannot work out what it's all about mainly because while trying to question him the Police are reluctant to divulge information. So, sensibly, he clams up and asks to see a lawyer. She arrives quite soon and, after talking to Police, is able to tell him that a 14-year-old girl student has lodged a complaint through her foster carer that he had raped her on the school premises not once but on two separate occasions during lunch breaks in Keith's main Geography classroom. And, this is supposed to have happened three months ago.

Keith is arrested, told of the charges he faces, and released on Police bail.[31]

He goes home confused and devastated.

Fellow teachers advise him to engage a top but likely expensive law firm in Townsville, Gordon and Brown. He takes their advice. The girl is one of his students, Jessica Brook, and she is already on a Child Protection Order (CPO) and in foster care. But, he cannot understand why she should make these allegations about him. She is a quiet unassuming moderately pretty girl who is not doing well academically but doesn't hang out with 'in' groups, although she tries to be with them. He has seen that she is subtly excluded by them. He even asks one of the 'in' group why. The frank answer is: "Oh, she's a pain, hangs around like a bad smell. She's in foster care". On one occasion Keith spent time with her during the

---

[31]   Section 382 of the *Police Powers and Responsibilities Act 2000* (Qld) allows a Police officer to grant bail.

first part of a lunch break in his classroom when she asked for help with an assignment. But, this support lasted only fifteen minutes as he felt he shouldn't give preferential treatment to one student. Several times after that she used to come to the Staff Room door and ask a teacher to give him a note which was usually about an assignment or asking for an extension of time. Why she didn't ask him in person he doesn't know. On two occasions the notes were about wanting to meet him in his classroom at lunch break and he assumed it was about an assignment. But, on both occasions he was tied up with other school meetings. In his naïvety he doesn't realise that she had a crush on him but other staff had noticed this and so had other students who used to giggle and snigger about her. He liked the girl not in a sexual way but in a nurturing way. Fully aware of foster care issues, he felt she was a kid needing support.

He is suspended from his job by the Education Department although he does have some moral support from the representative of the National Teachers Union representative at Fulham State High, a fellow teacher.

It takes nearly two years for the case to finally come to a trial before the District Court in Townsville and he is approaching 67. There is a seemingly endless series of 'mention' hearings and then a one-day Committal hearing before a Magistrate in Townsville who reviews the evidence before Keith is sent for a trial in the District Court.[32] On the advice of his solicitor who is also his barrister, Margaret Matheson, he pleads not guilty. So, it is to be a full trial before a jury.

All this is very distressing for Keith. Of course, he is not allowed to contact the girl. He just has to wait and wait. As a nine-year-old child he was sent to boarding school. Life there in the 1950s taught him to bottle-up his feelings and be stoic. And, that is what he does.

---

[32] Before a trial on a serious matter there is a Committal hearing before a Magistrate who, on examination of most of the evidence, decides whether there is sufficient evidence that could convince a jury in a full trial to convict the accused. If the Magistrate decides there is sufficient evidence, then the accused is sent for a full trial. If the Magistrate decides there isn't, then the accused is discharged and is free. Child sex abuse allegations are notoriously hard to prove and so these days the complainant is assumed to be traumatised and therefore accorded the respect of having their allegations taken seriously by the Court system. For this reason, a Magistrate is under pressure to send the accused to trial.

Another teacher comes to visit him at home. She explains some of the reality of his situation. The girl must have felt rejected or hurt and now, out of pique, has made these accusations. The teacher tells him, several other teachers have agreed to appear in Court and be witnesses for his defence. She reminds him that during lunch break, specialist classrooms like the Geography Room and Science Labs are out of bounds to all students. He should not have been alone there with the girl. Students can meet with teachers in the classroom during timetabled classes and immediately before or afterwards. Corridors and verandahs are patrolled by rostered duty teachers. In any case, the door is supposed to be always locked at lunch break unless there was a supervised academic activity. These restrictions are to protect the school against vandalism and theft as well as to protect students as in some rooms there is dangerous equipment. It is also for the protection of teachers from students and accusations like the one Keith now faces. He knows about this but, in his caring attitude towards his students, had given in to the student's request for help. He now realises his naïve stupidity which has got him into such deep trouble.

Outside the school community there is widespread public anger about child sex offenders in general, something which as gripped Australian society for at least a couple of decades. Now, the local *Townsville Chronicle* and tabloid Brisbane paper *The Daily Mirror* give almost salacious coverage to the case. The girl concerned is in foster care and thus is seen as vulnerable. And, of course, she cannot be named and nor can the school. However, after the committal hearing Keith is named in the press. And, in typical press jargon it is reported that "on each occasion the attacks were alleged to have taken place in a classroom during lunch breaks". Use of the word 'attack' even when qualified by the word 'alleged' is sensationalist but the press do this regularly and it only heightens public interest and angst and props up sales. Many in the community discuss this "dirty old man" who "groomed" a vulnerable teenager. As in many cases of child sexual abuse, Townsville people are sceptical about trial outcomes and believe Courts support offenders rights, are too lenient and don't consider the victim. So, there is widespread belief in Townsville that Keith is guilty. And, because he is suspected of having sex with or having raped a 14-year-old child the press and media use the word paedophile indirectly not directly. That is because they do not want to compromise a court case. So, typical of popular views about paedophiles, many in the public they want to see him put away.

There is another growing and widespread imperative in society and that is that we must listen to and believe alleged child sex abuse victims. So, there is a general air of sympathy in the community for the girl and corresponding negativity about Keith.[33] This is an increasingly common perspective as seen in Victorian Premier Daniel Andrews' response to the acquittal of Cardinal Pell following his trial for allegedly sexually abusing alter boys: "I have a message for every single victim and survivor of child sex abuse: I see you. I hear you. I believe you."[34]

During the trial he had rave reports from fellow staff members. His diligent caring approach to all his students was emphasised by six fellow members of the school teaching staff in affidavits tendered to the Court. This included the school principal, Dr Michael Ambrose, who also appeared as a witness for Keith. Although he was quite rigorously cross-examined by the prosecution, he was steadfast in his support for Keith and in his belief that it would be totally out of character for Keith to do such things. He also emphasised that with the low windows and a busy thoroughfare alongside the class room, it was virtually impossible for such things to go on in that Geography room during lunch break without anyone noticing.

In contrast, the prosecution claimed Keith "groomed" the child over several months and that he used the excuse of coaching her privately. He focussed his attentions on a vulnerable child and influenced her to trust him. Afterwards, he put pressure on her "not to tell". These were the allusions which prosecution barrister made skilfully with his

---

[33] Suzanne Moore, "Believe the victims of child sexual abuse? If only we did". *The Guardian*, London, 08 March 2019. https://www.theguardian.com/commentisfree/2019/mar/07/child-sexual-abuse-victims-michael-jackson She says: "If there is one thing we should have learned from all the recent child abuse scandals it is simply this: listen to the victims. Believe them."

[34] Lower, W., "'I believe you' Premier Andrews issues cutting statement". *Daily Mail*, London, 07 April 2020. https://www.dailymail.co.uk/news/article-8194475/Premier-Dan-Andrews-issues-cutting-statement-George-Pell-acquittal.html The Premier of Victoria told child sex abuse victims: "'I have a message for every single victim and survivor of child sex abuse: 'I see you. I hear you. I believe you.'" He said this immediately after the High Court of Australia unanimously acquitted Cardinal George Pell of all child sex abuse charges.

subtle questioning of witnesses as well as during his summing up.

The trial before a jury does not go Keith's way.

The girl told the Court via a video link that on two separate occasions Mr Todd had invited her into his classroom during lunch break and then raped her. At times she seemed nervous, which is understandable, and there were long

This is part of Fulham State High. Keith's Geography room is on the ground floor to the left of the photo. The low windows provide a full view into the classroom from the verandah.

pauses. But, she did not cry or in any way become emotional. She had a Court-ordered support person sitting next to her. She, of course, remained silent and did not prompt the girl in any way.

Keith's lawyer and barrister did not put him on the stand to be cross-examined. She had felt that his evidence was so clear that he could not have raped the girl where she said he did. And, of course, Keith knew he didn't and expected the justice system to prove it. Keith had some public animosity directed at him and putting him on the stand to be cross-examined by the aggressive prosecution might have made matters worse.

Despite these rapes supposedly having taken place in a building with dozens of students passing by on the verandah, apparently no one could be found who saw or heard anything untoward at any time. Like the school Principal, Keith's barrister again pointed out that there are large windows at that classroom and anyone walking past could have seen.

A psychiatrist gave evidence and described exactly what the other teachers had told Keith: that the girl had a crush on him. She often pursued him for advice on her studies and he would retreat into the staff room to avoid her. Yet, she persisted with frequent knocking on the staff room door whereupon she would ask a teacher to give note to Keith. Staff understood what was going on and avoided letting Keith answer the door. The girl was eventually upset at what she had seen as his rejection of her. However, the Department of Public Prosecutions barrister implied that this was a situation that Keith had then exploited to achieve his own sexual gratification. Thus, a vulnerable teenage student was an easy target to groom. Subtly mocking Keith, the barrister asked the jury: "Did grooming this vulnerable child stimulate his declining elderly libido?"

At the end of the trial, Keith's aggressive defence barrister urged jurors to resist a public "atmosphere of hysteria" surrounding the issue of child sexual abuse when considering her client's fate. She went on to characterise the evidence relied upon by the Crown as "vague" and "inconsistent" and accused prosecutors of using imprecise terms when describing the alleged conduct to put a "salacious gloss" on the uncorroborated evidence. She compared his case "to the execution of witches at Salem".

However, her aggression did not go down well with the jury who tended to see a need to stand up for a vulnerable child who bravely faced the camera in the video link.

In summing up for the jury, the prosecution barrister painted Keith as a dirty old man lusting after an easy prey and vulnerable foster care child. He then cast aspersions about the supporting teachers as being "typical cheer squad you so often find in a trial of this nature. Therefore, their views should be discounted." Moreover, assuming Keith's guilt, he criticised him for showing no remorse.

After three days of legal argument and testimony, the jury adjourned. They returned after only an hour to find Keith guilty of all charges.

Of course, Keith was devastated and in complete disbelief. "How could they!? Where's justice? How could this happen to me?"

The Judge would pass sentence in five days while Keith could remain on bail until then in order to have further consultation with his solicitor and put his affairs in order. The Judge had told Keith: "Take it from me. Your sentence will involve a considerable period in custody."

During this time, Keith arranges for all his furniture and personal possessions to be packed up and put into storage. Of course, he has to pay for this. But for how long, he doesn't know. And, he arranges with a real estate agent to let his house.

Next week at the sentencing hearing, during summing up and sentencing the rather imperious Judge told Keith:

Your premeditated offending had poisoned and eroded the sense of trust in the complainant's life. It is likely she will for ever have to live with the horrors which you inflicted upon her. In effect, you have ruined her life. Your employment at the school encouraged parents and carers to trust you as a devoted teacher. You encouraged and built up that trust. The victim herself trusted you. You were her teacher entrusted with her care. Instead, you exploited that rôle and used it to attack her. You were supposed to protect her and yet you did the opposite compounds the crime and only adds to the aggravation.

In view of the gravity of your offending against a vulnerable child and your position of trust as her teacher, I have disregarded the statements of support from your colleagues.

Our society will not tolerate the type of attack which you inflicted upon one of its most vulnerable citizens particularly with the aggravation involved. Therefore, you are to receive a long sentence not only as a means of ensuring your correction but also to protect other children from you.

He then sentenced him to nine years in jail with eligibility for parole after five years.

Keith is dumbfounded. His lawyer did her best to console him by telling him she will appeal. In the few minutes she was able to talk to him while he was still in the dock, she told him: "I believe you are innocent and I will fight this. At the moment, I see there are two grounds for an appeal. The main one is that there was clearly reasonable doubt and that should have acquitted you. Secondly, I do not believe the girl was a credible witness."

Then, Keith was taken away hand-cuffed in a Police paddy wagon to Stuart prison to begin serving his nine year sentence. He is stunned.

Next morning, the dramatic front page of Saturday's *Townsville Chronicle* was dominated by the sentence. The headlines read:

Pedophile rapist teacher gets only 5 years
Victim devastated - Ruined for life

(The paper's headline referred to the time to be served before Keith is eligible for parole. This was used to emphasise the "shocking" short sentence for such a heinous crime.)

There was a slightly blurred photo of Keith's partly obscured face as seen through the rear door of the Police paddy wagon when the car left the Court Building for the Stuart Prison. The newspaper article continued:

This creature should have been locked away, not to see daylight again for decades. Mandatory indefinite sentencing for serious child sex offenders is essential and urgent. Our Courts need to protect the children of Queensland from these perverts who groom vulnerable children. And, if the Courts will not do it, Parliament needs to legislate. Enough is enough. The community will no longer accept that these monsters be allowed to roam free in our suburban streets, to frequent schools, playgrounds, and shopping malls and to exploit internet social media. Are our children ever going to be safe from animals like this? Civil libertarians should listen to the community. Our children's safety must come first. Anne Christian, prove that you are worthy of being Queensland's Premier and do something about this!

"Brave rape victim speaks up" The newspaper banner reflected public thinking.

These sentiments about perverts, creatures, and monsters were echoed in the Saturday edition of the big Brisbane *Daily Mirror* and other regional Queensland papers. A state-wide commercial TV station breakfast news show took the same line, going over the same ground *ad nauseum* with the presenter sombrely shaking his head in shocked disapproval every time the item was run. Well-known Brisbane-based child safety campaigner, Anne McLeod, was interviewed and said: "Electronic tagging of all sex offenders is vital and mandatory indefinite sentencing for repeat offenders must come ... and the sooner the better. Forget the rights of paedophiles. Our children must come first."

As for local Townsville social media, *Facebook* in particular, public anger and vigilantism were fired-up with comments such as "there is no place in society for this scum", "this monster should be tortured and killed before being allowed to rot in hell", and "this creepy animal must be strung up and publicly castrated". Another post said: "death penalty please!" One cyber-vigilante said: "He should have a knife slowly inserted into every orifice of his body before he is left to die a slow lingering death". It seems many believe that in cyberspace people can unleash their basest feelings with impunity.[35] Social media can reveal some of humankind's worst characteristics.

Of course, the girl's identity was by law never revealed. But, because she was known at her high school in Townsville, the Department of Child Safety moved her to another foster care placement in Brisbane. This was done even before the trial started. The video link during the trial was filmed in Brisbane in the comfort of the new foster carer's house.

Newspapers had a field day branding Keith like Cardinal Pell was when he was found guilty. Coverage was similarly malicious and destructive for Keith. But, unlike Pell, he did not have a high powered and very expensive legal team. And, unlike Pell, he went to jail with no public support at all. But, like Pell, he had to wait at nearly two years for an appeal to be heard. Meanwhile, he was bashed in prison. Pell was well protected.

Essentially, Keith had been found guilty by accusation rather like Cardinal Pell was. Like Pell, the prosecution did not establish guilt "to the requisite standard of proof".[36] The probability of him being able to rape the girl in the exposed place was way beyond the bounds of reasonable possibility, especially as there was a much used public thoroughfare outside the classroom, no curtains, no corroborating witnesses, and there was no DNA profiling.

The case also bears similarities to one where a teacher in Victoria was accused of having sex with two eight-year-old boys. Apart from the fact that they were too young to ejaculate, it was understood they had colluded to make up the story and only made a complaint twenty seven years after the alleged rape. Then, after more than two years in prison, the Supreme

---

35   These are real comments reported in the press. For sensible discussion about vigilantism in the press, media and in cyberspace see: Minogue, C.W. (2009), "Burning the law and celebrating violent vigilantism". *Alternative Law Journal*, Monash University, Melbourne, 34(2), pp 118-117 & 136. https://journals.sagepub.com/doi/abs/10.1177/1037969X0903400210?journalCode=aljb The article cites numerous serious examples in Australia where vigilantism has gone beyond "idle talk by emotionally wrought hot heads" and resulted in violent action which has lead to arson, torture and murder by individuals and mobs. Sometimes a person has not even been charged let alone been to trial when vigilantes attacked. These actions are described as "trial by media and vigilantes".

36   "George Pell ... wrongfully jailed for child sexual abuse". *ABC News*, Sydney, 14 April 2020. https://www.abc.net.au/news/2020-04-14/cardinal-george-pell-andrew-bolt-sky-news-interview/12146594?

Court quashed the conviction and she was released.[37] The original complainants were not charged with perjury or with trying to pervert the course of justice.

On arrival at Stuart Prison, Keith had to listen to a recorded description of what was to happen to him and how he should behave. He was told to remove his clothes and place them in a large box together with all the personal belongings with him, such as his wallet, watch, and iPhone. He was then made to have a shower after which he had to squat and cough to make sure he had nothing hidden in his rectum. He was weighed and measured and asked questions about his health by a prison doctor. After dressing in the brown prison track suit, he was given a short interview with a prison psychologist. She asked him: "Do you want to be placed in the protective wing? I can assure you that if you are placed with mainstream prisoners, they'll make mincemeat of you."[38]

So, carrying a bag of prison issued items such as a brown track suit, soap, tooth brush and tooth paste, he was lead to one of the protective wings of the prison. Here he was placed in a room for about an hour with another longstanding inmate who then talked to him about prison life. The man was helpful. He told Keith: "You are not going to be in here as long as me. You haven't done anything like as bad as what I've done. He was very cordial and nice to Keith. (Later, Keith was surprised to find out he was doing life for raping and brutally murdering two prostitutes.)

Next, Keith was locked in an isolation cell for 48 hours where there was a bright blue ceiling light on all day and night. This "Blue Light Cell" is a special suicide watch cell. Finally, he was let out and given a cell in the main part of this protective wing. He now had to get used to a strict regime of meal times, cell inspections and roll calls. But, on his third day after he is placed in the protected wing of the prison with other protected prisoners, some of them corner him just out of view from CCTV cameras. Prisoners know where the blind spots are. He is enticed behind a flight of stairs where he is attacked. These men are some who are also protected, many of them having been charged with or convicted of very serious

---

[37] Ugur Nedim, "Teacher's wrongful conviction finally overturned." *Sydney Criminal Lawyers*, 25 June 2015. https://www.sydneycriminallawyers.com.au/blog/teachers-wrongful-conviction-finally-overturned/

[38] An actual statement given during induction to a newly arrived prisoner by a female prison psychologist.

violent child sexual abuse offences. He is kicked repeatedly in the groin and his testicles swell badly. He is bashed on the face with a sock with a cake of soap inside it. One tells him: "Go kill yourself, now." Eventually, some guards intervene and he is taken to the prison hospital where his cut forehead is treated with sutures. But, their delayed intervention was suspicious.

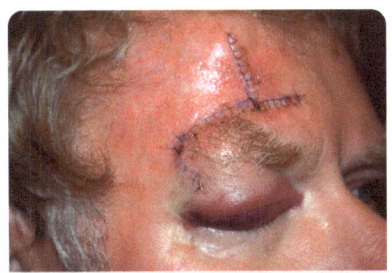

Some of Keith's injuries after being bashed up in prison. (*iStockphoto.* Posed by model)

Luckily, Keith was not attacked like another man was with boiling water with jam in it to make it even more painful. And, the man was in a protected wing of the prison and not yet convicted. His attacker was also a prisoner in the protected wing.[39]

Whenever there were school holidays Fiona made a point of visiting him in prison. This would cheer him up. He even had separate visits from other teachers at Fulham State High and they all told him his conviction was very wrong.

After six weeks he was given a job in the prison kitchen, mainly washing dishes every morning. He does this for 18 months. He is lucky. This is regarded as a plum job. Other jobs are harder such as cutting up rags and sorting and cutting up old house timber. Probably, his age is taken into account. However, he feels abandoned by society. Yet, he didn't do anything wrong and certainly didn't rape that girl or even groom her. However, his childhood boarding school life means that he remains strong and has no thoughts of suicide.

His lawyer, Margaret Matheson, diligently lodged an appeal before the 28-day deadline. Typically, it took nearly two years for the Supreme Court (Court of Appeal) to consider his case.

He had been in prison for just over 15 months when the 'victim', who is living in Brisbane and is now 18, has just dumped a boyfriend. He is upset and contacts the main Brisbane tabloid newspaper, the Brisbane *Daily Mirror*. On the phone, he tells a reporter that Jessica Brook told him no such rape occurred and that she had made it all up. He is interviewed by the paper but they can't find Jessica. She has gone to ground. Thus, this revelation is not published by the tabloid.

---

[39] "Man accused of being Australia's worst-ever pedophile allegedly attacked in prison by fellow inmate", *Courier Mail*, Brisbane, 07 October 2023. https://www.news.com.au/national/queensland/man-accused-of-being-australias-worstever-pedophile-allegedly-attacked-in-prison-by-fellow-inmate/news-story/215fa7f0e57fa60f6634921aa9f783c9.

But, within a week, Police have tracked her down, arrested her, and charged her with perjury. Nothing appears in the press and media about this. And, the whole issue is simply not publicised. She goes to trial six months later and is convicted but gets a suspended sentence because she was a minor when the perjury occurred. This trial result is still not reported anywhere in the press in either Brisbane or Townsville because she was a minor and also in foster care at the time of the offence. Newspapers will not publish anything about it. Indeed, under sections 185 to 194 of the *Child Protection Act* they are not allowed to. It was Keith's lawyer, Margaret Matheson, who told him during a prison visit about the girl's conviction for perjury. She has advised the Appeal Court.

Two months later, the Appeal Court hands down its decision. The entire conviction is quashed and he is acquitted. His immediate release is ordered.[40]

Margaret told him: "Now you know for certain that your acquittal was definitely not on the basis of a legal technicality. Legally, people have to believe you now but probably won't."

The Appeal Court Judges said the evidence against Keith, namely the location and openness of the Geography room where the alleged rapes were supposed to have occurred, was so weak that more than reasonable doubt should have acquitted Keith. And, there was no corroborating evidence or witness statement. The trial Judge also erred in not reminding the jury of this. The unanimous statement from the three Appeal Court judges said: "There is a significant possibility

---

[40] An example of deliberately fabricated rape allegations: Pidd, H., "Eleanor Williams jailed for eight and a half years after rape and trafficking lies". *The Guardian*, London, 15 March 2023. https://www.theguardian.com/uk-news/2023/mar/14/eleanor-williams-jailed-lying-rapes-trafficking

And, a Queensland case case of an 11-year-old Toowoomba girl's claim that a man sexually abused her and penetrated her with his penis convicted the man. When the man appealed, the appeal Court threw out the convictions because the girl had later admitted that she had fabricated the allegations. Nolan, M., "Sex conviction quashed". *Courier Mail*, Brisbane, 15 November 2022, page 4.

Also: Hickey, P., "'I kept repeating I did nothing wrong': man's child sex abuse conviction quashed". *Sydney Morning Herald, Sydney*, 24 May 2019. https://www.smh.com.au/national/i-kept-repeating-i-did-nothing-wrong-man-s-child-sex-abuse-conviction-quashed-20190523-p51qil.html. After spending 15 months in jail, the man's conviction was thrown out by the High Court after lower courts had rejected his appeal. The complainant admitted telling lies. He had the money and perseverance to go all the way to the High Court. Few are in that position.

McClure, T., "New Zealand court quashes child sexual abuse conviction in landmark ruling." *The Guardian*, Auckland, 07 October 2022. https://www.theguardian.com/world/2022/oct/07/new-zealand-court-quashes-peter-ellis-child-sexual-abuse-conviction In this case, the man died before the Court ruling but the Court decided to continue the case so that in death his name would be cleared.

A *Google* search will find many other cases of child sexual abuse convictions being quashed.

that an innocent person has been convicted because the evidence did not establish guilt to the requisite standard of proof. It should be noted that the alleged victim has since been convicted of perjury in relation to this case. As a result, the Appeal Court has no option but to acquit."

Significantly, like the Cardinal Pell case, the Appeal Court does not order a re-trial, which is a measure of the way it felt about Keith's original conviction and the pressure Keith had been subjected to by the public and the press and media. Likewise, the Department of Public Prosecutions accepted the Appeal Court's decision. Moreover, the Appeal Court also specifically ordered that any record of Keith's criminal charges and conviction be removed.[41][42]

---

[41] Similar cases of teachers falsely accused:

Duell, M., 'School teacher accused of repeatedly raping a pupil in a geography classroom'. *Daily Mail*, London, 21 July 2016. http://www.dailymail.co.uk/news/article-3699606/Girlfriend-private-girls-school-teacher-accused-repeatedly-raping-pupil-geography-classroom-pregnant-arrested-court-told.html

Rawstorne, T., "Teacher's career lies in ruins after he's acquitted in less than half an hour of raping a troubled pupil". *Daily Mail*, London, 26 July 2016. http://www.dailymail.co.uk/news/article-3707840/The-outstanding-geography-teacher-dreamed-headmaster-career-lies-ruins-accused-rape-millionaire-s-girl-flew-New-York-week-therapy.html

Coletta, F., "Private school teacher found NOT GUILTY of fondling the" *Daily Mail*, London - Australian Edition, 29 August 2016. http://www.dailymail.co.uk/news/article-3763138/Private-school-teacher-not-guilty-fondling-testicles-four-students-lawyer-compared-case-execution-witches-Salem.html

Nedim, U., "Teacher's wrongful conviction finally overturned". *Sydney Criminal Lawyers*, 25 June 2015. http://www.sydneycriminallawyers.com.au/blog/teachers-wrongful-conviction-finally-overturned/ This teacher spent more than two years in prison awaiting trial and waiting for an appeal Court decision to acquit.

Anon, "Being a male teacher was my dream - until I was falsely accused". *Stuff NZ*, Auckland, 24 November 2017. http://www.stuff.co.nz/life-style/life/98942078/being-a-male-teacher-was-my-dream--until-i-was-falsely-accused

On this issue, see the brilliant 2012 Danish film *The Hunt* starring Mads Mikkelsen as the teacher and Annika Wedderkopp as the little girl he is accused of molesting. https://en.wikipedia.org/wiki/The_Hunt_(2012_film)

See also: "False allegation of child sexual abuse", *Wikipedia*: https://en.wikipedia.org/wiki/False_allegation_of_child_sexual_abuse

A simple *Google* search of "falsely accused of child sex abuse" will find many pages of examples.

However, for several years a teacher avoided prosecution by fleeing overseas: McNeill, S., "Malka Leifer: Australian principal accused of 74 child sex charges walks free in Israel". *ABC News*, Sydney, 03 June 2016. http://www.abc.net.au/news/2016-06-03/australian-principal-accused-of-74-child-sex-charges-walks-free/7473246 In 2021 she was extradited from Israel to Australia to face child sex abuse charges. In 2023 a Melbourne court convicted her. Silva, K., "Malka Leifer found guilty of rape and child sex abuse". *ABC News*, Melbourne, 03 April 2023. https://www.abc.net.au/news/2023-04-03/malka-leifer-sex-abuse-trial-jury-verdict-principal/102061290?utm_source=sfmc&utm_medium=email&utm_campaign=abc_news_newsmail_pm_sfmc&utm_term=&utm_id=2062204&sfmc_id=238639983

[42] Olding, R., "Man wrongly accused of sexual assault sues police". *Sydney Morning Herald*, 19 June 2014. http://www.smh.com.au/nsw/man-wrongly-accused-of-sexual-assault-sues-police-20140627-zsefw.html

A few hours later when Keith was released there was a bevy of reporters at the prison gate photographing him and pestering him with loaded questions like "What are you going say to your victim now that you've been released on a legal technicality?" Stunned, Keith didn't know what to say. His lawyer ushered him away as quickly as possible into her car.

Margaret Matheson arranged for him to stay in a motel. His current tenants have just a month left of the lease agreement for his house. However, rather than moving back in, he decides to put the house on the market and move out of Townsville. The city has been too hurtful for him. This is especially so now when the local *Townsville Chronicle* editorial even states that he got off on a technicality.

> He got off because of the legalistic concept of 'reasonable doubt'. He had the benefit of the doubt. Sadly, the victim did not. As a result, a civil case could eventuate. The paper then suggested that the child victim is likely to be devastated and she will need massive support for a long time, not only for what is alleged to have happened to her, but also for what she has been forced to endure in this convoluted Court process. He has not been held accountable.

So, despite this turn-around, Keith's name is still mud.

Then a day later, as Keith walked from his solicitor's car to her office with her, a reporter approached and pestered him about how he felt. Taking his solicitor's advice, he ignored the reporter. Some are now openly sceptical of the verdict. A common refrain is: "He got the benefit of the doubt. She should've got that benefit." Courts are accused of defending sex offenders' rights. "Courts need to put victims' rights first. He groomed her to bend to his will and then stole her innocence. She's been ruined for life."

In Margaret Matheson's office, she warns him very frankly of the likely repercussions. "The truth is that from now on you will always still be suspect in the eyes of many. People will say 'where there is smoke there is fire' and 'he got off on a technicality'."

Keith: "That's not right. I didn't do it. And, the Appeal Court agrees I didn't do it. They knew about her perjury. The Judges also had my original conviction expunged."

She told him: "Look, I know, the Appeal Court knows, the so-called 'victim' knows and most importantly, the public should now accept that you did not do it but many will not accept that. Simply put, you were originally found guilty by accusation. You are not guilty. Yes. But, the public likes to find villains. Before the trial you were seen as a child rapist. They like that. I suggest you find a DVD copy of that Danish film *The Hunt*. In it a primary school teacher is accused of molesting one of his pupils. In the end he is totally exonerated but not everyone accepts that. Some still like to have a villain and somebody tries to … . Well, see the film for yourself and you'll have an idea of what I'm saying."[43]

Later, he borrows a DVD from the local library and views the movie at home. He is impressed by the last few scenes where the hero realises that society will never accept his innocence. Some will always want a demon.

Margaret: "Look, these days, mere allegations of sexual assault of children attract publicity. In the press and the wider community people are guilty until proven innocent and that can be impossible to prove conclusively. This was a vulnerable child in foster care. So, in the public eye your innocence has not been proven. And, it's not as if there is a sudden increase in child sex offences. There were just as many decades ago but in the current climate victims are believed straight away and so a fair trial can be difficult. In the press and media there is usually no presumption of innocence any more. In all states sex offenders may legally be named even as soon as they have been charged.[44] Gone is the presumption of innocence until proof of guilt. And, with internet social media it is open slather."

---

[43] In the Danish film *The Hunt,* a male teacher is eventually exonerated from child sex abuse charges. But, a year later while still living in the same community, somebody tries to shoot him. Starring in the film are Mads Mikkelsen as the teacher and Annika Wedderkopp as 5-year-old Klara, who he is accused of abusing. See the official trailer at: https://www.youtube.com/watch?v=ieLIOBkMgAQ.

[44] By May 2023 legislation existed in all Australian states allowing the naming alleged sex offenders immediately they are charged instead of having their identities hidden to protect them from reputational damage because they may later be found not guilty.

Keith feels like a pariah. This sense of being an outcast now dominates his life.[45]

Margaret: "That Judge should not have accepted the prosecution's branding your supporters' character references as just 'cheer squad'.[46] It just shows how fallible Judges and jurors can be."

She continued: "But, listen carefully to me. Many want kudos for publicly identifying evil perverts. Some see you as one and no amount of contrary evidence will convince them otherwise. So, please be careful in future. No publicity was given about the girl's conviction. So, even when informed of it many in our society will still want to see you as a pervert."

He makes a point of emailing a copy the Jessica Brook's conviction to Fiona and the loyal fellow teachers who had visited him in jail. They all responded that they were very happy for him.

He begins to think sometimes that he might be a bad person. Why else would all this be happening to him? When he is in a shopping mall or some other public place, he sometimes wonders if people see him as a sex fiend? Yes, the mud thrown was washed off him when the conviction was quashed and he was acquitted but is there still some mud on him? Oft-heard

---

[45] An example of deliberately fabricated rape allegations: Pidd, H., "Eleanor Williams jailed for eight and a half years after rape and trafficking lies". *The Guardian*, London, 15 March 2023. https://www.theguardian.com/uk-news/2023/mar/14/eleanor-williams-jailed-lying-rapes-trafficking

And, a Queensland case case of an 11-year-old Toowoomba girl's claim that a man sexually abused her and penetrated her with his penis convicted the man. When the man appealed, the appeal Court threw out the convictions because the girl had later admitted that she had fabricated the allegations. Nolan, M., "Sex conviction quashed". *Courier Mail*, Brisbane, 15 November 2022, page 4.

Also: Hickey, P., "'I kept repeating I did nothing wrong': man's child sex abuse conviction quashed". *Sydney Morning Herald, Sydney*, 24 May 2019. https://www.smh.com.au/national/i-kept-repeating-i-did-nothing-wrong-man-s-child-sex-abuse-conviction-quashed-20190523-p51qil.html. After spending 15 months in jail, the man's conviction was thrown out by the High Court after lower courts had rejected his appeal. The complainant admitted telling lies. He had the money and perseverance to go all the way to the High Court. Few are in that position.

McClure, T., "New Zealand court quashes child sexual abuse conviction in landmark ruling." *The Guardian*, Auckland, 07 October 2022. https://www.theguardian.com/world/2022/oct/07/new-zealand-court-quashes-peter-ellis-child-sexual-abuse-conviction In this case, the man died before the Court ruling but the Court decided to continue the case so that in death his name would be cleared.

A *Google* search will find many other cases of child sexual abuse convictions being quashed.

[46] During 2024 there was widespread public pressure for Courts to reject character references for those accused of sexual crimes. Kyriacou, K., "Rapists never good people". *Courier Mail*, Brisbane, 28 May 2024, page 15. What if the accused person's guilt is overturned on appeal as in Keith's case?

catch phrases in the newspapers like: "This creature must be locked away, not to see daylight again for decades" which appeared in the press when he was first convicted tend to haunt him. And, after his acquittal, one newspaper said:

> The legalistic concept of 'reasonable doubt' gave him the benefit of the doubt. The victim's life is ruined. He's not been held accountable. This man could be on your street.

The press and media do not know about the girl's conviction for perjury. So, even with her conviction, he wonders whether the smell of child sexual abuse would ever leave him? As we shall see, it doesn't leave him.

As time passes, he lapses into strong feelings of wanting to retreat from society, which is what he does. This attitude dominates his thinking and drives what he does for a long time until one November morning years later something really dramatic happens. He is jolted out of his depression.

In the meantime, his lawyer applies for compensation for wrongful conviction. There are no legal provisions for this and he is dependent upon the goodwill of the government of the day for an *ex gratia* payment. These payments vary considerably but four years after his conviction was quashed, he receives a payment of a seemingly arbitrary amount of $100,000 for the wrongful conviction and a further $30,000 for the injuries he received and the psychological trauma he suffered in prison.[47] Yet, he gets nothing for the loss of his reputation. And, there is no publicity about these payments, again because of provisions of the *Child Protection Act* (at sections 185 to 194, especially sections 189 and 194 which protect identities of children and others involved).[48] With his conviction being quashed

---

[47] See: "Compensation for wrongful conviction": https://www.aic.gov.au/publications/tandi/tandi356

[48] These days legal fees mount up considerably. While Keith's defence cost him nothing like the defence of Cardinal Pell, legal fees can be astronomical. Some have put Pell's legal costs at "over five million" (Kelso Lawyers in 2017) with $50,000 a day during Court hearings. Keith's solicitor and barrister charged $490 per hour for a consultation and there were other expenses like preparation of materials, disbursements like conference fees, Court fees, search fees, lodgement fees, correspondence and what lawyers call "petties" as well as travel and accommodation expenses. The list goes on. For attendance to his defence in Court the basic fee was around $7,000 a day. There were around seven days of Court hearings in total. He also had to pay for a psychologist's assessment. So, the *ex gratia* payments probably only covered some of his expenses. Without those two payments, it would have been an incredible and unjust burden imposed on an innocent person. But, this type of injustice is not uncommon.

after his so-called victim's perjury, he is just pleased that he has been acquitted. Yet, unlike Cardinal Pell, he does not have public support. So, he is still motivated to retreat from society. Allegations of child sexual abuse, true or not, are invariably devastating. The stain never goes away.

CHAPTER 3

Keith starts to move on

Fortunately, Keith is able to sell his house for a good price because of the then current mining and resources boom. He pays the legal bill but is pleased that he engaged a top Townsville legal firm. He knows he would have been swamped by the legal processes had he not done so and possibly he could have ended up an innocent man remaining in prison. Still, he is upset that through no fault of his, he has been so penalised financially and emotionally. His time in prison was a nightmare.

Now, retired and with time on his hands, he does a lot of soul-searching. He reads a little on the internet about child sexual abuse and paedophilia. Much of it is new to him. He's never before had an interest. He has been put off by all the psychology. He is too sceptical of psychology, especially anything to do with Sigmund Freud who he sees as a quack. He distrusts psychology and sees it as not as worthwhile as the practices of a witch doctor or *sing'anga* among the Chewa people. In his undergraduate years he read of terrible things done in the name of psychology during Hitler's *Third Reich,* in post-war Sweden, and the USA. He thinks particularly of the medications, castrations and lobotomies. He knows that New Zealand novelist Janet Frame had been subjected to repeated electroconvulsive therapy and was only saved from a lobotomy at virtually the eleventh hour when her first novel won a major literary award.[49] He has read Ken Kesey's novel and seen the film *One Flew Over the Cuckoo's Nest* [50] where a totally sane man is given a lobotomy. He also reads in the press where Philip Zimbardo's[51] famous research

---

[49]   See: "Janet Frame", *Wikipedia.* https://en.wikipedia.org/wiki/Janet_Frame
[50]   Kesey, K. (1962), *One Flew Over the Cuckoo's Nest.* New York: Viking.
[51]   Zimbardo, P. (2007), *The Lucifer Effect.* Random House: London.

on how good people in society can so easily turn evil has recently been torn apart by critics.[52] Likewise, he has also read about the questioning Stanley Milgram's obedience experiments, something he had learned about many years ago in his undergraduate teacher education at University. Milgram used his experiments to show how we can be convinced by those in authority to commit evil. This was particularly relevant to the 1961 trial of Adolf Eichmann in Israel. Now, after decades of believing in the efficacy of Milgram's research, he finds that there are fundamental flaws in Milgram's work and many are now also questioning it.[53]

His scepticism about psychology is already deeply embedded and he now almost feeds upon these examples of where psychology is questioned.

Then, one day he borrows a copy of Nabokov's novel *Lolita*[54] from the Townsville library. He had known about it since his university years in the 1960s when it was banned in Australia until 1965. So, he had not read it and had not seen the film. Now, he finds the book tame and almost boring at times. He wonders what all the fuss was about. Next, he discovers a little book of short stories with a story in it called *Lust*. It is not fiction. It is true. Rather like *Lolita*, it is about a 12-year-old girl who has a sexual affair with a man in his

---

[52]   For example: Perry, G., "Inside the prison experiment that claimed to show the roots of evil". *New Scientist*, 10 October 2018. https://www.newscientist.com/article/mg24031990-200-inside-the-prison-experiment-that-claimed-to-show-the-roots-of-evil/#ixzz6IbOsASKQ. The Stanford University prison experiment was the classic demonstration of how power can bring out the worst in us. But, now it seems it was more about showbiz than science.

[53]   For example: Perry, G. (2012), *Behind the Shock Machine: the untold story of the notorious Milgram psychology experiments*. Scribe: Melbourne.
        Also, Hannah Arendt (2006), *Eichmann in Jerusalem: A Report on the Banality of Evil*. Penguin: London.

[54]   Nabokov, V. (1995), *Lolita*. London: Penguin. Originally published in America in 1955, the novel is the story of a late middle-aged man who crosses boundaries and has a full-on sexual affair with a 12-year-old girl, Lolita. The man openly admits that he fancies prepubescent girls or what he calls "nymphets" aged between nine and fourteen (page 16) and describes himself as a "nympholept" (page 17). As for Lolita, she took the sexual relationship quite casually even teasing the man about it (page 140) and was sometimes jealous when he looked at other "nymphets" (page 190). Shocking when first published, today it is tame and studied in literature courses at universities.
        See also the National Archives of Australia website at http://blog.naa.gov.au/banned/2013/10/09/lolita/

fifties.[55] The girl, who lived in the up market bayside Sydney suburb of Darling Point, had a steamy secret sexual relationship with a much respected District Court Judge. Keith loves the author's subtle and frank use of language. She wrote: "I loved the thrill of the secret rendezvous" and "I always felt that my relationship with the judge continued according to my will not his, and that he was doing me a favour in initiating me into the world of sin I was so eager to know."[56]

He also reads about the controversy surrounding Lewis Carol, author of *Alice and Wonderland,* and his relationship with young girls and the dozens of photos he took of them naked.[57] (And, before his death he destroyed many of them.) Many deny that Carol was a paedophile. This leads him to the question of what a paedophile is. It is all new to him. Naïvely, he had never thought about these things before. Now, he notices in newspapers what seems a continual flow of popular statements about paedophiles. He really hadn't paid much attention to them before. There are the usual statements about locking these men up and throwing away the key or chemically castrating them. There are statements by child protection activists that "they always re-offend" and "once a pervert always a pervert". He feels he is very lucky his conviction was overturned but this worries him, especially society's attitude. He has always tended to empathise with the underdog in society. As an undergraduate at University, he and his ex-wife had supported Aboriginal rights. This had motivated him to study Hitler's Third Reich and the persecution of Jews. So, he later visited Auschwitz where naturally he was shocked.

Decades ago when homosexuality was illegal and seen as abhorrent and evil by society, men so inclined were denigrated and punished with severe jail sentences. He thinks of

---

55   This is a true story by Blanche d'Alpuget, now in her 80's and was married to former Australian Prime Minister the late Bob Hawke. From the age of 12 she had a relatively long and lustful sexual affair with a respected 54-year-old District Court Judge who she originally used to meet at the bus stop on her way to school. Yet, he was known for the harsh sentences he used to hand down to sex offenders. See: d'Alpuget, B. (1993), 'Lust' in Fitzgerald, R. (ed.), *The Eleven Deadly Sins*. Melbourne: Minerva. Blanche feels she was not a victim and she has never publicly revealed the learned Judge's name. However, many have criticised her for seeing her relationship with the Judge not in terms of the horror of child sexual abuse but more as a useful learning experience. At the time of publication some attacks on her in the press were quite vitriolic.

56   d'Alpuget, B. (1993), 'Lust' in Fitzgerald, R. (ed.), *The Eleven Deadly Sins*. Melbourne: Minerva, page 105.

57   See: http://en.wikipedia.org/wiki/Lewis_Carroll where the debate over Lewis Carroll's sexuality is considered.

playwright and novelist Oscar Wilde and how he was pilloried and jailed. Crowds jeered and spat at him. Until very recently homosexuals were not allowed to teach or join the forces. Some were treated with so-called "aversion therapy" using electric shocks administered to men when shown sexy images. Some were treated with castrating chemicals. Did all this change them or just drive them underground? Despite his own personal homophobia because of an experience at boarding school when he was ten-years-old, he empathises with them. A teacher had anally raped him. On the other hand, he has never thought about lesbians especially not in the context of female sex offenders. He is like the rest of society: women don't do such things. They are protectors and nurturers.[58]

He reflects on how he loved his own children and never sexually abused them. He loved being a parent, especially a full-on intimate parent. In fact, he misses not having little children to care for. It was fulfilling having his children grow up and he still likes little

---

[58] A "culture of denial": For those who find the notion of female child sex perpetrators improbable, see: Townsend, M. & Syal, R., 'Up to 64,000 women in UK are child-sex offenders'. *The Guardian*, London, 04 October 2009. http:// www.theguardian.com/society/2009/oct/04/uk-female-child-sex-offenders

Charlotte Philby, 'Female sexual abuse: The untold story of society's last taboo'. *The Independent*, London, 23 October 2011. http://www.independent.co.uk/life-style/love-sex/taboo-tolerance/female-sexual-abuse-the-untold-story-of-societys-last-taboo-1767688.html If child sexual abuse is usually tied to male aggression and power, what is this?

Snyder, H.N. (2000), *Sexual Assault of Young Children as Reported to Law Enforcement: Victims, incident and Offender Characteristics*. Washington DC: Bureau of Justice Statistics, US Dept of Justice. http://bjs.gov/content/pub/ pdf/saycrle.pdf Of all sexual assaults against children aged 6 and under, 12% were committed by women (page 8). These statistics are based on convictions only. And, that report was in the year 2000 when people were even more unable than today to accept that women can sexually abuse. Two decades later, it is likely the percentage has grown as child sex abuse by women is increasingly acknowledged and reported to authorities.

Deering, R. (2006), *Female Perpetrators of Child Sexual Abuse: Impact, Professional Perspectives and Management*. PhD Thesis, School of Psychology, Deakin University, Geelong, Australia. Rebecca Deering said at least 20% of child sexual abuse is committed by women and female child sexual abuse is "more prevalent and more damaging to the victims than is recognised by society".

See the short comment by Michele Elliott: 'Women can be abusers too'. *The Independent*, London, 02 October 2009. http://www.independent.co.uk/voices/commentators/michele-elliott-women-can-be-child-abusers-too-1796374.html

Recently: Tozdan, S., Briken, P. & Dekker, A. "Uncovering Female Child Sexual Offenders—Needs and Challenges for Practice and Research". *Journal of Clinical Medicine*,8(3), March 2019. https://www.ncbi.nlm.nih.gov/pmc/articles/ PMC6463078/ "The 'culture of denial' surrounding women who are sexually offensive conceals their acts as 'silent crimes'. Moving beyond traditional gender stereotypes seems to be necessary to get over the confusion that women considered so far as caregivers, guardians, and defenders are able to be just as sexually abusive to children as men."

children. It's the nurturer in him. And, as a teacher this was reflected in his approach to his students. As a parent he was never a blokey man. At barbecues he didn't like hanging around with the fathers, beer can or stubbie in hand, talking sport and cars, while some of them cooked sausages. Yet, he used to find he was not really welcome with mothers while they talked breastfeeding, cracked nipples and children as those mothers sipped on white wine or Claytons. So, at these social gatherings he would sometimes spend time with his own girls until, of course, they got involved with other kids. Then, he would walk away and look at the garden by himself. And, he has never felt any sexual interest towards any of the many school kids he has taught over the years. He knows of other male teachers who did and succumbed to their teenage girl students' advances and got into trouble. Sometimes, other male teachers in the staff room laughed quietly between themselves about the sexual interests of the immature teenage girls. He didn't get involved with that but he knew. So, not enjoying barbecues and staff room banter, he always saw himself as a bit of a social outsider or even a misfit or, in modern terms, a 'nerd'. Many assume a loner is not just a misfit but somebody unable to "make it with a woman" and even a pervert.[59] He wonders if, as a loner, his unwillingness to mix well is why he has now fallen so foul of society. And, because of this, he feels very browbeaten by the opprobrium which still lingers around him despite his acquittal and the girl's perjury. It lingers especially because his acquittal has not been taken seriously by so many in society who still see him as having "got off because of a technicality". And, of course, his supposed victim's perjury got just zero publicity.

Depression is getting to him. He begins to think that society will never accept him again. In truth, in the eyes of so many, child sex offences are the pits. No crime could be worse. He keeps noticing comments by people in relation to other people who commit

---

[59] This is a popular view at one time which used to be backed up by academia: Marshall, W.L., 'Intimacy, loneliness and sexual offenders'. *Behaviour Research and Therapy*, 27(5), 1989, 491-504. "The history of sexual offenders illustrates why they fail to develop the attitudes and skills necessary to attain intimacy, and why this failure leads to sexual abuse." (page 504)

Yet, as a teacher, Keith certainly does not lack empathy though he is a loner. Some child sex offenders are not loners, have excellent social skills, and have been popular figures such as some singers and comedians (e.g. Rolf Harris). For a positive view of loners which include Michelangelo, Isaac Newton and Ludwig Wittgenstein, see: Rufus, A. (2003), *Party of One*, Cambridge, USA: De Capo Press.

child sexual abuse crimes. Thus for example, he reads a report in a newspaper where child protection advocate Hetty Johnston said of child sexual abuse: "This is probably one of the most serious crimes you could commit against a child. In fact, it is."[60] He thinks about the massive crimes committed against children by Nazis like Josef Mengele and other SS officers at Auschwitz and by Pol Pot in Cambodia and other tyrants and their henchmen elsewhere. Most of those victims died *en masse*. Child sexual abuse of individuals pales into almost insignificance by comparison. Yet, he did not commit any child sex offence. He realises that the mud thrown at him before and during the trial is sticking. He can't get it off him. He wonders: "What if I did commit child sexual abuse? I would be really 'up shit creek without a paddle'. I don't think redemption, let alone forgiveness, would ever come my way. Yet, I have not committed any sex offence and the smell of child sex abuse surrounds me."

Then, he sees an item in the news about how an innocent man in Victoria was suspected, abducted, tortured, and ultimately murdered by a group of men.[61] He is shocked. What can he do to avoid that sort of thing happening to him?

The opprobrium he felt from the community in the long twenty-four months leading up to the trial has affected him deeply. Now, even after his acquittal, it is still worrying him. He feels he must retreat and isolate himself from society. He wants to escape totally. He decides to go and live somewhere as a hermit. So, with his house in Townsville sold and now having reached seventy-one, he goes for a long drive south in his VW campervan. He must go far from Townsville, the city which he feels has rejected him. He doesn't want to bump into people in the street who might know him, even if they are supportive of him. He is in a search for a quiet, peaceful place to live, away from people but a place where he can be embedded in nature. As a Geography teacher, that has for along time been his

---

60   This is what Australian 'Bravehearts' director Hetty Johnston said at a press conference: Kehren, K., 'Man caught in bed with boy walks free'. *Courier Mail*, Brisbane, 05 August 2014. http://www.couriermail.com. au/news/queensland/ man-caught-in-bed-with-boy-walks-free/story-fnihsrf2-1227013826341

61   To read about this ghastly vigilante torture and murder: "Albert Thorn found guilty of executing Bradley Lyons in shallow bush grave after vigilantes tortured him". *ABC News*, Melbourne, 17 June 2023. https://www. abc.net.au/news/2023-06-17/albert-thorn-guilty-of-bradley-lyons-murder-lakes-entrance/102426248

ideal. He also wants a climate that is cooler than Townsville's. He is tired of the hot sweaty humid tropics.

Keith is especially depressed because he sees that his life seems to have gone nowhere. He wants to retreat into reclusive isolation. He would like to find a little house isolated from people but not too far from civilisation. Preferably, it should be surrounded in natural bush.

As he travels further south he feels he has had enough of the heat and congestion of life in the growing city of Townsville. Inland from Mackay he spends several days at the Eungella National Park which is up to about 1,300 metres above sea level. He loves the cool climate but at the moment there is nothing suitable for sale. He continues even further south past the town of Graniteville, a town in a valley among gorgeous granite boulder outcrops and in the middle of a fruit and wine growing region not far from from the NSW border.

Then, he finds an isolated little house only about twenty kilometres south of Graniteville. He buys this very secluded modern little house on 40 hectares almost covered in dense bush, wonderful granite boulders, and rising up to hills behind. It is just over 1,000 metres above sea level. His research tells him it snows here in winter at least every two years or so. Nevertheless, usually by mid afternoon all trace of snow has gone. Lovely!

Keith's secluded house at the end of the long driveway.

Granite rocks at the back of the house.

He loves it. And, it is so secluded and isolated. Nobody will know who lives here.

There is no electricity connection with the main national grid. So, the house is self-sufficient with many solar panels and battery storage or what is called "off-grid". For cooking, there is bottled gas. His water supply comes from water tanks which collect rain water from the roof. Nevertheless, he has to be careful with water as sometimes it might not rain for a couple of months.

The house is about two kilometres from the little settlement of Kinross along a minor road to the east. At the village there are a shop, post office, petrol station, chemist shop, and a small state primary school. It is surrounded by several vineyards and wineries. Once a day a bus passes by on its way north to Toowoomba. This little village is about 20 kilometres by road north of the border with New South Wales. On a clear day, Keith can even see NSW from his front verandah. From the road there is a long steep driveway up to this hidden house which he now jogs up and down each morning. He also maintains his fitness with some rock climbing.

Nevertheless, being only two kilometres from Kinross there is a broadband connection by line of sight to a tower at the village. So, he is able to continue occasional e-mail contact with his friend Fiona in Yarrabah. Their messaging is good for him in his isolation.

Aware of the loneliness which comes from isolation, he buys some Rhode Island Red chickens and four Guinea Fowls to keep free range. The chooks and guinea fowls become central to his life. He corrals them at night to protect them from foxes. Whenever he returns home, the chooks run out to greet him. He thinks it is charming. And, he has names for each of them.

His little house, isolated and secluded in the bush yet still handy by car to basic amenities, is just what he was looking for. He feels he is happy. Or, perhaps he feels he should be. Yet, despite his poultry, he is still feeling lonely. Thus, his depression is not improved but made worse by his isolation from other people. The chooks don't really help. He knows this. One day, he finds himself talking to them: "My chooks, I love you, respect you, and care for you. But, you are just chooks. I'm a human. We are different."

Keith is now especially cautious and suspicious of the Police. In fact, he knows he is lucky he didn't suffer the way Bill Spedding did after the disappearance of three-year-old

William Tyrrell in 2014. Bill Spedding was a totally innocent man who was questioned aggressively and spent more than 50 days on remand because Police had a mere suspicion that he was involved in the boy's disappearance.[62] He was also pilloried and abused publicly. News outlets across the country reflected this. Some *Facebook* comments were just awful, for example: "Now castrate, then hang the grub."

---

[62] "Person of Interest: Four Corners", *ABC TV News*, Sydney, 04 November 2019. https://www.abc.net.au/4corners/person-of-interest/11670066 This is about Bill Spedding's ordeal as a naïve and totally innocent man. He sued the NSW Police for false imprisonment. In 2022 a Court ordered compensation of $1.5 million. https://7news.com.au/news/crime/former-suspect-in-william-tyrrell-case-bill-spedding-wins-15-million-after-suing-nsw-Police-c-9024413

CHAPTER 4

Bolivia Hill

After four years living alone at his gorgeous little house and now 74, Keith decides that he needs a break from his lovely secluded environment. He can't go on living in isolation. The company of chooks is not enough. So, he goes away on a camping trip in his Volkswagen campervan. He hasn't been camping for ages. He erects an electric fenced off area for the chooks. He is able to get the kind elderly neighbours to check up on his chooks every day. The also have chooks.

As it is early November and with warmer summer approaching, he decides to travel to cooler parts for a short break. He drives to the national parks of the New England Tablelands. He loves the forest there. And, at over 1,200 metres, he is assured of cooler nights in the Cathedral Rock National Park.

Although very pleasant and interesting at this National Park, it's further isolation. Still not the best for him. There are some other campers who are also enjoying the peace and the bush. He meets some like-minded retired people or 'grey nomads'.[63] He even accepted an invitation to join the couple for dinner in their big Mercedes motor home. He found he enjoyed the evening. They live in Melbourne and they invited him to call in and stay when he is next down south.

He spends a further two days in the National Park enjoying the forest and creeks and doing some quite long hikes all by himself.

---

[63] "Grey nomads": in Australia, these are retired people who travel independently and for an extended period within Australia, particularly in a caravan or motor home. They have invested some of their superannuation in an expensive motor home or caravan and enjoy their twilight years "spending their children's inheritance".

Then, he is on his way home north towards Queensland along the New England Highway. He left fairly late and he is driving through the night. The weather is calm and the sky is clear. He is feeling a bit sleepy. So, sensibly, at about 11:00 p.m. he stops for the night at a roadside clearing in wild bush on the southern slopes of Bolivia Hill some 40 km south of Tenterfield. It isn't a proper designated rest area and the turn-off track to it was hard to see. He only noticed it as he passed. He had to stop and do a u-turn to go back to it. It's a clearing used in the past by Main Roads Department maintenance workers to stockpile road metal aggregate, gravel, and quarried blue metal. Though, sometimes passing motorists have also occasionally stopped here and some have left rubbish: old tyres, coke and booze cans, nappies, fast food containers, and other rather horrible human detritus. There is grass and some trees between this Main Roads Department stockpile area and the highway. So, it is fairly secluded. He keeps the windows closed but pops up the campervan's roof for ventilation, makes up the bed, and settles down to sleep.

At around 3:00 a.m., he wakes up needing a toilet trip. It's a cool and calm windless night outside. The jet-black sky and clear bright stars are awesome. He snuggles back into bed.

Then, he thinks he can hear a cat fight. "Bloody feral cats!" He covers his head with a blanket to try to keep out the distant noise of the cats. The cat fight noise dies down.

He is alone and feels at peace, the only human for miles around.

At least, he thinks he is alone.

He isn't worried. He has camped alone at the roadside and in the bush many times before. However, he could not have predicted what was about to happen next.

As dawn approaches, he hears the not too distant howling of a dingo.

Keith loves the wild.

He gets up out of bed. All is serene and calm and the early morning is nice and cool. The soft light of dawn is beautiful, even though the air is crisp and cool.

He takes his 12volt electric car kettle out of a cupboard, fills it from the campervan's sink tap, and boils some water for a cup of coffee.

While it is coming to the boil, he gets out of the campervan and looks around at the site he had chosen to camp at in the dark.

"It's a nice spot. And, it's off the highway. I was lucky."

The sun hasn't yet risen. He takes out his iPhone and takes a photo of the clearing and his campervan in this soft early morning light. Then, he looks at the photo he has just taken. He is pleased. It's not spectacular but it's a pretty photo.

On the left is the photo he takes at sunrise. Later, after he has downloaded his iPhone photos onto his computer at home, he clicks on the little marker at the top right corner. It shows the iPhone has recorded exactly where and when the photo was taken: **Bolivia Hill, 16 November 2018 at 5:36:28 am**. This iPhone facility is important in the story.

He returns to his campervan for his cup of coffee. He takes his time and watches the crows in the distance some 30 metres ahead from where he is parked. On the ground and in low bushes, they are making lots of "arr … arr … arr … arr" noises, their aggressive call. They must be arguing over something.[64] Nearly two hours later, when he has finished his breakfast, brushed his teeth, and listened to the radio, he is sitting in the driver's seat ready to drive off. The sun is beginning to warm up the place. Mildly interested in animal behaviour, he is curious about the crows. They've been making a fuss for a longer time than he would expect. So, he decides to investigate. He gets out of the car. Perhaps, there's a roadkill kangaroo carcass.

---

[64] To hear a recording of this aggressive Crow call, see: 'Torresian Crow' in *"Bird Calls/Torresian Crow* at https://www.graemechapman.com.au/library/sounds.php?c=85&p=15 On the right, click on "692 Strong Advertisement".

This is what Keith sees from his car. He gets out and walks towards the entrance to the clearing. The clearing has not been used recently by Main Roads Department trucks or heavy road making equipment. He can just see a plastic Coles re-usable grocery shopping bag next to the bushes.

Crows are making a lot of noise near it. A car zooms past. As he approaches, the crows take off. He looks at the area of grass, bushes, and trees between the clearing and the main road. This is where the crows' interest is. There's the usual human rubbish: Coke cans, a beer bottle, a Coles plastic grocery bag, an old used baby's nappy, McDonalds chip packets, and a worn out car tyre. He feels disgusted. "How can people be so horrible about this pristine environment!"

He turns to the Coles plastic shopping bag which has also been dumped there. He wonders: "Is this what the crows are interested in? Perhaps, there is rotting food in it? Do they think I'm about to rob them of their breakfast."

(*Above*) Now closer to the source of the crows' interest, he sees some usual roadside rubbish in the grass: cigarette butts, an empty beer can, empty drink bottles, and KFC packets. He is disgusted. And, there is that Coles re-usable plastic grocery bag which seems to have something in it. Is it rotting food?

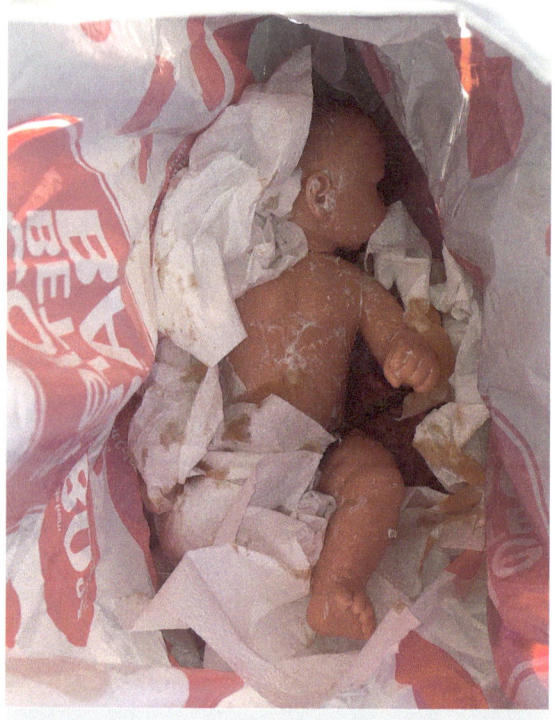

(*Right*) He picks up two short sticks and uses them to gingerly prise open the top of the Coles grocery bag.[65]

He looks inside the bag.

He is stunned and recoils in horror. It's a distressing sight.

No wonder the crows were making a fuss.

He photographs its contents.

Inside the bag is what appears to be a dead human baby.

There is still drying vernix on it. So, he reasons that it must be a fairly recent birth.

He looks closer. He can just see part of a placenta next to and under the baby. And, he can see part of an umbilical cord. The scene in the bag is messy with paper tissues and some blood.

---

[65] As this is a story of fiction but aiming to be as realistic as possible, the photo of the baby inside a Coles re-usable plastic grocery bag is actually a doll. It has been made up to look like a new born baby which still has now drying vernix on it. Part of the placenta can be seen at the lower right (actually hamburger mince from the butcher's) and the small section of umbilical cord seen near the baby's hip is a short length of nylon rope. Moreover, the baby in this story is thinner than this doll would suggest.

He looks at the photo he has just taken. It is gruesome and quite tragic.

His phone also records the time and place of the photo: **Bolivia Hill, 16 November 2018 at 8:15:23 am**.

He decides to do the right thing and phone the Police on '000'. He'll report that he has found a dead baby. But, that is when he notices the message at the top left corner of his phone's screen: '**NO SERVICE**'. The time is **8:16 am**.

"Oh, bugger! I'm outside the mobile phone coverage area. I can't phone them from here."

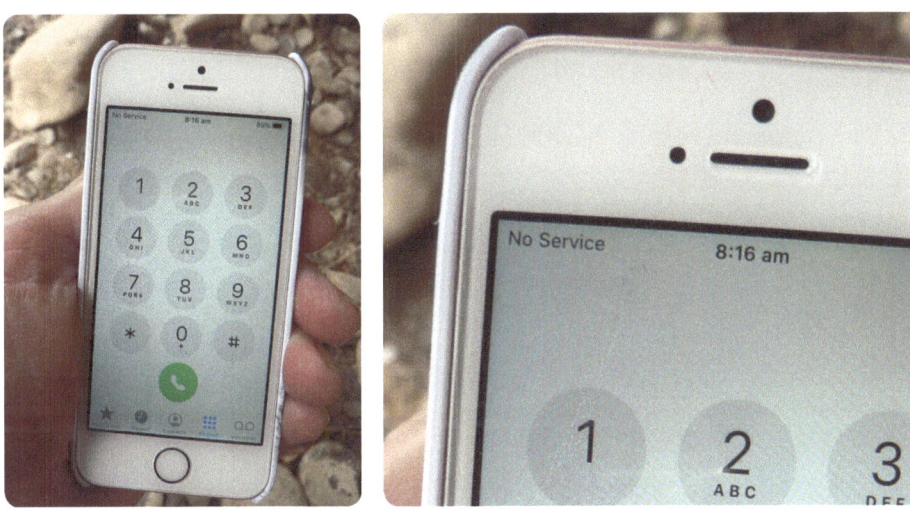

So, he doesn't dial '000'.[66] He believes he can't. He puts his iPhone back into its pouch at his belt and decides to go back to his car and drive further along the highway up to the

---

[66] Mobile phone coverage with Telstra, at present (2024) the best coverage in Australia, is G4 in cities and towns and in some areas G5. In more distant rural areas coverage in 2018 was by G3 (phased out in 2024) which was widespread and good but does not have the speed of G4. Yet, there are still areas not even covered by G3 which is what Bolivia Hill was like at the time this story is set in. On the edge of a G3 coverage area, coverage deteriorated to "SOS Only". Outside that coverage area, the phone tells you "NO SERVICE". If you try dialling a number, the phone is silent. This part of the story was set in 2018 and coverage in the Bolivia Hill area has since been improved to G4.

Note also that even when in a "NO SERVICE" area, an iPhone still knows where it is and, when you take photos, those photos are still able to indicate and record exactly where and when each photo was taken. The iPhone camera is not dependent on mobile phone coverage like the service provided by Telstra or any other phone service. It independently uses the GPS or the space satellite based Global Positioning System. (Thus, Keith's iPhone has recorded the exact time and place where the photo of the dead baby in the plastic grocery bag was taken: **Bolivia Hill Nature Reserve, New England Highway 16 November 8:15:23 am** which is about a minute before he tried phoning the Police at 8:16 am.)

highest point of Bolivia Hill and phone '000' from there. He'll meet the Police and bring them down the hill to show them this dead baby.

(*Left*) The Main Roads Department stockpile site where this baby was born.
(*Right*) Blood and amniotic fluid still soaking on the ground next to the bag. This is proof that the baby was born at the Department of Main Roads stockpile site number ST50079.

Upset, he realises that the oil patch on the ground next to the plastic bag must be amniotic fluid and some blood, not oil. He photographs it.

He walks back to the car and gets in.

Deep in thought, he is still feeling upset and very sad about this baby. "How could they do this? Even to a dead baby! Just abandoned! Dumped in the bush with rubbish?!! Why?"

Then, about to start the engine, he looks up through the car's windscreen. He sees that a dingo has walked right up to about two metres from where the dead baby is still in that bag. It has stopped and and is sniffing the air.[67]

---

[67] There are pure dingoes in this area. The author has seen one in the Bolivia Hill Nature Reserve near the old railway line and also photographed a fresh dingo carcass at the side of the New England Highway. See also the distribution map in the *Australian Museum* article in the next footnote.

Keith looks through the windscreen before driving off to phone the Police. He notices a well camouflaged dingo close to the grocery bag and it's sniffing the air. It doesn't seem to be worried by occasional passing cars.

He turns off the ignition, jumps out of the car, and runs full tilt at the dingo, shouting: "Whaaah! Whaaaah!"

As he runs, he grabs an old bit of tree branch lying on the ground and hurls it with all his might at the dingo. It hits the animal. It yelps and backs off but only a little. After all, this human is preventing him having his breakfast.

Keith picks up another longer and heavier dead tree branch and, holding it, he continues to shout and walk slowly and aggressively in a slightly crouching and menacing stance towards the animal.[68] This is bluff but it works. The dingo backs off into some nearby grass. It sits down a short distance away and watches him.

---

[68] This was risky behaviour by Keith. Dingoes are usually solitary creatures but sometimes operate in packs. If there were other dingoes nearby, Keith's threatening stance might have emboldened the dingo if it knew that it had back-up. Fortunately, this dingo was alone but Keith didn't know that. See: "Dingo attack", *Wikipedia*, https://en.wikipedia.org/ wiki/Dingo_attack Also, Sue Burrell, "Dingo", *Australian Museum*, 19 March 2019. https://australianmuseum.net.au/ learn/animals/mammals/dingo/

The dingo sits in the grass and watches Keith. (*iStockphoto*)

Standing between the dingo in the grass and the baby in the bag, Keith is protective of this dead baby. He thinks: 'Even though it's a dead baby, that bloody dingo is not going to have it!'

Of course, Keith is well aware of what happened to baby Azaria Chamberlain and this crosses his mind. And, she was not dead when taken by a dingo.[69]

He photographs the dingo sitting in the grass just metres from the dead baby.

(His iPhone records details of the time and place this photo of the dingo was taken: **8:25:42 a.m. 16 November at Bolivia Hill**. So, he has a record of the dingo's presence and silently waiting for a chance to take the dead baby.)

He is now even more upset, especially because of what the dingo's intentions were.

"Still-born or alive, how could anyone do this?!!! Where's the dignity in being dumped with rubbish?!! Why? And, left to be a dingo's breakfast! … Well dingo, you're not having this baby for breakfast, even though it's already dead."

He turns and has another look at the baby inside that plastic bag.

He is feeling sad and a bit peeved: "If it was still-born or if it was born alive and died, how could anyone do this?!!! This was once a life to be respected. Where's the dignity in being dumped in the bush like all this other rubbish?!! And, in a grocery bag, too! A dead baby is not rubbish!"

Then, he realises that if he drives up to the top of Bolivia Hill in order to phone the Police, that dingo will take the dead baby while he is away. He is in a quandary. "What should I do.? … Okay, I'll put the dead baby still in the bag into my car. I have a photo of where I found it before moving it. And, I have a photo of the hungry dingo. They are proof of the situation. Yes, I won't leave the dead baby here."

Before picking up the bag with the baby in it, he looks more closely inside it.

---

[69] Most Australians will know of the case of two-month-old baby Azaria Chamberlain who is understood to have been dragged from the family's tent and eaten by a dingo at Uluru (Ayers Rock) in 1980. Cunneen, C., "Chamberlain, Azaria Chantel (1980-1980)". *Australian Dictionary of Biography*, Vol. 13, 1993, Melbourne University Publishing. http://adb.anu.edu.au/biography/chamberlain-azaria-chantel-9719

He thinks: 'It's such a sad sight. All alone and dumped in the bush!'

Upset, his eyes well up with tears, clouding his vision.

He says aloud: "Oh, you poor little thing."

Suddenly, he freezes. He thinks he may have seen an arm move! 'Did it move?'

He takes out his handkerchief and wipes his eyes to see better.

'Am I just seeing things? Is it just my imagination?'

The arm moves again.

'Hell! It's alive! Oh my God! Shall I pick it up? Do something! You can't leave it like this … in the bush. It'll be eaten! Dingo's breakfast! It'll die. Pick it up! Help it! Now! Get yourself together! Come on! That dingo is waiting! Imagine being eaten alive. This baby may be newborn but it's still a living sentient being! Come on!'

Ignoring the dingo, he picks up the plastic bag and carries it over to his campervan and puts it on the floor in the back. He carefully lifts the baby and placenta out. He puts them onto a clean towel on the floor. The baby is a girl. She is quite messy with drying vernix[70] still all over her. As well as bloody paper tissues, there is also some other material under the baby in the plastic grocery bag. It looks like a pair of woman's underpants. But, they are messy with blood and amniotic fluid. He leaves them in the plastic bag.[71]

'Now, what must I do? Yes, the umbilical cord. It's not pulsating. It's dark in colour and a bit shrivelled. It doesn't look like the cords I saw when my daughters were born all those years ago. They were sort of full and almost pulsating.' Taking a vegetable knife and

---

[70] *Vernix caseosa* is a white, creamy, naturally occurring biofilm covering the skin of the fetus during the last trimester of pregnancy. Vernix coating on the neonatal skin protects the newborn skin and facilitates extra-uterine adaptation of skin in the first postnatal week if not washed away after birth.

[71] A *Google* search of "Abandoned baby found" will find dozens of examples of abandoned newborns. Here are just a few more recent examples from across the world:
https://www.timesofisrael.com/newborn-baby-found-abandoned-in-cardboard-box-on-acre-street/
https://www.theguardian.com/us-news/video/2019/jun/26/georgia-newborn-baby-found-alive-plastic-bag-video
https://www.mirror.co.uk/news/uk-news/body-tiny-baby-found-bin-22806177
https://www.wvlt.tv/content/news/Newborn-found-alive-abandoned-inside-plastic-bag-569120461.html
https://www.dailytelegraph.com.au/she-was-crying-on-my-doorstep/news-story/93e6479f78951b30174a1e5afdc6aa78
https://thenewdaily.com.au/news/2023/04/22/newborn-baby-abandoned-sydney/?
Other places where babies have been found abandoned include dumpster bins, public toilets, buried alive in a shallow grave, drains, including one found alive in a sewer pipe after being flushed away in a toilet.

a clothes peg out of a draw, he clamps the cord close to the tummy and cuts it. It is tough and not easy to cut. But, he succeeds. There is no flow of blood, probably because the cord has been inactive for a while.

Keith puts the placenta and cord back into the plastic bag on top of the panties and tissues. But, he has noticed that the placenta seems to have been torn or to his untrained eye that's what it looks like. It doesn't look whole or complete. He remembers when his daughters were born, a nurse put the placenta on a tray and picked it over to make sure it was complete and nothing was left behind inside the mother. But, he doesn't think more of this at the moment.

Leaving the peg in place, he picks up the baby. He sits down on the back seat and lies her on his lap. Remembering when his second daughter was born, her mother had trouble with some of the afterbirth or placenta not coming out. So, the baby was given to him to cuddle while the doctor attended to Mum. He just loved that moment, the first person ever to cuddle her.

On Keith's lap. She is partly wrapped in a towel and with vernix still on her. (*Dreamstime* photo.)[72]

Now, he looks at this baby: helpless, vulnerable, naked, and lying on the towel on his lap.

She is quiet. Even though her face is screwed up, she is so tiny and fine featured. Her dark eyes look up at him. He looks back at her.

'But, why's she not crying? I reckon she's exhausted. Yes, I think she doesn't have the capacity to cry, now. I reckon that cat fight I heard in the middle of the night was her crying. She must be drained, running on empty. I reckon she's nearly cactus.' Then, he looks into her open eyes. 'Oh God, I hope I've got you in time.' She is quiet. This worries him. But, despite her screwed up little face, he thinks she is so exquisitely beautiful.

---

[72] This photo is of a real newborn baby, not a doll. The baby is used here as a model for the story.

Mother Nature is pulling on his heart strings. It's a natural survival technique by a baby.

For a minute or two, he sits there just admiring her. Yet, she is looking at him.

He thinks: 'Newborn babies are often screwed up and ugly looking. But, this one is actually quite sweet.'

Then, he says to himself. 'Don't just sit looking at her. Sort her out! Warm her up.'

He feels her tiny little cold legs and arms.

'Oh, your limbs are cold! It was a cool night last night.'

He thinks: 'Her body's only a little warmer.'

Now, he does something he believes is very important.

He remembers that he and his ex-wife used to discuss Kangaroo Mother Care (KMC) as practiced in South Africa.[73] She was involved with a breastfeeding group and so he is well aware of the importance of skin to skin contact for all newborns, not just pre-term babies. And, he has been the father of previous babies.

He undoes his jacket zip, undoes his shirt buttons and opens out his shirt. He lifts her off the towel all naked and covered in vernix. He holds her close right up against his bare chest. He closes up his shirt and jacket around her. He wraps his arms around her. She is cold.

Now, he also wraps that towel around her to try and make her more snug and warm.

He can feel her rapid heart beat against his chest.

'It's been a cold cloudless inland night and you've been exposed with hardly any cover all night long. No wonder you're cold. No wonder you're worn out. You were probably crying well into the night. Now, tired out, you can't cry any more. You've been here since before I arrived last night. Oh dear, I'm so sorry, little one. I thought your crying was a feral cat fight. I should have investigated. I would never have expected to find a newborn baby all alone out here.'

As she is nuzzling up to his chest, he is stunned by her instinctive reaction. Her tiny cold but clammy little hands cling to his chest hairs. It's sore for him as she holds tightly

---

[73] Nils Bergman, 'Fathers and skin to skin contact'. *Kangaroo Mother Care*, Cape Town, 2018. https://kangaroomothercare.com/about-kmc/fathers-and-skin-to-skin-contact/

Ruiz-Palaez, J.G., "Kangaroo Mother Care, an example to follow from developing countries", *British Medical Journal*, 11 November 2004. 2004;329:1179 https://www.bmj.com/rapid-response/2011/10/30/kangaroo-mother-care-importance-skin-skin-contact

onto them. He doesn't flinch. She doesn't relax her fingers. 'Oh my God. She wants me and won't let go.'

He tenderly strokes her mucky head still with vernix on it.

Then, he recalls that her head needs warming, too. They put beanies on newborn babies. So, he completely encloses her, pulling up that towel to cover her some more with just a small gap for her to breathe.

He holds her like this for ages. He becomes all emotional. It's magic: cuddling a brand new baby who is snuggling into his chest. Smitten, he is bowled over by her and overcome with feelings of love.[74] He starts humming Brahms' *Lullaby* and slowly rocks this baby from side to side.[75] [76]

---

[74] See: "Oxytocin" in *Wikipedia* at https://en.wikipedia.org/wiki/Oxytocin Oxytocin is a peptide hormone which plays a vital rôle in bonding in the period after childbirth.

Typically, recent research has shown that high levels of oxytocin produced at the postpartum period were related to a clearly defined set of maternal bonding behaviors, including gaze, vocalizations, positive affect, and affectionate touch.". Feldman, R., et alia. "Evidence for a neuroendocrinological foundation of human affiliation: plasma oxytocin levels across pregnancy and the postpartum period predict mother-infant bonding". *Psychological Science*, 18(11), November 2007, pages 965-970.

Ruth Feldman, Leckman, J., Orna, Z., & Gordon, I. 'Prolactin, Oxytocin, and the development of paternal behavior across the first six months of fatherhood'. *Hormones and Behavior*, August 2010, 58(3), pages 513-518. "The neuropeptides Prolactin (PRL) and Oxytocin (OT) in processes of maternal bonding have similarly been shown to play a rôle in the neurophysiology of fatherhood." https://www.sciencedirect.com/science/article/abs/pii/S0018506X10000991?via%3Dihub.

Thus, Keith's immediate attachment to this foundling is not conjecture. And, for this baby, he is the first caring human contact. Their combined oxytocin levels are already creating a maternal/infant bond between them. As the next few days pass, the bond is strengthened.

[75] These days in maternity birthing rooms, as soon as the umbilical cord is clamped and cut, the midwife places the newborn baby on the birth mother's chest. This stimulates bonding for both mother and baby and is done before the newborn is cleaned up. Keith doesn't quite realise it but this is what is happening to him. The baby is instinctively bonding with her mother who just happens to be an old man and the first human contact she has had.

This practice of placing a newborn on its mother's chest immediately after birth is likely derived from what is commonly known as 'attachment theory' which was promoted by John Bowlby shortly after World War 2 in his *Maternal Care and Mental Health*, commissioned by the World Health Organisation and published in 1951. His main conclusion was that "the infant and young child should experience a warm, intimate, and continuous relationship with his mother (or permanent mother substitute) in which both find satisfaction and enjoyment" and, without that, the infant may have significant and irreversible mental health consequences. Keith studied and read Bowlby's *Maternal Care* at Armidale University during his graduate diploma of education course. So, quite apart from pheromones, oxytocins, and the like, his reaction to this newborn foundling is also subconsciously influenced by Bowlby.

[76] For a lovely rendition, Johannes Brahms - Op.49 No.4 Wiegenlied / Lullaby (original composition) https://www.youtube.com/watch?v=t894eGoymio

Mother Nature is really getting to him.

After a while, he moves the towel away from her face for just a little look. She looks up at him. 'Oh God, she's adorable! How could somebody abandon her?'[77]

He covers her up again. As she snuggles more up to his chest, he feels her slowly warming up with heat from his body. This lasts for ages.

He realises she is capturing him. 'After being left alone in the bush for so long, she has finally found somebody. And, afraid of more aloneness won't let go of me.'

He uncovers her face again and looks into her eyes once more. She stares back at him. He is besotted.

He wonders what to do next for her. 'Feeding a newborn isn't urgent. I arrived here at about 11:00 p.m. last night. She was already here. So, she must be at least nine or ten hours old.'[78]

He undoes the towel a little more again and touching his finger on her lips, he checks her 'rooting reflex'. She doesn't immediately try to suckle. 'Maybe it's because she's so tired.' He tickles her lips more. She tries to suckle but it's not strong. He places his little finger in her palm and her hand closes up on it. He can't see anything abnormal about her, though

---

[77] Patty, A., "Newborn in drain: How a baby can survive for six days without food or water". *Sydney Morning Herald*, 24 November 2014. https://www.smh.com.au/national/nsw/newborn-in-drain-how-a-baby-can-survive-for-six-days-without-food-or-water-20141124-11sg2a.html

This baby was born in a hospital but dumped in the drain when a day old. Kembrey, M., "Sydney mother jailed for leaving baby in Quakers Hill drain". *Sydney Morning Herald,* 21 July 2016. https://www.smh.com.au/national/nsw/ sydney-mother-jailed-for-leaving-baby-in-quakers-hill-drain-20160721-gqaa64.html The mother was originally charged with attempted murder but this was later reduced to a lesser charge of "abandoning a child under seven causing it to be in danger of death and recklessly cause grievous bodily harm". She was given a sentence of three years and six months with the possibility of parole after 21 months. The baby was placed in foster care.

So, if the mother of Keith's baby is found, there could be very serious consequences for her and the baby. As her baby was abandoned in New South Wales, it is very likely that she and her baby would have faced similar consequences: jail for the Mum and foster care for the baby with the possibility of forced adoption after just two years. Lu, A., "NSW Government's adoption law changes to create a two-year deadline for re-homing". *ABC News*, Sydney, 25 October 2018, https://www.abc.net.au/news/2018-10-24/ nsw-government-adoption-law-overhaul-proposed/10422140

[78] Keith doesn't know how long this baby has been alone in that plastic grocery bag. He arrived at 11:00 p.m.. Abandoned newborns have lasted for a long time especially in warmer climates. But, a factor not in this baby's favour was the cool cloudless night and 1,200 metre altitude. However, she was partially sheltered in that plastic bag.

she is tiny and skinny. He can't see any hernia, no *hydrocephalus or* swollen head and no cleft palate. He knows what *spina bifida* usually looks like.[79] She doesn't look jaundiced and doesn't have a flat face and other typical Down syndrome features. 'From what I've seen, she's a thoroughly normal little baby, quite small and skinny but seems to be all okay. Though, I'm not an expert.'

He asks her: "Where is your Mum, little one? … Do you know who she is? … Why were you dumped here? … What was her trouble? … I don't suppose you know."

He admires her fine features and cute screwed-up little face. Holding her close again, he looks down at her. "Oh, you're just beautiful!" He covers her up again.

Again, he wonders what to do with her. 'Take her to Tenterfield Hospital? It's half an hour away. They'll know what to do. … But, she'll go into foster care! No way! A succession of paid foster carers. And, abuse by carers. I've taught dysfunctional foster care kids … and that poor kid who accused me of raping her, she was quite dysfunctional. … But then, I don't really know what I'm letting myself in for. Could I cope? … Okay, it might be best if I hand her over.'

Cuddling and sorting her lasts more than two hours. He loves it. Some would say this is purely a biological response.

Anyway, he is overcome by the intimacy.

It is now 9:30 a.m. and, with his car in the sun, he puts his baby all wrapped up on the floor and moves the car to some shady trees.

After well over another hour, more cuddling, and wondering what to do with her, he decides to leave. He wraps her well in those towels and puts her securely on the floor in front of the passenger seat. Without a proper baby seat, the floor is the safest place.

Finally, it's about 11:00 when he sets out for Tenterfield. He'll hand her over at the hospital.

On arrival at Tenterfield, he drives through the town and up Naas Street to the Tenterfield District Hospital. He parks in the car park at the Emergency section at the back near where ambulances arrive. He picks up this little baby. He unwraps her and holds her on his lap.

'Oh, she's a darling.'

---

79   https://en.wikipedia.org/wiki/Spina_bifida

He cuddles her more. "I'll have to say good bye to you now, my dear."

Even though he has known this baby for only a few hours, he is crying. He puts a CD on which plays an old favourite of his.[80] He tells her: "Little one, it breaks my heart to leave you. I'm so sorry." He is crying so much that he has to eject the CD.

Then he thinks: 'No! No! I'll not abandon her to bureaucracy. I'll care for her. I owe that to her. I found her. … Actually, she's found me. … Perhaps, it's as if she was sent to me. … Yes, I'll keep her! … I'll drive home with her. … But, first, I'll drive into town for provisions.'

Then, still holding her, he makes a list of things to buy: towelling nappies (he and his wife were against disposables), Napisan, safety pins, bottles, teats, Milton sterilising tablets, a baby car seat, and Newborn milk powder. He knows that human breast milk is by far the best for her but he can't produce it and what hospital is going to supply him with stored human breast milk? He just has to compromise.[81]

Thinking of milk, he checks her tongue. It's normal. No sign of being tongue tied.[82]

He wraps her up again. He washes his hands and puts on a clean shirt.

Then, after climbing into the front of the car and driving off, he thinks of some of the kids he taught who had been "in care" as they say. Many were quite dysfunctional and drifted from one foster home to another. Some were physically and sexually abused. 'So, no way! I can love her just as much as paid foster carers.'

He stops wavering and decides to drive home with her.

He remembers a teacher at Fulham State High told him he was born premature in the 1950s on a rural property out west, was fed on milk from one of the farm goats and survived well. If he could find some newborn human baby formula milk powder made from goat's milk he'd buy some. It should minimise any reflux problems with cows milk formula.

---

80 "The carnival is Over". *The Seekers*. https://www.youtube.com/watch?v=z4ZipKdI1sY

81 The author's youngest daughter has had two full-term babies. Both were fed formula milk right from the start. Despite the adage that "breast is best" and convinced of it, the author has been surprised that they survived well and are now healthy active children without problems.

82 See Mayo Clinic at: https://www.mayoclinic.org/diseases-conditions/tongue-tie/symptoms-causes/syc-20378452

As he drives, he thinks about where he found her: 'If Main Roads Department workers were to make use of the old gravel at this clearing today, it is more than likely they would have been here around the start of work at 7:00 a.m. But, I don't think they would have used some of that gravel. Those gravel heaps and crushed blue metal piles haven't been used for a long time. And, with the grass coverage at the entrance to the cleared area, I don't think Main Roads Department trucks have been there for at least six months or so. There were weeds growing on some gravel heaps. When I left, no workers had come. And, no other tourists or passers-by have driven into that clearing. So, if I had not found this baby when I did and had simply driven on, nobody would have found her by the time I left at around 10:30. She was in that grocery bag with diminishing shade. In this November weather, the sun would have started cooking her by lunch time, that is if the dingo hadn't eaten her. I think she is lucky. I'm also lucky I found her: one man's trash is another's treasure.'[83]

At the shops in Tenterfield, he undoes his shirt buttons and puts her inside his shirt again, held in place with the towel wrapped around both her and him and tucked in on itself. It's Kangaroo Mother Care style with that all-important skin to skin contact. He does up his shirt buttons and jacket zip. He looks like a man with a beer-belly.

He throws away the placenta, umbilical cord, and the woman's pants which he left in that Coles plastic grocery bag. There is a commercial dumpster at the end of the carpark.

In the Coles supermarket at the shopping centre he can't find towelling nappies. He tries at the Target Country shop next door. Couldn't find any there either. They must have gone out of out of fashion. So, he buys tiny 'newborn' size disposable nappies for the journey. Maybe he'll find towelling nappies later on in Graniteville. He buys a pair of tiny dolly size singlets. He buys her a little beanie and two pairs of full length 00000 size onesies, the smallest ones you can get. Next, back in Coles, he looks at tins of Newborn formula. On the label of one it stresses the need for vitamins, especially vitamin K. Yes, he remembers one daughter having an intra-muscular vitamin K injection at birth. And, he was told why

---

[83] An early foundling story is the Old Testament account of Moses in the bulrushes. In *Exodus*, the abandoned baby Moses is found among the bulrushes on the banks of the River Nile by the Egyptian Pharaoh's daughter who brings him up as her own.

it was so important: because of the danger of haemorrhaging during the first several days after birth. Vitamin K is vital in clotting and is not in breast milk. He wonders whether the vitamin K in the formula milk is enough. Then, he finds some goat's milk formula and it's for newborns and it has that vitamin K. 'Yippee! Just what I want. It's *Karicare* Goat Newborn 1, although at $40 for a 900g tin, it's nearly double the price of some regular tins of cow's milk formula.

Pleased, he buys a tin.

He thinks: 'At least she'll get some Vitamin K from the formula milk. I hope it's enough.'

Apart from towelling nappies, he feels has bought everything he needs, including bottles, Milton, teats, and wipes. He takes his loot back to the car.

He returns to Target and buys a baby car seat.

On return to the car, he fits the child seat to the front seat of the campervan. The child seat he has bought for her can be used forward facing seat for 0 to 4 years old. There are no seat belts in the back.

He drives off with his new baby safely strapped in.

He stops a few kilometres along the road under a shady tree.

He climbs into the back and sterilises the bottles and teats in Milton.

As they are sterilising, he heats up some of that already boiled water in the electric jug left over from his morning cuppa. He uses that to mix up the formula milk. He doesn't let it come to the boil. It would be too hot and he'd have to wait too long for it to cool down. His campervan is very handy. While waiting for the water to heat up, he again has second thoughts: 'This is difficult. I should go back to Tenterfield and do the right thing by handing her in at the Hospital. They're better equipped with skills and knowledge. Am I being reckless with her life? They'll know what to do. No! They'll farm her out into foster care! And, if they found the Mum, she'd be facing charges and possibly jail for attempted murder or recklessly putting her baby in danger. No, we can't have that. There must be a reason for throwing away her baby. I wonder what it was? But, foster care? No way! I can love and care for her just as well as foster carers doing it for money. On the other hand, she could be

HIV positive. She could have Hepatitis. She could be deaf. She could have Down Syndrome. She doesn't look it. Although you can't always tell for sure with a baby without a blood test. She could have Foetal Alcohol Syndrome. Although I can't see the classic FAS signs like a small head, epicanthal folds, a low nasal bridge, short perky nose, a thin upper lip and a flat 'philtrum'. But again, they don't always have those characteristics. Yes, it might be best if I hand her over. I don't really know what I'm letting myself in for.'

He looks at her warm in her capsule. She seems to be looking up at him.

Again, he thinks of her : 'She is a darling … and I love her. Oh God, I'll not abandon her to bureaucracy. No, I owe it to her to care for her. It's as if she came to me or was even sent to me. It's as if I was destined to prevent crows and dingos from eating her. It's as if I was destined to remove her from danger. Oh God, this is a dilemma. … Yes, I must keep her.'

He starts making excuses for himself. 'She's tiny but looks healthy. She's survived overnight exposure to the elements and is breathing well. She can have a healthy and happy childhood with me. I've had kids before. I was a teacher, too. If she suffers a medical downturn in the next few days, I can always hand her over at the Graniteville Hospital. After all, I didn't throw her away. I'm not the guilty one.'

He lifts her out of her seat and sits on the back seat with her. He tries feeding her.

She doesn't suckle. He tries squeezing milk into her mouth from the bottle teat. Only a little goes in but much goes all over her face and on to the towel he has wrapped her in.

What can he do?

He tries something really innovative.

From his involvement with his ex-wife's research into breastfeeding, he knows that breast milk and saliva both contain *Immunoglobulin A* (IgA)[84] which is beneficial to a baby's developing immune system. He also knows that during birth as the baby passes through the birth canal, it picks up large quantities of usually beneficial microbes from the mother. And, quantities of the mother's microbes are also naturally transferred to the baby via breast milk or even just with the birth mother's intimate care like handling, kissing,

---

[84] "Immunoglobulin A", *Wikipedia*. https://en.wikipedia.org/wiki/Immunoglobulin_A

cuddling, breathing, and so on. These activities help build up the baby's immune system, thus increasing its survival.

Moreover, modern medicine accepts the inevitable transfer of such beneficial microbes to a newborn.[85] So, he reasons that some of his saliva mixed with the formula milk, should not be harmful or, perhaps, even be beneficial. He knows that this baby collected microbes from her mother during the birth process. He will now continue that natural process. In effect, he is becoming this baby's mother. However, that is not his considered intention. He didn't think of it like that. While he has some knowledge of birthing and breastfeeding because of his presence at his daughters' births and involvement with them afterwards, he has been thrown into this current situation by being presented with a newborn baby abandoned in the bush. His basic motivation is survival of this baby. This is inadvertently coupled with Mother Nature's capturing him through that natural part of maternal bonding via pheromones.[86] The oxytocins produced by both this baby and Keith started doing that before he tried to feed her. Mother Nature has already been bonding them.[87] Now, the bonding is becoming physical with the transfer of microbes.

Still holding her, he has an idea. He is cautious about it. So, he gets a cup of water, takes out his dentures, and rinses his mouth out. He opens the sliding door and spits the mouthful of water onto the ground outside. Then, he undoes the teat on the bottle, takes swig of formula milk, puts a finger in her mouth to open it, holds his lips against hers, and gently squirts milk from his mouth into her mouth.

It works! She swallows!

'God! I hope I haven't given her any infections. At least, with my dentures I don't have rotten teeth.'

Keith repeats the process four times. A little bit of milk goes in each time.

---

[85] Weule, G., "Babies receive essential microbes from their mum even when born via caesarean section." *ABC News*, Sydney, 09 March 2023. https://www.abc.net.au/news/health/2023-03-09/babies-microbiome-mothers-birth-caesarean-section/102059396?

[86] "Pheromone", *Wikipedia*. https://en.wikipedia.org/wiki/Pheromone

[87] "Oxytocin", *Wikipedia*. https://en.wikipedia.org/wiki/Oxytocin Oxytocin is a peptide hormone which plays a vital rôle in bonding in the period after childbirth.

Then, he tries the bottle again. He tickles the teat on her little lips. She opens her mouth. The teat goes in. He moves it around. She doesn't suck.

'Oh well, at least she's got something in her.'

He straps her back in the baby capsule and drives off.

After a few minutes, he stops and looks at her. She is asleep.

'Oh! How beautiful a peacefully sleeping baby is!'.

Within the hour, he is home. He takes her and the baby things inside. She wakes up and starts crying. Yes, she's hungry. She didn't get much milk. Now, with her crying, he feels under pressure. She needs more food in her new tummy. Again, he starts feeding her the formula milk directly from his mouth. After half a dozen successful squirts where she swallows, he tries the bottle again. This time, she tries to suckle but weakly. He tries putting the teat right into her mouth and squeezing it to squirt milk in. Only a tiny bit squirts in each time. He perseveres. He is elderly and patient. Eventually, she has taken in a little.

Then, all of a sudden, she starts pumping. Soon, she is pumping well.

'Yippee! Hooray! You're up and running on all four cylinders!'

After and hour or so, she passes some meconium. It's almost odourless.

He is pleased because her systems are now working.

Later in the afternoon, he baths her, getting rid of the last of that dry flakey vernix.

'Now, I have to get used to baby poo, reflux, wind and then teething. And, baby waking at night, nappy changing, feeding and demanding attention day in and day out. When she is a toddler there may be tantrums. When she is a teenager ... oh, well. ... And, there's no other parent to lend support and carry some of the load. I'm in my seventies, well past retirement age. Not the best time to start parenting. And, alone! With a newborn baby! Perhaps, I should have taken her to Tenterfield Hospital after all. Yes, I could now take her to Graniteville Hospital.'

After drying her, he weighs her using his electronic kitchen scales. She is a fraction over 1,500 grams. He looks up newborn baby weights and dimensions on the internet. 'Yes, she's under weight. It says here she should be 2,700 to 4,100 grams. But, all babies lose a bit of weight in the hours after birth. And, I reckon out there in the cool night for so long she lost a quite bit.'

He found it difficult to measure her from head to heel because of her curled-up legs. So, he measures her length from 'crown to rump'. 'Gosh! At around 28 cm she is well undersize, too. She should be 31 to 35 cm. I reckon she could be a 'premmie'.'

He picks her up off the scales and holds her close. He looks down at her. He is still besotted. In his eyes she is exquisitely beautiful. He is filled with love and tenderness: 'I can't hand her over. Not into foster care! No way! … She was not wanted. She was discarded, dumped, and thrown away like a piece of roadside rubbish! Left for crows' or a dingo's breakfast! Well, that didn't happen. She's mine, now. There's no going back. I've taken her on. I have to accept that. She's my obligation, my commitment, like a burden. Yes, she's my shiralee.' He thinks of D'Arcy Niland's famous novel about an itinerant farm worker or swagman who travels the country with his four-year-old daughter in the 1950s doing odd jobs along the way like shearing.[88] 'But, she's not going to be a burden for me. I love her already. That's not a burden. She's a different shiralee.'

He is also reminded of George Eliot's 1861 novel *Silas Marner,* a text which he studied during his first year English Literature course at University. Silas Marner, a social outcast bachelor in nineteenth century rural England, found an abandoned baby in the snow outside his little house. He took in baby "Eppie" and raised her successfully on his own. When told by villagers that he should hand baby "Eppie" over to a woman, he protested: "No! No! I can't part with it. I can't let it go. It's come to me. I've a right to keep it." [89]

So, Keith decides on the name "Eppie".

Meanwhile, he wonders about this baby's mother. He simply does not know the circumstances but that's not the issue now. Saving this baby is. I think she's been sent to me. So, it's my duty to care for her. I really love her. … But, I'll have to keep her secret. Horrible things have happened to kids in foster care. I don't want her removed by zealous

---

[88] Niland, D. (1955), *The Shiralee.* Sydney: Angus & Robertson.
Also: https://en.wikipedia.org/wiki/The_Shiralee_(1987_film) A superb *ABC TV* film of the novel.

[89] George Eliot (actually Mary Ann Evans) (1861), *Silas Marner: The Weaver of Raveloe.* This quotation is from a 1999 edition published by Wordsworth, Herts., page 99.

bureaucrats just because I'm male or too old. I can care for her. I can parent her just as well as any foster carer. I can parent her just as well as any woman. I really loved my daughters. They grew and blossomed with me around. Now, this little one is my new baby daughter.'

He makes a personal commitment to himself: 'If her life is ever threatened by illness or injury, I will risk taking her to a hospital even if it means losing her. To me, her life is paramount. That's why I took her on when I found her at Bolivia Hill. And, if her life is threatened with violence, I will defend her to the bitter end.' Little does he know that in a few years that last commitment will be put to the test. He will almost lose his own life defending her.

Five years later: An elderly Keith and little five-year-old Eppie on the bridge across the Condamine River at Canning Town.

With her cradled in his arms, he looks at her, this gorgeous tiny exquisitely formed little baby. He tells her: "Your are just beautiful. And, yes, you're my little 'Eppie'. Welcome to my world. It's our world, now." Tears are running down his face. **This has been our first day, my darling. As you grow, I'm going to hold your hand and help you along the road. I'll do my best to guide and protect you until you're grown up and ready for the world. Then you can fly away from the nest with my blessing and goodwill. That's my promise to you.**"

Mother Nature, in her primal way, has truly got to him.

CHAPTER 5

Fiona's Advice

Next evening Keith phones his friend Fiona who now lives at the Aboriginal community of Yarrabah south of Cairns and tells her what has happened. He needs advice. She is astonished but is very supportive. "The baby has survived well so far and the Department does not know of her existence. So, if you really want to parent her, keep a low profile with her. Even keep her very existence on your property secret. Living there you're away from prying eyes."

She warns him: "The Department will without a doubt remove her from you under sections 21 and 22 of the *Child Protection Act.*" She explains: "If they find out, they will remove her straight away claiming they are doing so because 'it is in her best interests'[90]. They always use that term and it is they who determine what her best interests are because they are the so-called 'experts'. Then, they'll come down on you like a tonne of bricks. They'll claim you are a single man and too old. They may even use against you the rape charges that were acquitted of."

Keith: "That's sexist! And yes, I was acquitted!"

Fiona: "Yes. But, that's the way they will see it and they have the power."

Keith: "And, it's ageism, too."

Fiona: "Yes, it is. But please be realistic, Keith. They'll also say you didn't report finding her and nor did you take her to a hospital. You put her life at risk. You denied her the necessities of life. You have not given her the appropriate care she needs. She missed out

---

[90] There is much debate and academic literature about 'the best interests of the child'. The issue probably began with the 1973 publication of Goldstein, J., Goldstein, S., Freud, A. & Solnit, A. *The Best Interests of the Child.* (1973), New York, Free Press. Two further volumes appeared later.

on the Vitamin K injection at birth as well as a range of tests given to new-borns at hospital like the little heel prick they give newborns to look for potential problems which can often be remedied if detected at birth.[91] She will also have missed out on the newborn hearing screening tests. They will determine that you have failed to protect a helpless newborn infant. You failed in your duty of care. Essentially, they will 'substantiate that you have subjected her to an unacceptable risk of suffering significant harm'. Note, please, they would have you up for the <u>risk</u> of harm which you subjected her to. For them 'risk' blends into 'harm'. And, therefore 'risk' is as good as 'harm' itself. Then, they would probably have you face criminal charges. They would have you charged under the Criminal Code Act."

She looks up the relevant section. "It's section 324 'Failure to provide necessaries'."

Keith: "I'm shocked. I've not done her any harm. Quite the opposite! I saved her life! Actually, I removed her from harm, from exposure, and from crows, and from foxes and dingos." Adding sarcastically: "Don't they know that dingos eat babies!"[92]

Fiona: "I don't think they would be concerned about that. It's what you did not do or should have done with her that will get them so off-side, especially that business of the necessities of life."

Keith: "And, as for Vitamin K, I especially bought a tin of formula milk powder already laced with Vitamin K."

Fiona: "Good. I'm glad to hear that. Well done!"

Keith smiles to himself, then facetiously adds: "And, so far I've protected her from harm likely to be caused to her by the Department of Child Safety!"

Fiona laughs. "I like that! But look, Keith, this is very serious. As I said, it is the 'risk' that you then subjected her to after rescuing her, the 'unacceptable risk of harm'. Now, you see some of the things I was up against in the Department. They lack both common sense

---

[91] "Neonatal screening test." *Health Direct*, Australian Government, Canberra. <u>https://www.</u> <u>pregnancybirthbaby.org.au/</u> <u>neonatal-screening-test</u> A midwife or nurse will perform the test by pricking the newborn baby's heel and putting a few drops of blood on a special filter paper. This blood sample is used to test for a number of conditions babies may be born with. It is not compulsory but really should be done.
[92] Dingos have been known to carry off human babies and eat them: "Death of Azaria Chamberlain". *Wikipedia.* <u>https://en.wikipedia.org/wiki/Death of Azaria Chamberlain</u>. (Just about every adult Australian knows what happened to baby Azaria Chamberlain at Ayers Rock/Uluru in 1980.)

and compassion. They are also prejudiced against all sorts of people, men, the elderly, former drug users, ex-convicts, social outcasts, the homeless, people struggling to make ends meet and so on. But, if you were a 28-year-old single mother who is wheel-chair bound with a little daughter they'd be all over you with support programmes and funding. You, like so many, are not in their sympathy categories. And, you represent a challenge to their preconceived notions of an ideal parent. You must be taken down. So, they'll drag up all sorts of reasons for their intervention, for their removal of this child, and for their prosecuting you." Then she adds: "Just remember this: there are a few shrewd and subtle Irma Grese characters in the Department.[93] Some of them are motivated by misandry because of past abuse inflicted on them by men and the pent up anger they feel.[94] You must be so careful. Engaging with the Department can be like walking through a minefield."

Of course, all this worries Keith. But, she reassures him that if he is sensible, cautious and private about her he should end up keeping her. In the meantime, he should simply lie low with her and attract as little attention as possible. Remember, failure to get her vaccinated is not depriving her of the necessities of life. Many first nations people don't get their kids vaccinated.

She reminds him that if he wants to get her vaccinated she needs a Medicare Card and to get that she needs a birth certificate. She will also need a birth certificate to go to school and by the time she is of school age she may need to have an up to date immunisation record. "So, at the moment getting a birth certificate for her is not something you should contemplate. In around five years time, yes. But, not now."

Keith is very subdued about this advice. But, he has to go and attend to Eppie who is now stirring. So, he thanks Fiona and asks if he can phone her tomorrow night. However, he decides to update his own whooping cough (pertussis) vaccination. He hasn't had a pertussis jab since 1944! He doesn't want to inadvertently give it to unvaccinated Eppie. His 'flu and COVID jabs are already up to date. Two days later a doctor in Canning Town gives it to him.

---

[93] "Irma Grese", *Wikipedia*, https://en.wikipedia.org/wiki/Irma_Grese Irma Grese was a notorious senior warden at Auschwitz, Ravensbrück, and Bergen Belsen concentration camps and known as the "Hyena of Auschwitz". Put on trial by the British army at Lüneburg, she was convicted of mass murder and hanged in 1945.
[94] An allegation once made to the author in confidence by former senior Children's Service Department officer and Anglican priest the late Rev. Illtyd Loveluck.

Next evening, it is Fiona who phones Keith. Fortunately, Eppie is asleep. She asks what he has called her. He tells her he has called her "Eppie" as in George Eliot's 1861 novel *Silas Marner*. She thinks it's a wonderful choice. "It's rare, almost unique. In the circumstances most appropriate, you know, your finding an abandoned baby."

She moves on to talk about baby Eppie. "Now, I've been thinking. You've told me she doesn't look to have spina bifida, doesn't look Down syndrome, and doesn't look Foetal Alcohol Syndrome but you don't know what other problems she might be born with. She may have been born to a heroin addict and will go through what they call "neonatal abstinence syndrome"[95], you know, withdrawal or "cold turkey". You'll find out in the next couple of days. She might have an STD, you know like chlamydia, herpes, gonorrehoea, or even syphilis. Her birth mother may have been on Methamphetamines.[96] I think you'll find out as time passes."

Coin: "Oh no! What have I let myself in for!"

Fiona: "Listen, you can do it. What you are doing with her so far is just right, couldn't be better. So, just hang in there for her sake."

A dejected Keith: "I suppose I have to."

Fiona: "Yes, please do it just for her. She really needs you. You are her mother, now. And, I mean that."

Keith: "Okay."

Fiona: "Another thing you have to accept is that this child is not a clean slate or a *tabula rasa*, you know like Rousseau's little boy 'Emile'. You know, from your teacher training."[97]

---

95 Neonatal abstinence syndrome. https://www.health.qld.gov.au/data/assets/pdf_file/0029/143579/c-psuneo-nas.pdf

96 Kennedy, E., "Babies born to meth-affected mothers seem well behaved, but their passive nature masks a serious problem". *ABC News*, Sydney. 03 January 2020. https://www.abc.net.au/news/2020-01-03/the-hidden-problem-of-babies-born-to-meth-affected-mothers/11829668

97 Rousseau, Jean-Jacques (1979) (Trans. Allan Bloom), *Emile, or On Education*. New York: Basic Books (First published in Paris in 1762.) Emile is a fictitious little boy educated away from the corruption of humankind. Rousseau wrote: "Everything is good as it leaves the hands of the Author of things; everything degenerates in the hands of man." (Page 37). Thus, a newborn baby is supposedly a clean slate ready for its parents or the world to shape and guide.

Keith: "I suppose we all now know a newborn baby is not a *tabula rasa*. So, what do you mean by this in relation to this baby?"

Fiona: "Although you have a brand new baby, there's probably many other more psychological things she has inherited from her mother or even from her father. You know, like autism, epilepsy, attention deficit disorder or ADHD, and even PTSD. Yes, even the effects of PTSD can be passed down. So, you are going to be like any other foster carer. You are going to have to manage somebody else's damaged goods. Sorry to say that to you but that's the challenge that all foster carers face to varying degrees."

Keith: "I know that but in my naïve idealism I haven't expected to face it myself."

Fiona: "Yet, in a way you are not like a foster carer. There's a difference. You can't just ring up a child safety officer and say: 'Take her away. She's too much for me to handle.' No, you're stuck with her. She's yours. She's your commitment. You're bonded, too. That's what happened to you when you found her. And, I think it is also what happened to her at that time."

Keith: "That's nice."

Fiona: "Another thing has crossed my mind: I think she was simply an urgent roadside birth.[98] Probably with no warning to go to hospital, not even earlier Braxton-Hicks contractions.[99] With her low birthweight, the birth may have been sudden and unexpected. Anyway, I have discussed your and Eppie's situation with the midwife here at Yarrabah.[100] Don't worry. I've not said anything about who you are and where you are. And, in our conversation, she thinks you are a woman. I was interested in what she says."

Keith: "Me too. Go ahead."

Fiona: "She says that newborns have been known to survive on their own for quite some time. So, the baby may have been abandoned in that old grocery bag for 24 hours or even more. The baby would have declined slowly at first but, after 24 hours, decline would

---

[98] For example: Daly, J., "Roadside baby Beatrix born next to highway", *ABC News*, Brisbane., 14 February 2022. https://www.abc.net.au/news/2022-02-14/maternity-services-shortage-chinchilla-leads-to-roadside-birth/100817374

[99] "Braxton-Hicks contractions", *Wikipedia*. https://en.wikipedia.org/wiki/Braxton_Hicks_contractions

[100] Gurriny Yealamucka Health Service Aboriginal Corporation, "Child and Maternal Health", Yarrabah, Queensland. https://www.gyhsac.org.au/child-maternal-health

have been rapid especially with a pre-term baby with minimal reserves of protective fat. When the baby was finally dead, other animals would have picked up the smell and come for a share of the carcass."

Keith: "Oh, my God! … I think she could have been in that 'after 24 hours decline'."

Fiona: "I think so. But there's more. She told me that if the mother went into labour in the car and the car had pulled over, she could have got out and the waters broke suddenly.

The midwife thinks this is probably the way Keith's baby was born at Bolivia Hill. The waters have broken, amniotic fluid is pouring out, and the baby's head is crowning. She is on her way out. The top of her head is just visible. (Courtesy *Cristiane Pereira*. Photo taken in Brazil.)

It would be natural for her to want to get out urgently. That would account for the blood and amniotic fluid on the ground next to the bag you found her in."

Keith: "Wow! That's a plausible scenario."

Fiona: "She said it was likely what they call a 'precipitous birth'. She also said pre-term births are sometimes not very active, not much crying or movement. They may have thought it was a stillbirth because of that lack of movement and no crying. So, the baby was simply dumped wherever they had been able to pull over quickly. So, I asked her about that. Yes, she said it was quite likely. And, she said everything that came out of the mother would have been discarded with the baby. So, I wondered if the mother might have then sought any medical assessment of her after the birth? She said often they don't. They just soldier on and that might especially be the case if they were travelling. If she was a teenager or Indigenous that would likely be the case. And so, the mother may have just moved on with life."

Keith: "Wow! I am stunned."

Fiona: "Me too. There was nothing else in the bag apart from the placenta?"

Keith: "Yes, there was. There were heaps of messy tissues. Underneath her, there looked like a pair of women's panties. They were soaked in amniotic fluid and probably some blood. So, I left them in the plastic grocery bag and dumped them in a dumpster at Tenterfield."

Fiona: "No other towels or clothing lying nearby?"

Keith: "No. I didn't look for anything else. I was focussed on this baby. But, I did realise what I had thought was engine oil was, in fact, amniotic fluid. So, I photographed it."

Fiona: "I think the driver pulled over into that rest area. The mother urgently got out of the car. And, out popped Eppie!"

Keith: "Maybe. I think you might be right. I even thought she was dead. You know, when I put her in my car on a towel on the floor and cut the umbilical cord, I noticed that the placenta was not complete. I've seen placentas from my own daughters when nurses checked them after the birth. I reckon there was probably less than half the placenta there."

Fiona: "That means one of two things. Either the last bit of the placenta ejected itself a little while later or the mother could have been in trouble with catastrophic bleeding or haemorrhaging and needing hospital treatment. I don't suppose we'll ever know. I hope it simply ejected itself."[101]

Keith: "I remember when my second daughter was born, after a nurse checked the palcenta, the doctor was in a bit of a panic because all the placenta didn't come out. I was given the baby to hold. The doctor put his hand right inside her. She cried out with the pain."

Fiona: "So, you understand. Anyway, there is something else which has crossed my mind and its a possibility. That is the so-called 'Cinderella syndrome'[102] where a man in a relationship with the birth mother who is not the biological father of the baby will kill the child. In this case, the man with the woman who gave birth could have forced her to abandon the baby, you know, when it was born at the rest area. It's a possibility. And, that could be a reason why the birth mother has not gone to a hospital: pressure from the man. He has dumped the offspring of his partner's previous relationship."

---

[101] See: "Placenta: how it works, what's normal." *Mayo Clinic*, USA 2024. https://www.mayoclinic.org/healthy-lifestyle/pregnancy-week-by-week/in-depth/placenta/art-20044425#:~:text=The%20placenta%20attaches%20to%20the,lying%20placenta%20(placenta%20previa)

[102] Much literature on the 'Cinderella syndrome'. See "Cinderella Effect", *Wikipedia*, https://en.wikipedia.org/wiki/Cinderella_effect . Also, Koubaridis, A., "Is the 'Cinderella effect' the reason why stepdads kill their partners' children?" news.com 30 September 2016, http://www.news.com.au/lifestyle/real-life/news-life/is-the-cinderella-effect-the-reason-why-stepdads-kill-their-partners-children/news-story/822c3dac9bf401da57f8e100f685dc00.

Keith: "That's sad."

Next day, Fiona phones Keith again. It is four days since he found Eppie. He tells her he is feeling is a little upbeat and there is no sign so far of any withdrawal symptoms or 'cold turkey'.

Fiona is very happy for him. "I think you might be lucky. Fingers crossed. Her mother probably had other reasons for dumping her. We don't know. She could have been a little teenager who just didn't know what to do. Maybe her boyfriend didn't know either. Maybe she didn't know she was pregnant and just panicked. A low birth weight can sometimes be a factor in a teenage birth especially with girls under 15. If she is a few weeks premature, then that might be a factor in her slow response to your trying to get her to suckle. But then,... Oh God forbid, slight prematurity might be … well, her boyfriend could have used a wire coat hanger or something like that … or he could have even beaten her on her stomach to induce an abortion. We can only speculate. But, look Keith, keep doing what you are doing with her. She is a living human being who desperately needed help. By chance, she found you. And, remember, you are just as good and capable as any foster carer, probably more so because of the commitment you have to her from the way in which you found her, you know, the physical and very intimate bonding you had right from the very start."

She then moves on. She says she has thought more about what to do. She tells him about a good way to get a birth certificate: "Once she is five or six years old and well settled with you, see a good but probably expensive lawyer in Queensland to apply for a birth certificate for her from the NSW authorities, using your iPhone photos as evidence. It should be fairly simple as long as the child protection departments in both states are not alerted. If all goes well, you should escape the Queensland Department of Child Safety's attention because there would have been no 'notification'. Generally, they will only act when somebody 'notifies' them and it then becomes what they call a 'matter of concern'. They cannot monitor every single child in the state. That's why you have to lie low with this baby for a few years and keep her out of the public eye. You will have to avoid seeing a doctor about her because, with no birth certificate, you cannot get a Medicare card for her. If it becomes necessary, you might have to see a doctor who does not bulk bill to the government and pay the full amount of the consultation up front. But, this might raise eyebrows."

So, Keith has to be careful to avoid situations where questions are asked.

She continues: "You just have to lie low with her for half a dozen years until you can demonstrate that you have cared for her well, in fact very well, better than normal and be able to prove with concrete evidence that it is in her best interests to remain in your care. Because of your gender and your age, this will always be an uphill battle. You will have to have a good really switched-on lawyer. Difficult, but it is possible."

Keith tells her he is still worried. "Why is the Department so like this? I've not harmed her. I saved her."

Fiona: "I'll explain further. Somebody else could have found her and taken her to hospital. In their eyes that would have been the correct thing to do."

Keith: "No other vehicles stopped there. It was a secluded spot. Crows were interested in her and I saw a dingo sitting in the grass."

Fiona: "Okay. But look, I'm being a bit of a devil's advocate pointing out what you are up against. They will argue that you should still have put her interests first and handed her over."

Keith: "But, I saved her life. If the dingo hadn't taken her, the crows were waiting. How long could she have survived being in the sun, after so long in the cold night? It wasn't a proper rest area and she wasn't in the shade. I was there with her in my campervan for over two hours sorting her out before I finally drove away with her at probably towards noon. So, I didn't leave for Tenterfield until at least two or more hours after I first found her and thought she was dead. No other vehicles came during that time. Having spent a night out in the open, she was already very cold and weak. She couldn't cry anymore. So, it's unlikely anyone else would have seen her before she would have been cooked in the midday sun or been eaten before that happened."

Fiona: "Yes, I'm sure that's true and the Department would accept that but they'd still argue that, in your misguided and selfish way, you then subjected her to an 'unacceptable risk of harm'. I'll repeat myself. Remember what I said before, they always take 'risk' a little further, linking it to 'actual harm'. And, they would 'substantiate' it, which really means 'in their professional opinion'. They use this as 'proof'. They sound so credible as so-called experts. But, their expertise is often flawed. Sometimes good lawyers who are not afraid of them do pull them down. Too often, they are zealous do-gooders devoid of common sense and compassion. It's that zealotry that you're up against. Yet, common sense and compassion are things that you have just proved about yourself."

Keith: "Wouldn't I get any credit for saving her?"

Fiona: "No."

Keith: "Why not?"

Fiona: "In their eyes what you've done after saving her is irresponsible and criminal negligence. That's rough but that is what you'd be up against. And, there is something else I must warn you about. Some of the CSOs are themselves victims of child sexual abuse. That is one reason why they have entered the child protection business. So, an unwritten knowledge among some of us CSOs was that, as a result, they are man haters.[103] What's the word? Yes, misandry. Those few will gun for you. You won't know who they are but if you ever have contact with CSOs, you should assume that the woman you are dealing with could be one of them. So, you must be cautious. Look Keith, I know how they operate. So, as I've said and I'll repeat it, I believe that if you lie low and don't attract attention, in six years you could be out of the woods. She would be so well settled with you that it could be argued successfully

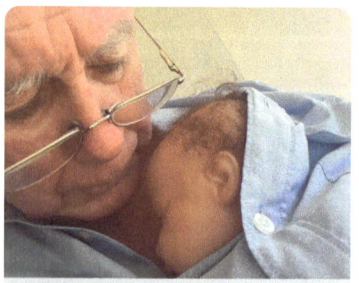

The selfie photo which Keith took of himself with now four-day-old Eppie.

by a good lawyer that it would not be in her best interests to be removed from your care. So, hang in there."

Keith is more re-assured. He thanks her very much for her frank advice. Then he e-mails her a photo of himself (a 'selfie') with tiny little Eppie in his arms. He sends her two other photos: the photo he took as he found her discarded inside the old grocery bag that morning and one of her on his lap still covered in vernix.

---

[103] Opinion given to the author in private by a former senior officer in the Queensland Families Department, university lecturer in social welfare, and ordained Anglican priest, Illtyd Loveluck, in Brisbane, 05 October 2004. A valued friend for fifty years, sadly he died in 2023

She phones back telling him the photos are excellent and Eppie is adorable. She also tells him "the photo of her in the grocery bag is vital evidence. Never lose these photos. Moreover, do not ever get rid of the iPhone that you used. It has recorded the time and place where you took those photos. Copies cannot show that evidence. If you download the photos to your Mac's photo library, those details are retained but not if you move the photo elsewhere, even elsewhere on your Mac like to your desk top. I suggest that, after downloading the photos to your Mac and without dragging the photo to your desktop, you should open and click on the tiny "info" key in the top right hand corner of each photo. This will open a little window in the centre of the photo which shows the exact place and date and time the photo was taken together with a little map of the area. Even though you and the iPhone were out of range and there was no service or no phone coverage, your iPhone still knew where and when it was that the photo was taken. It uses GPS technology, not the phone Telstra company coverage. And, it recorded all that info. Also, that little map with the precise location will only show up whenever your computer has WiFi access to the internet. So, take a screen shot and save that. Then you will have a permanent record. From time to time the iPhone operating system is changed or "updated" and the little map may disappear and be replaced with something less precise. That's another reason why you should take a screen shot. Later on, if necessary you can print out that screen shot for evidence used in a Court. And, of course, never get rid of that iPhone. It will always contain proof that your photos are real and not photoshopped concoctions."

Later, that's what Keith does. He does it for several of the photos.

Five days later and still worried but pleased with himself at having got his baby up and running, he decides to record more things about her. He photographs her. He measures her. She is between 28 and 29 centimetres from crown to rump. He knows that is small. He takes the kitchen scales out and weighs her again. She now weighs in at 1700 grams or about two tubs of yoghurt. She has gained 200 grams compared to when he weighed her five days ago - a good sign. She probably would have weighed a little more at birth and lost a lot through dehydration during her night in the open. Passing the meconium was also a factor in the low initial weight. He remembers his second daughter weighed 3200g and lost about 350g. So, he reasons: "This little Eppie is very definitely an underweight baby if not premature. But, I reckon she's a tough survivor."

Next day, he drives into Canning Town for groceries. With her inside his shirt, he calmly does his shopping. Nobody notices. And, he finds towelling nappies and some nappy liners. The price of disposables had shocked him. Back at home, he discovers he has not forgotten how to fold towelling nappies. He even automatically runs the tip of the safety pin through his scalp to grease it before doing up the nappy with it. It slips through the towelling material more easily like that.

In the evening while she is asleep, he is still worried about the Child Safety Department removing her from him. He does some internet surfing. He learns more about section 22 of the *Child Protection Act* which enables officers to remove new-born babies.[104] Will he face criminal charges for not reporting her birth and for not handing her in? He reads about a 64-year-old grandmother with an impeccable record who was denied a rôle as a kinship foster carer merely because of her age.[105]

He thinks: 'I'm seventy-four. What chance do I have? It's just not fair! Well, Fiona suggested I just have to 'go dark' as teenagers say, perhaps until she is older, can read and write and is ready for school. Yes, that's what I'll do. When she's five or six and well settled in life with me, I'll get a lawyer to fight for custody.' He is mildly optimistic and expects that by then fairness and decency will prevail for a six-year-old.

---

[104] In each Australian state there is legislation which permits the state government department responsible for child welfare and safety to remove babies at birth. It happens often and in Queensland on average once a week. In Queensland, the current relevant law is the *Child Protection Act* at section 22. During 2004 to 2009 in Queensland alone, some 250 newborn babies were removed or an average of 50 a year. Viellaris, R. (2009), 'Drunk mums give birth; babies seized from unfit parents'. *Courier Mail*. Brisbane, 27 August 2009, pages 1 & 5. https:// www.couriermail.com.au/news/drunk-mums-give-birth-babies-seized-from-unfit-parents/news-story/ cd256dddf33461472866f0eaf8d2ed28 This item sets out to be negative about a few drunk mothers. It does not mention mothers who are not drunk and the harmful distress and trauma for parents and the baby caused by the removal.

Overington, C., 'Department makes early call on child protection'. *The Australian*, Sydney, 20 February 2009. This item is about child protection departments across Australia removing babies at birth and the disastrous consequences. Sometimes Child Safety Officers arrive with a Police escort.

[105] Gregg, N., 'Grandmother told she is too old to care for grandchildren'. *Courier Mail*, Brisbane, 13 February 2010. http://www.news.com.au/national/gran-battles-to-care-for-grandkids/news-story/3c4d133ffc911d 9f0382efe0f1b31990

Ten days later, he drives not to Graniteville, which is just 30km away, but 60km further on to Canning Town. He has to have his car serviced at a garage where the owner has a VW like his. He has had his car serviced there before. So, he leaves his car at the garage and walks about a kilometre to the shopping mall. Eppie is safely tucked inside his shirt and he carries a shoulder bag with nappies, formula milk already prepared in bottles, other things like baby wipes and a change of clothes for her. He is well organised but it is cold.

While still in the shopping mall, he buys a small pram for her from baby section of the Target shop. He puts her in the pram and tucks her snuggly in with a small pink baby blanket he has also just bought. He didn't choose to buy a pink blanket. That was just the colour of the first one he saw on the shop's shelf. In fact, he is opposed to the 'pink-ification' of girls.[106] He was not concerned with the colour. He just wanted a baby blanket.

She is awake and calm. He pushes her around the shopping mall for a while. At one point he stops and looks at her. He makes sure she is properly tucked in with the new little pink blanket he has wrapped her in. She is staring up at him. It is that fixed stare of wonderment and adoration that new babies give to their mothers.[107] "Oh, Eppie. You are a darling. I never knew I would ever receive that gaze from a little baby. I am so privileged. Thank you, thank you."

(*Dreamstime*. Posed by model.)

He bends over, tenderly touches her cheek, and kisses her briefly on her forehead.

He tells her: "Dear, I love you so much. I am your's. I will do my very, very best for you. I will care for you, nurture you and protect you 'till my last breath, come what may."

She is still staring at him.

He remembers that 1961 Elvis Presley song *I can't help falling in love with you*:

---

[106] Valenti, J. "Let's end pink-ification: must the 'girls' aisle be full of sexist toys and clothes?" *The Guardian*, London, 05 August 2014. https://www.theguardian.com/commentisfree/2014/aug/05/girls-aisle-sexist-toys-clothes

[107] As a natural part of maternal bonding, the oxytocins produced by both Eppie and Keith have done it. That connected gaze with the mother increases the baby's heart rate. Ishikawa, M. & Itakura, S., "Physiological arousal predicts gaze following in infants". *Proceedings of the Royal Society*, London, 06 February 2019. https:// royalsocietypublishing.org/doi/full/10.1098/rspb.2018.2746

Wise men say
Only fools rush in
But I can't help falling in love with you
Shall I stay?
Would it be a sin
If I can't help falling in love with you? [108]

He thinks: "Why is this? Is it wrong? The song says: 'Would it be a sin'. I'm a grown man in his seventies and this is happening. At my age, love is supposed to grow. Am I a fool? An oldman like me doesn't crash into love. I'm not a teenager. Yet, I've crashed into loving a little baby! Has being on my own for so long done this to me? … No. I think you've done it, Eppie."[109]

He wipes his eyes more. He is very emotional. His eyes are still watering. And, her little hazel eyes are still fixed on him. He smiles at her and touches her cheek again. She seems to know he really, really loves her.

There is another psychological aspect to what is happening between Keith and this baby and that is 'imprinting', in particular 'filial imprinting' which has been explained succinctly:

> Filial imprinting refers to the most basic form of imprinting when a deep bond is built between two animals, usually a newborn and a parent. This imprinting is critical for the young animal's survival.[110]

Imprinting from birth is very well known especially in terms of birds but it is now widely accepted as having a significant effect on human behaviour early in life. It is likely that the effects of pheromones and peptide hormones, such as oxytocin, are involved in this filial imprinting which has occurred.

---

[108] To hear Elvis Presley singing this song: https://www.youtube.com/watch?v=vGJTaP6anOU

[109] Feldman, R., *et alia*, "Natural variations in maternal and paternal care are associated with systematic changes in oxytocin following parent–infant contact." *Psychoneuroendocrinology*, 35(8), September 2010, 1133-1141. https:// www.sciencedirect.com/science/article/abs/pii/S0306453010000296 Oxytocin continues to be the vital ingredient in the growing relationship between baby Eppie and her 'mother' Keith.
    Weismann, O. *et alia*. "Oxytocin shapes parental motion during father-infant interaction", *The Royal Society Biology Letters*, 23 December 2013, https://royalsocietypublishing.org/doi/10.1098/rsbl.2013.0828
    Feldman, R. & Bakermans-Kranenburg, M., "Oxytocin: a parenting hormone". *Current Opinon in Psychology*, Vol. 15, pages 13-18, June 2017. https://pubmed.ncbi.nlm.nih.gov/28813252/ Essentially, Keith's taking on this abandoned baby has been determined by a peptide hormone triggered when he found her at Bolivia Hill.

[110] Heyl, J.C., "Imprinting in Psychology", *Verywell Mind*, 09 June 2023. https://www.verywellmind.com/imprinting-in-psychology-7504676

CHAPTER 6

Growing with Eppie

K eith finds he absolutely loves being a mother to this baby. It is hard work and at times frustrating. But, his sense of connection with her and his feelings of fulfilment in the evenings is wonderful when, worn out, he looks at her peacefully asleep. Then, he finally crashes asleep. Then, she wakes two more times during the night and wants more feeding. Night after night like this wears him out.

(*iStockphoto* Posed by models)

There are times when he is at the end of his tether especially during the first six months. After days of rain, he is tired, has run out of clean nappies and is low on disposables when he loses it. He explodes smashing a large plastic nappy bucket full of nappies soaking in Napisan. Nappies, Napisan, and bits of plastic go everywhere, flooding the laundry. He howls with despair. Fortunately, Eppie is asleep. After a few minutes he tidies up. He sits down with a cup of coffee.

Keith's previous children were co-sleeping babies, especially when their mother was breastfeeding. However, that was decades ago. Society has become much more aware of the dangers of Sudden Infant Death Syndrome. He tended to think this occurred when a mother, especially an overweight mother, rolled over onto the baby during the night or when she fell asleep on the couch tired out and watching television. Now, like the rest of society, Keith is more aware of the dangers. He searches the internet and decides that he just does not want to take any risks with Eppie. So, after co-sleeping with her for three nights, he travels into

Wrapped up snugly in her portable cot which he has placed right next to his own bed.

Keith took this photo of himself holding Eppie while he prepared a bottle for her at 2:00 a.m.. (He put his Panasonic Lumix camera on a tripod and used the self-timer.)

Graniteville and buys a portable cot for her at the Target Country shop. It's walls are like mosquito netting and it has a hard flat surface with a quite thin mattress. He also buys a zip-up swaddle for her which allows her to sleep on her back. And, it has no loose fabric to interfere with her breathing. She responds well to it especially as he sits next to the cot, strokes her temple, and sings to her to sleep.

When Eppie is six weeks old, as they get close to Canning Town on a grocery shopping trip, he is caught in road works traffic just as she wakes up and wants a feed. He can't attend to her immediately. Then, she starts that stressed rapid tremulous crying: "Waa! Waa! Waa! Waa!" When he pulls into the shopping centre car park she is going full steam. Flushed in the face, she is in a sweaty tizz. He worries about attracting attention. Fortunately, with a campervan he is able to climb into the back, draw the curtains and comfort her as he prepares her bottle. Finally, she vigorously sucks milk into her tummy. Peace! What bliss! Silence, except for the pumping sounds of a hungry little mouth. Then, she needs burping. Then, some reflux. After more milk, she starts emptying her bowels. Fortunately, there is a stove, water on tap and a sink in the campervan, and curtains for privacy. These are typical of the stresses Keith faces and handles alone.

Yet, Eppie grows and develops quickly. She goes through all the normal developmental milestones on cue: tummy time at 19 weeks, starting to crawl at six months, and her first steps just after 12 months. Keith finds he is totally engrossed in parenting Eppie.

Based on his past experience, he makes up his mind right from the start that he will not baby-talk her. He will always talk to her in an adult way and will always explain things to her and even discuss issues. He believes this will mature her in a sensible way and promote her self-esteem. He also decides to be very physical with her with lots of hugs, cuddles and kisses. She responds likewise and it is very fulfilling for both of them. She is a happy little girl full of confidence, trust in, and love for Keith. She is a success story for him but a secret one.

(*Left*) Eppie starting to crawl.

(*Right*) At two-years-old, a happy Eppie loves the company of this 'parent' and friend who she adores. (*iStockphoto*. Posed by model.)

With a background of university studies in Education and a closely involved parent with two babies before, he developed rather idealistic views about children growing up. Then, he also lived in India where some in the Hindu tradition believe that, because of reincarnation, children grow up not as little innocents but as little adults reflecting their previous life of good or evil.

So, while he is steeped in current Western values and the Rousseau *tabula rasa,* he still sees children as basically innocent at birth but realises that some factors are probably inherited. A clear example of this is that PTSD can be passed on to the unborn child.[111]

One evening, while on the phone to his friend, Fiona, she reminds him that Eppie is an unknown quantity. "I think you are still seeing her through Rousseau's rose coloured

---

[111] Costandi, M., "Pregnant 9/11 survivors transmitted trauma to their children". *The Guardian,* London. 09 Sep 2011. https://www.theguardian.com/science/neurophilosophy/2011/sep/09/pregnant-911-survivors-transmitted-trauma

spectacles. You don't know how her innate personality is likely to develop and how she will really turn out despite all your idealism about a *tabula rasa* and so on. She may turn out to be schizophrenic and start beating you up. And, coupled to that, she may grow into a big physically strong young woman who will give you a hard time. This might be in spite of all the love and devoted care I know you are giving her. This is a risk you are taking."

Keith's response is to basically agree with her. "I understand what you are saying about the risk but I cannot help my feelings towards this little baby that I have found or, yes, this baby that I have saved. I absolutely adore her. And, I confess, sometimes I dress her like a little doll. In a way it is infatuation but I am totally committed to her. I suppose it could be like a man who finds an abandoned leopard cub in the African bush and takes it home and nurtures it with devoted love only to find it turns on him one day and mauls him."

Fiona: "Yes, a good but extreme analogy. But, I am just being a 'Jobe's Comforter'. I also have faith that she will turn out to be a Godsend for you and you for her. Just make sure that in a quiet non-patronising way you always let her know about her origins. She needs to know that. Another thing, you and I mean <u>you</u>, Keith, are so bonded to her that if she is taken from you by the Department, well I think you will be broken. So, please, please be so careful and vigilant."

Eppie at about 18 months and still in nappies.

During the hot summer months Eppie is often "bare arsed" during the day with no nappy and just a T-shirt especially outside when the nappy is a bit cumbersome for her. (Of course, their house is secluded and very private.)

At around her second birthday, she no longer wears nappies during the day. She is very proud of this. Of course, Keith is very pleased, too. Nevertheless, she very occasionally still has accidents even when she has turned three. In this photo, taken while they were in the bush on a camping trip, she had wet herself during the night. Keith has taken her down to a creek just to sluice her groin area. She is pleased: "I don't wanna be stinky."

Often, when he looks at her, he cannot help feeling she is so very beautiful. This is a parent's natural adoration. She senses his feelings and loves his loving her. So, the love is mutual.

At this time, he introduces Eppie to caring for the chooks. She is eager to look after them. Soon, she learns to feed them, provide them with water, clean out their pen,

Keith takes a naked Eppie down to a creek.

release them each morning and every evening she rounds them up and locks them up in the pen. There are foxes about. Eppie even has a favourite hen which she calls 'Henny Penny'. Despite Eppie's sometimes rough handling, Henny Penny is very tolerant and likes her. Every time they return from a trip to town the chooks run out to greet them. Eppie and Keith love this and make a fuss of them whenever they return.

As a slightly old-fashioned 'parent', he encourages her to help around the house, with their little vegetable garden and looking after the chooks. By four she has responsibility for caring for the chooks on a daily basis.[112] If she forgets, he rouses on her. All domesticated or pet animals suffer if they are not cared for. In the same way, the house would become stinky and messy if we didn't tidy up. He believes

2-year-old Eppie learns to feed the chooks.

that in parenting you also have to teach. Not everything comes naturally. You also have to let children experience hardship and calamity. He believes parents shouldn't 'helicopter' their kids.[113] They need to learn some tough lessons to build independence and resilience.

---

[112] See how another little girl takes on responsibility for livestock: Brown, S.L., 'Meet Emily, the six-year-old farming lambs for pocket money'. *ABC News*, Melbourne, 05 October 2017. http://www.abc.net.au/news/2017-10-05/meet-emily-the-six-year-old-farming-lambs-for-pocket-money/9014266.

[113] See: 'Helicopter parent' in *Wikipedia* at https://en.wikipedia.org/wiki/Helicopter_parent

One night she forgot to lock up the chook pen. She left the door ajar. He saw this but did nothing. It was a chance for her to learn the hard way. So, he sat up late. At about 11:00 p.m. it happened. Eppie was woken by the commotion as a fox raided the coop near her bedroom window. They both rushed out but weren't quick enough. It was worse than Keith expected. Two hens were killed before the fox was chased away. She was very upset and next day they had a special funeral service for the dead chooks at their burial.

Keith is also aware that some of the problems faced by some children are due to a lack of attachment to a parent. If there is no real parent figure who is a rôle model and who is there to guide development towards adulthood, there could be problems. And, of course, he and Fiona had discussed foster caring as not real committed parenting. So, he gradually introduces growing Eppie to issues around foster care. By the time she is four, she knows that he fears her being taken into foster care. She doesn't really know what it is but he explains that "government ladies would come and take you away for ever and give you to some other people you just don't know. Some little kids in foster care are very badly treated. Some even die."

Many kids are brought up in their early years to see the world a good and kind place with nice people everywhere. This is despite 'Little Red Riding Hood' stories which are seen as merely fairy tales. But by the time she is just two, Eppie already knows that the world is not necessarily a nice kind place. She knows that she was dumped and left to be killed by the hot sun or eaten by a dingo. He even tells her about Azaria Chamberlain at Ayers Rock.[114] She also knows who her saviour is. She is bonded to him, trusts him implicitly, and really loves him. So, the threat of foster care and its possible outcome for her is taken seriously by this still very little girl.

As she gets older, he explains why the government ladies would come and take her away, essentially for three reasons: the fact that he is an old man on his own with her, because he didn't hand her in, and she has not been vaccinated. He believes he must always be up front, open and honest even if what he tells her is a little too advanced for her age. He stresses

---

[114] "Death of Azaria Chamberlain" *Wikipedia*. https://en.wikipedia.org/wiki/Death_of_Azaria_Chamberlain. In 1980, 9-week-old baby Azaria Chamberlain was dragged from the family's tent by a dingo at the Ayers Rock-Uluru camping ground, taken away and eaten by the dingo. Chamberlain, L. (1990) *Through My Eyes*, Mandarin, Melbourne.

those reasons are why they are living almost hidden on this lovely little property and why he is so protective. Because Keith is her 'parent' and mothering figure, she accepts what he says. She understands the gist of it and is accepting of a need for semi-fugitive life. It's even a little exciting.

With his experience from teaching and from his previous children, Keith is determined to be a full-on parent for his baby, a rôle model, a guide, and a protector. He feels he owes it her. It's what parents must do. He also remembers the wonderful fulfilling time when his previous children were little. He was close to them because he and his ex-wife agreed on shared parenting. Thus, he feels his rôle as a 'parent' is essentially as a protective facilitator <u>but</u> with the vital ingredient of committed love. So, he has come to believe that mothering is not gender specific. For him, it is a rôle which is not necessarily gender based and, more than that, he loves being a mother.

One of Botticelli's many Madonna paintings. But, this Madonna is clearly not too happy about her baby.

Also, he knows there are women who are reluctant mothers. Perhaps, Eppie's biological mother was one. He is reminded of a very telling Madonna and child painting by Italian Renaissance artist Sandro Botticelli which he had once seen at The Louvre in Paris.[115] Most of his Madonna paintings are typical adoring mother and baby portraits. But, this Madonna is different and seems to view her child as a tiresome burden.

So, Keith doesn't accept that women have a monopoly on the ability to mother. He feels it's an entrenched part of the way society operates or what he calls a 'Madonna social construct'. He is adamant men can also mother. He feels our society tends to have a sexist view of women as mothers, where all women are capable of being caring and loving virgin Marys and men can't. Thus, that recent guru of child rearing, Penelope Leech[116],

---

[115] See this unusual portrayal of a Madonna at: https://en.wikipedia.org/wiki/List_of_works_by_Sandro_Botticelli (Scroll down to the 'Madonna and child with five angels'. Then, click on it to enlarge it.)

[116] Leach, P. (1997), *Children First*. London: Random House, page 48.

superciliously describes a man who takes on full daily care of a child as merely a "pseudo-mother". In contrast, he remembers three authors he read over a decade ago shortly after his ex-wife got sole custody of their children and he was very upset bout it. And, there on his bookshelves are the three books. He opens up one by Shari Thurer at a pencil mark he made many years ago: "Mother love is a stubborn, hardy emotion in both men and women. … Any human being in her or his right mind, when presented with a hapless infant, will tend to provide for its care".[117] Then the same thing with the book by Rosie Jackson: "The idealised 'Mother' is one of the most comforting fantasies of all." and "Mothers need not be biological nor must the continuous adult figure needed for the child's emotional stability and maturity be female. Men can mother as well." [118] He reads Ann Dally's 1982 comment which he also marked: "motherliness is a human quality and by no means confined to woman … many men have motherly qualities and many more could develop them if society and circumstances would permit." [119] These are quite dated books but he still feels vindicated.

Now, through the internet he comes across several more recent books and academic research articles which seem to back his view. These are new to him and he is very interested.[120] As he eagerly reads the abstract of one of the research papers, he wonders: 'Perhaps the

---

[117] Shari Thurer (1995), *Myths of Motherhood: How Culture Reinvents the Good Mother*. London:. Penguin, page 6.

[118] Rosie Jackson (1994), *Mothers who Leave*. London: Pandora, pages 281 and 284.

[119] Dally, A. (1982), *Inventing Motherhood*. London: Burnett Books, page 200.

[120] McKie, R., 'Male and female differences down to socialisation, not genetics'. *The Observer*, London, 15 August 2010. http://www.guardian.co.uk/world/2010/aug/15/girls-boys-think-same-way

Fine, C. (2010), *Delusions of Gender: How our Minds, Society and Neurosexism Create Difference*. New York: W.W. Norton. "Our minds, society and neurosexism create difference. Together, they wire gender. But the wiring is soft, not hard. It is flexible, malleable, and changeable." (page 239).

Carothers, B. J. & Reis, H.T., 'Men and women are from Earth: Examining the latent structure of gender'. *Journal of Personality & Social Psychology*, 104(2), Feb 2013, pp 385-407. "Average differences between men and women are not under dispute, but the dimensionality of gender indicates that these differences are inappropriate for diagnosing gender-typical psychological variables on the basis of sex." Abstract: http://psycnet.apa.org/journals/psp/104/2/385/

Feldman, R. et alia, "Prolactin, Oxytocin, and the development of paternal behavior across the first six months of fatherhood." *Hormones and Behaviour*, 58(3), 513-518, 07 October 2010. https://ruthfeldmanlab.com/wp-content/ uploads/2019/06/Oxytocin-prolactin-and-paternal-behavior.HB2010.pdf

Abraham, E., Feldman, R., et alia. "Father's brain is sensitive to childcare experiences." *Proceedings of the National Academy of Science,* Washington DC, USA, 111(27), 08 July 12014. https://pubmed.ncbi.nlm.nih.gov/24912146/ Studies caregiving fathers without maternal involvement.

biological necessity of caring for a little baby has brought out the mothering instinct in me?' And, he knows his inner feelings: he loves his baby like anything, feels extremely physically close to her and knows he would die to save her. He is her nurturer, protector and her mother. For him, it is unconditional love. He is steadfast in his belief that men can mother. He doesn't

want to prove it. He knows it. He feels society's rôle norms are merely a social construct.

Nevertheless, he continually worries about what others might think, especially because he is male and old. An old man with a baby attracts attention. And, the Child Safety Department is often in the back of his mind. So, during the first year he keeps trips away from home to a minimum. He drives all the way to Canning Town (85 km) or even Glen Innes in NSW

As a toddler she is very bonded and clingy with him. He loves this. (*iStockphoto*. Posed by model)

(125 km) for groceries where he thinks there is less chance of people noticing him and Eppie.

She is a happy baby and typically loves him blowing raspberries on her tummy. He is physical with her. She begins walking at twelve months. At two, she is toilet trained and soon doesn't need a nappy at night. He reads to her every evening and when she is in bed he tells her a special 'dark story' which he makes up each night. It is a special time. At one stage, it is a story is serialised about a big water rat called 'Ratso' who has learned to speak English and makes friends with some people in town. He continues the nightly 'dark stories' for a few years even when she is six-years-old. Occasionally, he falls asleep during the story and she has to wake him up. Sometimes, he tells her real life true stories about his time as a child in the then Northern Rhodesia where they lived in a house with no electricity and running water. The outside toilet was a well with a wooden seat over it. Before you sat on it you had to wait and listen to make sure there were no wasps down there. They made their nests on the edges of the well. One story was about when as a six-year-old the family was living at Livingstone in Zambia. His father was the manager of a government-run barge service which operated up the Zambezi River (ZRT). 'My father took me on one trip. We stopped at a remote village and moored the barge to a tree. The village headman came to see my father. They exchanged greetings. The headman asked him if he could solve a problem for the village. A crocodile was regularly taking women when they came down to the river to collect water. Late that afternoon, my father lay on the steel deck of the barge with his rifle and waited. Eventually, he saw just the crocodile's eyes poking above the water. He carefully took aim and fired. He got the croc! It leapt up in the air and fell back into the water dead. Upside down, it floated downstream. There were loud cheers from the villagers who had been watching quietly. That evening the village celebrated with a 'beer drink' and lots of drums and dancing well after midnight. I went to the village with my father. He was given a hero's welcome. I'll never forget the beat of those drums: 'bonga bonga bonga bonga' all night long.'[121]

Another African story he tells her is about the family going on a trip into what was then the Belgian Congo. They used to sleep in the car because villagers told them they were in 'lion country'. One moonlight night, they woke up to the sound of grunting outside the car. Looking out through the windows, they saw lions prowling around.

Eppie loved these true stories. There were many more he told her.

Around her first birthday, Keith's friend Fiona comes to visit for a day. He is very pleased to see her and for her to meet Eppie. It is also a landmark occasion because Eppie is just starting to walk.

This tantrum is an early example of Eppie's defiant streak which will occasionally cause problems for Keith. Later, it will become one of her assets.

Eppie has a mind of her own. At around a year old, she is starting to walk. Here she is taking her early steps along their driveway but she stubbornly resists Keith as he tries to pull up and re-fasten her nappy which is falling down. He gives up and removes it altogether. (Fiona took the photo.)

---

[121] This is a true story which happened for the author in about 1951 upstream from the village of Katima Mulilo. The story about lions in the Belgian Congo is also true.

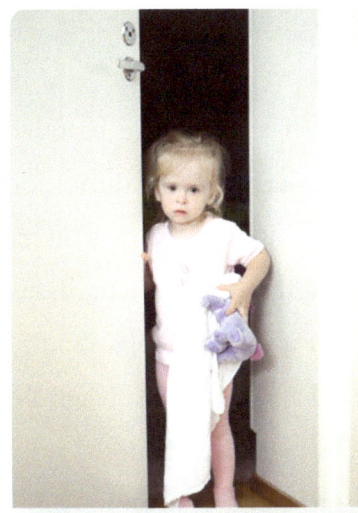

Eighteen-month-old Eppie has already been put to bed for the night but has woken up and wants to sit with Keith on the couch in the living room as he watches some TV. He cuddles her while she falls asleep again. (*Getty Images*. Posed by model.)

Eppie with her iPad. (*Shutterstock*. Posed by model).

For her second birthday she gets an iPad. She quickly gains internet expertise, like finding episodes of *Peppa Pig*, *Bluey*, and *Fireman Sam* on *YouTube*. Then, by herself she discovers how to take photos with her iPad. She spends ages taking photos of all sorts of bizarre things which Keith later has to delete. But, early on he teaches her about safety and not putting photos of herself anywhere. "Bad people will see you and want to find you." He warns her about this even though she doesn't have any social media access.

For her third birthday she gets a small trampoline which she also loves. Keith doesn't like it because it makes him giddy. For her fourth birthday she gets a bicycle with trainer wheels. She quickly learns to ride properly in the driveway outside their house.

She likes sitting with him in the evenings after dinner watching the TV news. They often discuss news items they've seen. And, he does not protect her from unsavoury things that go on in the world. Instead, he explains. Yet, she develops her own opinions. Her innate social conscience emerges even at a very young age and he encourages this.[122] She was upset

---

[122] A 5-year-old girl has a strong opinion about former British PM Theresa May: 'Five-year-old gives Theresa May a telling-off about the homeless'. *ITV News*, London, 05 October 2016. https://www.youtube.com/watch? v=xncfOR1X9n4

and angry when she read about the death of a five-year-old Yazidi girl in Iraq the same age as her.[123]

At her initiative and encouraged by Keith, together they built a make-shift cubby house in the bush among the boulders.

Their wild bush and granite boulder property is a wonderful playground for them. They have hide and seek games there. Sometimes, he plays the 'baddie' who hides behind rocks and jumps out to gobble her up. Typically, she shrieks with delight when he grabs her and gobbles her up. Then, she runs off calling: "More! Catch me again! Again! Again!"

Together, they build a cubby house in the bush among some granite boulders. It is made of old planks of timber, plastic sheeting, and other junk, most which she chose to use. She enjoyed building her "special place". They sometimes use it as a hide to sit together and watch birdlife. With pretend swords they sometimes have to fend off bad people attacking the cubby. She also has time out alone in the cubby house where she pores over her little books about the flower fairies. She talks to the fairies who live among the boulders in the surrounding bush. Some of the giant rocks are part of a tribe of rocks she calls "Bargens". They come alive at night. She tells Keith that they do things like roll down a hill at night and crush the bull-dozers that clear bush for residential land. They once discussed urban sprawl and clearing of bushland after the evening TV news.

---

[123] A 5-year-old Yazidi girl captured by ISIS fanatics in Iraq and kept as a slave died of thirst in the hot desert sun while chained outside for wetting her mattress. Reuters, "German court jails ISIS woman for Yazidi girl's death in Iraq." *The Guardian*, London, 25 October 2021. https://www.theguardian.com/world/2021/oct/25/german-court-jails-is-woman-for-yazidi-girls-death-in-iraq

As a four-year-old, Eppie is standing on one of the 'Bargens' in their back yard. She talks to them.

Inside their house, Keith and Eppie have been playing having a tea party with her dollies.

A Strangler Fig slowly killing its host tree. (*Wikimedia Commons.* Keith Woodward)

While visiting rainforest in the Bunya Mountains National Park they discuss a Strangler Fig which is killing its host tree.[124] He explains how a seed left by a bird in an upper branch germinates and as it grows it sends roots down to the ground eventually killing the host tree.

Whenever they are out in the car, she sits in the front and they talk as he drives. She asks about things they see, like a car with yellow number plates. He explains that it is from New South Wales and that's the style of number plates they have there. Of course, he reminds her that she was born in NSW. One day he shows her very clearly the different states as they cross the Queensland border at Wallangarra into NSW at Jennings.

She asks about some trees that seem to have leaves on some branches which are different to those on the rest of the tree. He explains that a parasite is living on that tree. He explains how it got there because the parasite has sticky fruit which birds wipe off their beaks onto a tree branch. The seed from that fruit then germinates and sends roots not into the ground but into the branch of that tree that it is on and sucks water and nutrients from the victim tree. She thinks that is horrible and a little like the Strangler Fig they saw in the rainforest. So, he reminds her of the threadworm he once removed from her vulva. It hatched from an egg inside her which she unknowingly ingested while at Play Group. She remembers it well. "It was so itchy and yukkie."

---

[124] See: *Ficus watkinsiana* in *Wikipedia*, https://en.wikipedia.org/wiki/Ficus_watkinsiana

As she gets older and starts reading and using her iPad more, he shows her *Wikipedia* so that she can find out things for herself. She will sometimes talk to him about books he has on his shelves. She finds his *Gray's Anatomy* and *Everywoman*.[125]

She is fascinated by the diagrams in them. He spends time explaining things to her and she learns correct terminology for sexual organs. And, of course, she learns about sex and human reproduction. He tells her about her vulva being strictly private. "Nobody must touch you there in a sexy way. Only if you want them to and when you are grown up. Your vulva is special and really private for you only."

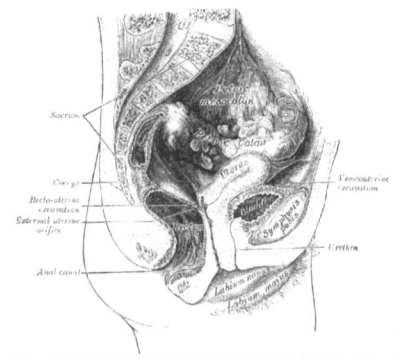

(Diagram from *Gray's Anatomy* 1858)

Later that day and at her curious initiative, Keith talks to her more about how her vulva is private and how he mustn't touch her in a sexual way at her vulva. He tells her, however, that only he and nobody else can look at her there or even touch her if there is something wrong, like if has a threadworm there. She remembers that. He adds that he can look or touch her there if she gets an infection and he then has to put cream on her vulva. He would do that because he is her 'parent' and has to look after her but she would always know the difference between sexual looking and touching and parent looking and touching. The sexy way would be rather like the smiling fox talking to Jemima Puddle-Duck, something she understands well.

She asks him: "So, if you're sick, can I look at your penis?"

Keith: "No, because you're not my parent."

Eppie: "Why not?"

Keith: "Because you're not caring for me. A doctor could if I was sick and if I asked him or her to. That's okay. And, as I'm your caring parent, I can also look at you if you're sick. But, any adult looking at a child's penis or vulva in a sexy way is just not on."

---

[125] Gray, H., (1858), *Anatomy: Descriptive and Surgical*. Parker & Son: London.
Llewellyn-Jones, D. (1990), *Everywoman*. Penguin: Melbourne.

When she was nearly three he plucked up courage to expose her to the outside world. He feels he would be remiss in not facilitating social interaction with other kids. He is beginning to worry that she could grow up a social misfit. Fiona reassures him: "Don't worry. She'll grow up with a healthy non-conformist streak. It will do her good in the real world."

Going back in time, at two years old he takes her swimming at the heated public swimming pool in Canning Town. He is no longer worried that she might do a poo at the pool. She'll tell him if she wants to and he'll take her to the Parents Room toilet. After two visits, he enrols her in a drown proofing class. She takes to it well. One day, after two sessions, the parent stands in the water at the edge of the pool and pushes their child through the water to the instructor sanding about two metres away. Eppie does well, dog paddling to the instructor who then praises her. She turns Eppie around and pushes her towards Keith with the words: "Swim to your Grandad". Keith catches her and praises her. But then, he turns to the instructor and tells her: "I'm not her Grandad. I'm her parent." The lady is apologetic and all the other Mums of toddlers at the class stare. Then, he has misgivings about saying what he said. Will people ask questions?

(*Shutterstock*, posed by model.)

Nevertheless, Eppie loves the pool and is soon swimming or dog paddling on her own. She especially loves diving to collect toys which have sunk to the bottom at the shallow end. She is a fearless little water baby. During these times at the pool she begins to engage with other kids. Keith is especially pleased to see her having a friendly giggling splashing match with another little girl of her age. Later, when she is five she has proper swimming lessons, learning correct strokes.

Keith also takes her to weekly Playgroup sessions at a Church hall in Graniteville. He feels she needs to learn to socialise more than just have swimming lessons. A totally secluded life is not good for her. He feels he must give her more social contact. Humans are social creatures and he would be remiss in his parenting duties if he didn't provide her with opportunities to meet and mix with other kids. Before he took her, he checked out Playgroup

Association membership on the internet. He found there is no requirement to present a birth certificate or vaccination evidence.

At first, Eppie is shy and apprehensive the first couple of times. Feeling different, she does not mix easily with other kids and is quite aloof: a clear down side of her isolation. He finds he is the only 'father' there but the mothers are soon supportive especially when they see Eppie's strong attachment to him. And, they seem to assume he is Eppie's grandfather who minds her while Mum is at work. And, although he is never questioned about his relationship to her, they talk to him as if that is the case. He does not enlighten them.

After two sessions, Eppie starts mixing more with another girl, Melanie Shaw, probably because she is the oldest kid there and thus a bit more mature. She even teaches Eppie how to do 'Hi Fives'.[126]

Playing in the sand pit. Eppie is on the left with Melanie on the right. (*Dreamstime*. Posed by models)

One day Keith is surprised when an astute mother, Belinda Shaw who is Melanie's mother, has noticed that Eppie always calls him 'Mumma' and wonders why. She asks Keith if Eppie is named after the little girl in George Eliot's book *Silas Marner* because it's such an uncommon name. Weary, he merely says: "I loved the novel when I studied it at University." He thinks she suspects Eppie is a foundling. Fortunately, nothing happens but he was worried.

Back at the house, he also uses the occasion to tell her how and why he was sent to jail and why some people still believe he actually did rape the girl despite her conviction for perjury. She gets the gist of what it is about and naturally supports her parent in what he is doing: "I don't want those bad ladies to come and take me away from you." [127]

---

[126] For an explanation of this common kids' thing: "High Five", *Wikipedia*. https://en.wikipedia.org/wiki/High_five

[127] On not keeping kids ignorant of the harsh realities of this world: Kasey Edwards, "Maintaining kids' innocence doesn't mean keeping them ignorant". *Brisbane Times*, 01 July 2001. https://www.brisbanetimes.com.au/lifestyle/life-and-relationships/maintaining-kids-innocence-doesn-t-mean-keeping-them-ignorant-20190629-p522ku.html She promotes the need for openness with children and this author agrees that ignorance is not bliss. It can be dangerous.

From her contact with other kids at Playgroup she comes down with some colds and coughs. He expected this and just hopes she does not get something really serious like whooping cough, meningococcal disease, and diphtheria. In a way he is pleased about this as it builds up her immune system. After her first day, he discovered that she has gained some threadworms. The first he knew about it was that she couldn't sleep at night and kept rubbing her vulva. Finally, he removed her pyjama pants, spread her legs, and had a close look inside with a torch. There, between her inner labia (and she is very small) was a tiny wriggling thread worm. He had to pick it out from the entrance to her vaginal vault very carefully with a wooden tooth pick. Needless to say, little girls are very soft and delicate in that area between their inner labia at the entrance to their vaginal vault. Then, he rinsed her vulva under a tap and put her in some fresh pyjama pants. She went to sleep straight away. Next morning, he bought some 'Combantrin' at the chemist's, dosed her and himself, and washed her pyjamas and their bed linen. Those measures fixed the problem.[128] Fortunately, there wasn't a second time and that was probably down to Keith's insisting that she wash her hands frequently especially while at Playgroup. Later, when she is at primary school he expects to deal with head lice. Then, when she is at high school it will be her first menarche, although she already knows what that is. Keith has already made up his mind to celebrate the occasion with her.

They often go camping at the Girraween National Park with its enormous granite rock formations. They play hide and seek among the boulders.

Despite her isolation, Eppie is an active and fit little girl at home with Keith. (iStockphotos. Posed by models.)

---

128 As a single male parent, the author had to do this with his twenty-month-old daughter after he first took her to Playgroup. Nine years later, he had help her with using a pad when her first period or menarche started.

On one camping trip, Eppie managed to get close to some kangaroos when a male mounted a female and started mating with her. She watched the preoccupied kangaroos closely. She asked Keith what they were doing. He explained in detail what they did. She was fascinated.

Trying to get close to kangaroos.

She watches some kangaroos mating. (*Wikimedia Commons* Sharon Beder)

At Girraween National Park, Eppie is standing on a granite rock playing 'King of the Castle'.

Their camping trips are usually full of interesting happenings. She learns a lot from him because he was a Geography teacher. In the national parks he explains so much about the animals, rock formations, vegetation and the damage done by feral pests like pigs. She loves the exquisite flowers at Girraween. They discuss why she shouldn't pick them. Disappointed, she understands. But, he always re-assures her with hugs and a kiss or two.

Keith has dressed her for the cold. It is exciting. Here she is scraping up snow to throw at him. He is not the winner of the snowball fight. (*iStockphoto*, Posed by model)

(*Right*) The view from their front verandah after the snowfall.

One cold winter morning, when she is four there is great excitement. It has been snowing gently overnight and still is. The bush around their house is a beautiful fairyland. They make a little snowman. Then, they have lots of happy laughing fun enjoying a snowball fight.

Keith makes sure she knows about housework. He tells her: "If the house is messy and dirty it becomes stinky and horrible." She understands and often enthusiastically helps.

When she is three, it is a hot Christmas holiday season. So, during the first week of January, he takes her to Brisbane to give her different experiences of the outside world. They go to the big shopping mall at Indooroopilly where there is lovely cool air-conditioning. She finds the crowds a little intimidating. She is fascinated by the escalators or moving stairs. She also likes pressing a button to call a lift to go up or down

Four-year-old Eppie on a sea-saw at Jubilee Park near the shops in Tenterfield during that winter. There is light snow cover on the ground. (*iStockphoto.* Posed by model.)

Here she is helping clean up mess on the kitchen floor. (*Dreamstime.* Posed by model.)

between floors. Because they are about to go to the South Bank water park, while at the mall he buys her her first pair of real swimming togs because she is growing. She chooses frilly pretty little girl's togs. It is clearly her taste. But, he wonders, is her desire for frilly girl's clothes because she spends so much time at home in shorts and doing things like climbing rocks and looking after chooks.

Next, he takes her to the South Bank water park for a swim. At first, she is too shy to wear her new pretty togs and wanders around just looking at other kids playing and splashing in the water. She is shy. He can see this and doesn't put pressure on her. Eventually, she lets him undress her and put her new swimming togs on. He does this in

The Brisbane South Bank water park. (*iStockphoto.*)

the open without going into the changing rooms. He is too worried about taking her into the men's changing room. Will some zealous person stop him or call the Police? Or, would they rush in and grab her to save her from being raped? And, as a man, he can't take her into the women's changing rooms. Changing her in public is the only thing he can do.

Once changed into her new swimming togs, he holds her gently at her shoulders. He looks at her. "Eppie, my dear, you look gorgeous in these togs. You are so pretty. And, I love you so much." He kisses her on her mouth. She smiles appreciatively.

(*Left*) At first, shy Eppie won't go near the water. Yet, she watches other kids splashing about.

(*Centre*) Keith manages to persuade her to let him change her into her swimming togs and she is tentatively paddling.

(*Right*) Finally, she has lost her apprehension and her hat. She runs in and out of the water. Note that she is still quite skinny. (All three photos from *iStockphoto* and posed by the same model.)

Finally, she has a paddle. It's all a new experience for this shy little girl. Then, she plucks up courage and runs into the water's edge. After a few minutes, she starts running in and running out again and again. She squeals with delight as she exchanges 'Hi Fives' with him. Keith just adores his little girl. His little foundling is growing into a pretty little girl. Petite and skinny with matchstick legs, she is intelligent, fit and healthy but remains undersized. She loves her trampoline, the bush and boulders around their house, and the interesting exploring walks they have in the national parks they often travel to. Sometimes, he feels age is catching up with him when, running ahead, she doesn't appreciate why he doesn't keep up. Sometimes when she is five and even six, she even mocks him. "You can't keep up because you're old." This happens several times but he never responds. Nevertheless, she is always excited when they load up the campervan for a trip away to a national park. She sits in the front with him and they discuss things they see along the way. They also play music and sing as they travel.

Before she could crawl he had been singing to her as he would cuddle her down to sleep for the afternoon or at night. Often he would play Brahms' *Lullaby*[129] on the CD player as he sang quietly to it using his own improvised words. He would also encourage her to sing with him at home or in the car while travelling to town to buy groceries or on a camping trip. It started with an old CD of ABC Television's *Playschool* songs such as *There's a Bear in There* and singing with the story told by Noni Hazelhurst of the *Sleeping Princess*. Together, they join in with the chorus: "And the princess slept for a hundred years"

Very early on, Keith has been reading to her, mainly from her books on fairies but also nursery stories like Beatrix Potter's *Jemima Puddle-Duck* and the old traditional *Little Red Riding Hood*. He explains the moral or message in each of these stories: the sneaky predator fox who cons Jemima into letting him have access to her eggs and the predator wolf Little Red Riding Hood met who set about tricking her so that he could eat her. Because she understands immediately, even at only three, he realises that she is like most children more mature than we give them credit for. So, he tends to talk to her quite openly about sex. He reasons to himself that for her own safety it is better to have her over-informed than under-informed. So, he decides to ensure that she knows about sex and sex predation on the basis that knowledge is an excellent defence. Then, he soon realises that there is more to this child than he expects. She, and probably all children are already innately developing sexual beings, although not developed sexual beings. When she is 4, they are having boiled eggs for

---

[129] Johannes Brahms, *Lullaby* https://www.youtube.com/watch?v=t894eGoymio "Wiegenlied" ("Lullaby" or "Cradle Song"), Op. 49, No. 4, is a "lied" for voice and piano which was first published in 1868.

breakfast. Halfway through the meal, Eppie tells him: "You know something? We're eating chooks' periods for breakfast."[130]

He laughs but congratulates her because she is right. She knows the difference between a fertilised egg and an unfertilised one. She has seen embryos when fertilised eggs have been cracked open. And, she has seen chicks hatch from eggs. So, he is pleased she understands. He thinks of something he read recently:

> Our mandate to protect children is couched in the language of responsibility for their frailty. But if we look back through the looking glass, through the fantasy of childhood innocence that organises these perceptions, we find children taking responsibility for our vulnerability by playing the part of humanity's infinite fragility.[131]

He realises that Eppie might try to unconsciously conform to his idealistic perceptions of her innate innocence. He doesn't want that. He wants her to be true to herself. And so, he feels justified in being very frank and open with her and treating her respectfully in an adult way in all aspects of their life even with regard to matters involving sex. So, they discuss things about sex abuse which they've seen on the internet. At one stage, when she is only just five, he talks about the damage that rape of a little girl like her does. He is frank. She listens attentively when he uses her iPad to show her an internet news item from South Africa a few years ago.[132]

The news item is about a case of a baby who had to have a *hysterectomy* and a 4-year-old girl who died of her injuries months after being raped. He feels he just has to explain quite frankly what a *hysterectomy* is and how and why a rape by a fully grown man would sometimes make this necessary for a little girl. He feels shouldn't avoid explaining it. He is mindful of what Desmond Tutu once said about not shying away from talking to kids

---

[130] This is what happened one day when having breakfast with the author's oldest daughters aged six and four.
[131] Faulkner, J (2011), *The Importance of Being Innocent,* Melbourne: Cambridge University Press, pages 60–61, 144, and 148. The passage cited has been reproduced here with permission of Cambridge University Press, Melbourne. For a similar perspective: Betts, H, "We can't shelter kids from sex entirely" *The Guardian*, London, 22 June 2013. https://www.theguardian.com/commentisfree/2013/jun/22/cant-shelter-kids-sex-completely
[132] "Baby has hysterectomy," *IOL News*, Johannesburg, 3 November 2001. http://www.freerepublic.com/focus/fr/562262/posts This news item makes shocking reading. So, he has to explain.

about rape.[133] She is hushed but most interested. He tells her what rape is: "when a man forces his penis into a girl's vagina. It's sex without her permission. When a man does that to a little girl it really damages her insides. She can die like that four-year-old girl". He uses the diagrams in his copy of that classic reference book *Gray's Anatomy*, which she finds fascinating. He tells her what was likely to have happened to the two girls internally when a man put his big penis through each little girl's tiny vagina. He tells her the need for one girl to have her internal reproductive organs removed was because of the severe damage and that it means she can never give birth to a baby. He explains that the 4-year-old's death was probably caused by rupture of her intestines during the rape causing *peritonitis*. This is advanced stuff for a 5-year-old but he is pleased his little girl is informed and at least realises the seriousness of it all for a little child like her.[134] Moreover, he has also discussed with her what to do if she is scared about a man.[135] They have looked at part of the Daniel Morcombe Foundation web site. Keith is critical of the site's advice about telling

kids to report the incident to a teacher, a carer, a Police officer, a counsellor, or a 'safety helper'. He told her: "If you feel worried about a man wanting to touch your vulva, you know, in a way that you don't like, there are things you can do. Tell him: 'No!' Then, if you can, run away or even scream. People who do those things to little kids don't like it if you scream because it attracts attention to them. Then, tell somebody about it. That's the advice of the Morcombe

Playing hide-and-seek. (iStockphoto, Posed by model.)

---

[133] Tutu, D., "To protect our children, we must talk to them about rape." *The Guardian*, London, 26 April 2013. http:// www.theguardian.com/commentisfree/2013/apr/26/protect-children-talk-rape-desmond-tutu. "We must not be squeamish about bringing this issue to the dinner table." Desmond Tutu was a former Anglican Archbishop of Cape Town and a recipient of the Nobel Peace Prize.

[134] Keith is on the right track. See Rock, L., "What parents can do to keep their children safe from abuse." *The Guardian*, London, 1 June 2014. http://www.theguardian.com/society/2014/jun/01/keep-children-safe-from-sex-abuse. Lucy Rock describes how a 3-year-old was sexually abused and so advocates early awareness and training in protective strategies even at the tender age of just 3. Keith's Eppie is not too young.

[135] Like so many, Keith assumes that child sexual abusers are men and not women or other children.

site. The problem is, what if one of those people is the abuser or potential abuser?"[136] Eppie listens attentively. She has a thirst for knowledge.

She has been engaged in many other activities. She loves playing hide-and-seek in their bush property. She becomes quite skilled at coping on her own in the bush and knows how to be careful about snakes and what not to do if she sees one sunning itself on a rock. She is also interested in the birds seen in their rocky bushland and one day excitedly brought Keith into the bush to show him a nest she found with eggs in it. She often refers to a book on Keith's bookshelves about Australian birds. She calls it the "Pizzey book"[137] and takes it in the car with them whenever they go camping. As a teacher, he has been teaching her to read. He does it not through 'phonics'[138] which is how teachers teach kids to read these days and taught him to read in the early 1950s but simply by reading nursery rhymes to her and letting her point out each word to him and say it to him. Thus she learns what words are pronounced by recognising them. Phonics would not be appropriate for words like 'thorough', 'palm', 'cabriolet', and 'croissant'. He concentrated initially her favourite 'Flower Fairies' books by Cicely Mary Barker.[139] Thus, she learned not sounds but words.[140] He also

---

[136] https://danielmorcombe.com.au/keeping-kids-safe-resources/ and https://danielmorcombe.com.au/wp-content/uploads/2023/10/DMF_React_2023.pdf and https://danielmorcombe.com.au/wp-content/uploads/2023/08/MyBodySafetyBooklet_Consent_A5.pdf Keith is critical of the site's advice about telling kids to report the incident to a teacher, a carer, a Police officer, a counsellor, or a 'safety helper'. What if one of those people is the abuser? That was the case when Gerard Byrnes was the child protection advisor at a Catholic primary school in Toowoomba. He was convicted of raping 13 girls in his classes (digital rape). He was so well respected that when a girl's parents complained to Police, the school took no action. Trenwith, C., "Ten years not enough for rapist teacher." *Brisbane Times*, 22 October 2010. https://www.brisbanetimes.com.au/national/queensland/ten-years-not-enough-for-rapist-teacher-attorney-general-20101022-16x37.html Also, Elks, S., "Dozen girls abused after report lapse". *The Australian*, Sydney, 18 February 2014. Veteran schoolteacher and student protection officer Gerard Vincent Byrnes was arrested for molesting or raping 13 of his students, aged eight to 10, in November 2008, 14 months after one of his Grade 4 students complained to the principal, the Royal Commission into Institutional Responses to Child Sexual Abuse heard. Later, the Principal was charged for not reporting the abuse. http://www.theaustralian.com.au/national-affairs/in-depth/dozen-girls-abused-after-report-lapse/story-fngburq5-1226829767670#

[137] Pizzey, G. & Knight, F., (1997) *Field Guide to the Birds of Australia*. Sydney : Angus & Robertson.

[138] "What is phonics and why is it used to teach reading?" *The Conversation*, Canberra, 20 June 2024. https://theconversation.com/what-is-phonics-and-why-is-it-used-to-teach-reading-232593?utm

[139] "Cicely Mary Barker", *Wikipedia*. https://en.wikipedia.org/wiki/Cicely_Mary_Barker

[140] This is how the author taught his eldest son to read at age four. He now has a PhD.

teaches her to write. During this learning to read and write period, she gets lots of 'Hi Fives' from Keith as she progresses.

She really loves having things explained to her. Her appetite is voracious. And, through her iPad, the internet has become an important tool for her. By age five she accesses *Wikipedia*.

One evening he is pleasantly surprised. They've been sitting together on the couch watching Keith's DVD of *The Shiralee*. Towards the end, the little girl Buster is badly injured when she is hit by a car on a country road. She is unconscious and her father takes her to hospital where she remains in a coma for many days. Keith notices tears running down Eppie's face. She has clearly been affected by the drama in

Learning to write. (*iStockphoto*. Posed by model.)

this video version of *The Shiralee*.[141] He is impressed that his little five-year-old is so caring and compassionate about what has happened. They discuss her feelings of sadness and compassion.

Several times, he has talked to Eppie about their need for secrecy. He has told her how he should have handed her in to the Department of Child Safety when he found her. He explained the fears he had for her future in foster care. As time passes, he alerts her to news items involving foster care especially where children have been abused while 'in care'. This may be seen as bias and manipulation. However, he sees that extolling the virtues of foster care would also be manipulation even deception. With his understanding of foster care that was influenced by his friend and former child safety officer, Fiona, and what happened to

---

[141] Niland, D. (1955), *The Shiralee*. Sydney: Angus & Robertson.

Also: https://en.wikipedia.org/wiki/The_Shiralee_(1987_film) A superb *ABC TV* film of the novel.

At first during the early 1950s, when swagman Macauley takes his 4-year-old daughter, Buster, with him across the Australian outback, she is a burden for him. He can't get or hold down jobs with her hanging around. Then gradually as they share hardships and adventures, her loyalty and affection bring him to realise that she is his only joy.

A "shiralee" is an old Australian slang word for a swagman's burden: the few heavier possessions an itinerant labourer has to lug around with him wherever he goes across the countryside as he looks for casual work.

Logan Marr in America[142] and other cases in Australia like what happened to Tiahleigh Palmer,[143] he feels it is his duty to protect Eppie from the inherent risks in foster care. He feels children need a committed parent to provide long term support and nurturing and he is providing that regardless of the fact that he is not her biological parent.[144] Without that kind of commitment, he feels that some foster care family members might take advantage of her.[145] So, she has to know about foster care and what it could mean for her if she was removed from him especially the all too common long term negative effects on her as a foster care child as she grew up.[146] When they see mention of Tiahleigh Palmer on the TV news, he doesn't hold back in explaining to her what happened. As we shall see, one outcome of their discussing foster care is that she begins to fear people she calls 'Child Safety witches'. This comes from her knowledge of the *Hansel and Gretel* fairy story where a little brother and sister find themselves lost in a forest and fall into the hands of a witch who decides to eat them.

---

[142] Frontline PBS, (2003), *Failure to Protect: The Taking of Logan Marr*. Portland, Oregon: Oregon State University Press. The full 52 minute programme may be viewed on *YouTube* at: https://www.youtube.com/watch? v=wT0p1KgJ7rE Five-year-old Logan Marr was killed by her foster carer who was also a senior child protection officer. In the *YouTube* item, Logan Marr was a real little girl. She was not acting. She suffered a horrific death.

See also: Simpson, T. "Logan's Truth". *Common Sense Independent*, Issue 1, Volume One. https://www.docdroid.net/ 1TRNCsj/comsens1a-1-pdf (28 pages)

[143] 12-year-old Tiahleigh Palmer was sexually abused and murdered while in foster care: https://en.wikipedia.org/wiki/Murder_of_Tiahleigh_Palmer It was so serious that it could not be covered up.

[144] This commitment is the 'permanency' many advocates of child removal and adoption promote for the benefit of children removed from their families but which Keith is now providing. Eppie is benefitting enormously from it.

[145] Because of secrecy provisions in all child protection legislation in every Australian state only a few cases of abuse have reached public view in the press or media. Thus, there is a general public perception that the activities of child protection departments are benign and in the best interests of children.

[146] There have been so many academic studies and official reports on this issue, for example:

Murray, G. (2003), *Final Report on Phase One of the Audit of Foster Carers Subject to Protection Notifications*, Brisbane: Queensland State Parliament.

Crime and Misconduct Commission, (2004), *Protecting Children: An Inquiry into Abuse of Children in Foster Care*, Brisbane: CMC/Queensland State Parliament.

These two public inquiries may seem out of date but twenty years later little has changed. Newcombe, M., "Our child protection system is clearly broken. Is it time to abolish it for a better model?" *The Conversation*, Sydney, 23 March 2023. https://theconversation.com/our-child-protection-system-is-clearly-broken-is-it-time-to-abolish-it-for-a-better-model-200716 She concludes: "Isn't it time we ditch an ineffective child protection system and instead invest in keeping children with their families and communities?"

Regarding internet safety, he alerts her to a problem: if he sets up an account for her with *Facebook* or other social media sites, she runs a great risk that she will be discovered. "Other users or 'friends' will ask questions and even if you don't give answers some could report to the Police or the Child Safety Department. So, please, please only use these sites with me. I have a *Facebook* account. She takes on board his advice. She already fears 'Child Safety witches'.

CHAPTER 7

Assertive Eppie

With her secret existence and him being an elderly sole parent, Keith has to be careful. He has to do often quite normal things like buying the weekly groceries, him having a hair cut, and a visit to a doctor for himself by going a long way from where they live so that he can maintain secrecy. They sometimes travel 130 km to Glen Innes or 160 km to Toowoomba for these purposes. While she was very little in the stroller with him, passers by comment to him: "Grandad helping out Mum?" He just smiles and says "Yes".

One day Keith is upset when he reads on the internet in a news item about a couple in Britain in their early sixties who had a their one-year-old toddler removed by officials because they were too old.[147] He is very upset and worried. He emails his friend Fiona. She responds by trying to re-assure him that it happened in Britain not Australia. Practices are different but she knows of relatives of kids in foster care in Queensland who were denied the possibility of caring for their grandchildren in a 'Kinship Care' arrangement because of their age.

Virtually since her birth Keith has been very aware of Eppie's small size. Although happy and fit, she is definitely undersized and skinny. He often feels as if she is like the proverbial runt of a litter of puppies but also feels that runts turn out to be the cleverest and most resilient. He thinks of *Jock of the Bushveld*[148] which he often reads to Eppie. She loves

---

[147] Burke, D., 'Britain's oldest new parents left 'devastated' after one-year-old child is taken away by Social Services'. *Daily Mail*, London, 29 April 2018. https://www.mirror.co.uk/news/uk-news/britains-oldest-new-parents-left-12449092? utm_source=mirror_newsletter&utm_medium=email&utm_content=EM_Mirror_Nletter_DailyNews_News_smalltease r_Image_Story3&utm_campaign=daily_newsletter

[148] Fitzpatrick, P., (1907), *Jock of the Bushveld*, Longmans, Green and Co., London.

these stories about Jock and gets him to read them to her many times. Jock was the smallest puppy and the runt. The odd little puppy grew into a great and fearless dog. Eppie loves the graphic drawings in the book. With his African heritage Keith loves the stories in it, too. And, they give her some African heritage.

This is one of the illustrations in the book.

When Eppie is four, they have a surprise visit from Fiona. It is the Christmas school holidays and she has travelled south from Yarrabah near Cairns where she teaches. She stays for two weeks. Eppie likes having her company and proudly shows her around focussing on things like the chooks and her favourite hen she calls 'Henny Penny'. She demonstrates her prowess on the trampoline and shows how she can now ride her bike in the driveway at the front of the house. She shows her how she can climb some of the granite boulders and how she jumps from one to another. Inside the house, she demonstrates her skills with her iPad and her ability to read some of her books. She especially loves the *Flower Fairies* books by Cicely Mary Barker. She is able to read passages to Fiona. She knows these little books by heart. Sometimes, she surprises Fiona by talking about items in the news, albeit in her own childish way.

During Fiona's stay they take her to the Girraween National Park for the day. Eppie shows Fiona many things about the park. Then, she excitedly and quietly waits with Fiona as they watch a Satin bowerbird[149] decorate his bower with blue objects like plastic clothes pegs, soft drink bottle tops and chocolate wrappers. Eppie has watched this before with Keith. Then, they see a female arrive. They watch quietly. The female briefly

A male Satin bower bird in his bower. (*Wikimedia Commons*, Joseph C. Boone.)

---

[149] 'Satin bowerbird', *Wikipedia*: https://en.wikipedia.org/wiki/Satin_bowerbird

inspects the bower but flies off. The male bower bird seems a little disappointed. He flies off. Then, to their surprise, while the male bower bird has flown off in search of more blue objects to decorate his bower, another male bower bird arrives, messes up the bower and steals some of the blue objects. Eppie breaks cover and chases him, shouting at him. But, Eppie then confesses to Fiona that she shouldn't have done that. "We should leave wild animals alone. It's their business." Fiona is very impressed with Eppie and can see Keith's influence.

Keith and Fiona discuss the Playgroup. He tells her how at one stage he was worried about one astute mother who knew the *Silas Marner* story and recognised the name 'Eppie'. Fiona tells him that while she thinks his desire to socialise Eppie is in her best interests, she feels that in the current circumstances it was a mistake. It could easily backfire. So, they decide that Fiona should take Eppie to the next Playgroup session and pretend to be her mother or give that impression. That is what happens during the second week of Fiona's visit. She is subtle and careful. Eppie is very excited about taking her to Playgroup. Keith stays at home. Eppie shows Fiona the toys and the activities they do. The subterfuge works. Eppie seems to understand the charade.

However, the woman who questioned Keith about Eppie's name, no longer brings her daughter, Melanie, because she has started her 'Prep' year at Graniteville State School.

During those few days, Fiona and Eppie talk. When Eppie asks her about her work, she tells her she's "a teacher just like your Mumma was. That's how I know him. We were teaching at the same school." During their conversations, she also explains that before she was a teacher, she was Child Safety Officer. Keith has told Eppie about foster care and Child Safety Officers. So, she asks Fiona what she did. Fiona confesses: "Sometimes my boss made me take kids away from their parents and into foster care. I hated doing it. That's why I stopped being a Child Safety Officer and became a teacher instead." During their talking, Fiona also mentioned that, "when some kids were very upset at being taken away from their parents, you know, crying and even screaming, the foster carer would give them a tablet to quieten them down. It made them all dopey and dreamy." Eppie asked: "Like a Zombie?"

Fiona laughed. She told Eppie that was a very wrong thing to do and it was another reason she stopped being a child safety officer.

Keith and Eppie are sad to farewell Fiona. So, the evening before her departure they explain to Eppie that she has to go back to her teaching job at Yarrabah. They tell her some of what teaching really is about and how both taught at the High School in Townsville. They explain that Keith has retired because he had been teaching for so many years and is old. Fiona tells Eppie that she wanted to teach Aboriginal kids who live a long way from a big town. Eppie has seen Aboriginal kids when she and Keith have been on shopping trips to Canning Town and they have talked about them. Keith had explained that Aboriginal people lived in Australia for hundreds and hundreds, even thousands of years. She didn't fully understand the numbers but still got the gist.

A week after Fiona's departure, Keith received a long e-mail from her. She was full of praise for Eppie and for Keith's parenting. This is part of what she e-mailed him:

> She is a healthy, fit and loving little child. The doctor's assessment of her speaks volumes. You even get her to brush her teeth properly every night and she does so without pressure form you.
>
> Having witnessed the loving emotional and physical interaction between you two, it is clear that she has unshakable trust in you and there is not the slightest hint of you wanting to sexually exploit her through that trust that she has.
>
> If you were a thirty year old single female parent and Eppie was your biological daughter, most in the Department would now see you as a shining example and even ask you if you wanted to become a foster carer. But, in your situation I think you should wait at least another year before getting a lawyer to apply for a birth certificate. It will still be risky but the extra year would reinforce the view that Eppie is bonded to you and that it would not be in her best interests to break that bond, despite your age. And, it would add even more weight to your successful parenting, you know in terms of her reading, writing, computer use, physical abilities like swimming and bike riding, etc. etc. However, the Department's holier than thou officers are unpredictable. Many have their own personal agendas despite official practice and procedure manuals. Simply put, three big problems for you are still that you are male, you are old, and you supposedly put her life at risk when you found her. You are still likely to face prejudice. But, as time passes you are proving that she has survived very well in your care and consequently those three problem areas are diminishing.

Your parenting is exemplary. Quite apart from the committed love you have for her, I see in you a clear example of the so-called "Westermark Effect".[150]

Keith is very pleased with this unofficial assessment and endorsement of his parenting by a qualified person. He shows it to Eppie and reads it to her, explaining as he does so.

She is happy, too: "She's a nice lady."

Keith: "Yes, I've known her for a long time."

When Keith watches Eppie on the trampoline or with the chooks or sitting with him at a campfire, he knows his feelings: he loves his little girl like anything, feels extremely close to her and knows he would die to save her. He knows his love for this child is deep, indelible and fundamental.

Eppie warmed to Fiona. (*iStockphoto*, Posed by models)

Even though he is not biologically related to her, he is bonded. He was smitten during the minutes after he found her. That was when he held that tiny dirty and cold but alive and helpless creature to his bare chest. He cannot undo the bond. He is tactile with her and cuddles her frequently, often just on a whim. And, it becomes reciprocal. She likes to catch him unawares, rushing up to him or leaping onto him, hugging and kissing him, telling

---

[150] The "Westermark Effect", *Wikipedia*, https://en.wikipedia.org/wiki/Westermarck_effect. The Westermark effect, also known as reverse sexual imprinting, is a psychological hypothesis that people who live in close domestic proximity during the first few years of their lives become desensitised to sexual attraction (e.g. parents and siblings).

Of course, it is not always the case that parents are unable to engage sexually with their children. Some parents, male and female, do exploit their own children sexually. And, when this happens child protection authorities and the press have a field day. However, research has shown that most parents' protective instincts usually or normally prevent them from abusing their own children. See: Parker, H. & P. (1986), 'Father-daughter sexual abuse: An emerging perspective'. *American Journal of Orthopsychiatry*. 56(4), October 1986, pp 531-549. http:// onlinelibrary.wiley.com/doi/10.1111/j.1939-0025.1986.tb03486.x/ abstract This is a very short abstract. The author has a copy of the full article. It is quite an old article but it has not been overturned since. Yet, the Parker perspective is not new. See: Westermark, E. (1921), *The History of Human Marriage*. London: Macmillan. (Originally published in 1891.) This has for ages been the common sense basis for our society's trust of parents. The belief is that close personal contact between a child and her/his parent(s) during a child's early years discourages sexual attraction. For decades there has been academic debate on this issue of 'reverse sexual imprinting' particularly as to whether this so-called 'Westermark effect' is an innate biological aversion or the result of a social construct. Maybe, it is both?

him: "I love you so much, Mumma." Of course, he loves this reaffirmation. This little girl has made his life so worthwhile.

On the basis of his always being honest with her, he tells her about his marriage and its failure, even when she is only four. He tells her why he thinks it failed but stresses that what he says is his view. He tells her about his two daughters, showing her the photo album he has of them. She is most interested and asks questions. He tells her how he misses them but they are grown up now. He also tells her that some of the things he does with her are what he did with them like the games they play and stories he tells. He tells her they are all married now and one has recently had a baby son. All this comes out, not in one big eruption, but little by little as she matures. He tells her how sad he is that he has virtually no contact with them, although he has their addresses and sends them Christmas cards each year but gets no response.

A day before each of Eppie's birthdays they leave for a short camping trip to northern New South Wales. They always camp their first night at the same un-official rest area where Keith found her. Every year, he photographs her sitting or then stranding where the Coles grocery bag was.

During the first year celebration, Keith also tidied up the area a little. He collected rubbish and took it all to an official rest area at Bluff Rock closer to Tenterfield where he put it all in a proper rubbish bin. He did this every year whenever they came to celebrate Eppie's birthday. And, Eppie happily joins him doing this tidying up. She doesn't want her birthplace polluted. On the morning of her birthday whenever he photographs her she usually stands next to the bushes smiling coyly for the camera. As the years pass, she starts posing and showing off during these birthday photo shoots. She's becoming a confident little miss.

For her fourth birthday, Keith was able to find a Coles reusable plastic shopping bag like the original one that he found her in. They place it at the same spot and photograph her next to it.

This is Eppie's fourth birthday photo next to a Coles plastic grocery bag like the one she was found in. She shouts "Yee Hah! Yay! Yay!" She is a happy intelligent little girl who is even beginning to show off about her origin with some pride as being rather special and unique. (*iStockphoto & PR Media Solutions. Posed by model.*)

He likes to ensure that they talk openly about her origins and these photos are a good basis for that. Moreover, they now have an enduring record of her as she grows. She will have a record for decades to come that she might be able to show her own eventual off-spring one day. But, for the moment she is proud of her origins found in an old grocery bag in the bush. She already realises that it is unique and sees it as special. These annual visits to her birthplace lead to an almost perverse pride in her origins such that she sometimes refers to herself as "the baby from the bush", a tongue in cheek image she even uses later during her school days.

They speculate about what her mother and father were like. But he never ever denigrates either of her biological parents no matter what they think their backgrounds might have been, usually finding possible explanations for why they abandoned her. In fact, he sometimes says things like: "You are so pretty. You must have got it from your mother" or "You are tough like your father probably was." He is always concerned that she should never think negatively about herself or her origins. This journey to her birthplace is an annual ritual that she loves. Each time they camp at the rest area they have a special birthday breakfast. She loves boiled eggs with 'dipper' cut-up bread pieces which they call 'soldiers'. Then, they celebrate with a birthday cake and presents. They also clean up the place a little because more rubbish accumulates each year.

While he is always honest and positive about her origins and never blames her unknown biological mother for abandoning her as a new born baby to be left alone in the bush, they sometimes speculate about what her mother looked like. When she is five, they are looking at a women's magazine. There is an article with photos of female movie stars past and present. They discuss who her mother might look like. She says she probably looks like Nicole Kidman. He tells her he thinks she would look like Ingrid Bergman. They have different but complementary ideals about her unknown biological mother.

Eppie has always known how Keith came into her life. And, she always sees him as her mother figure. As she began to vocalise and then start the early stages of talking as a one-year-old toddler, her name for him spoke volumes. Her calling him 'Mumma' came naturally but it was at her initiative, not his. He didn't coach or teach her. Nevertheless, he feels flattered.

When she turned five, Keith gave her a new more advanced *iPad 9th Generation*. It was expensive but with her ever increasing skills she really appreciated it. In fact, she just loved it. They spent time loading apps of interest to her like *YouTube, ABC Kids*, and even *Google Maps*. However, a condition he set was that it should have a security app downloaded onto it. Then, they discover that both his iPhone and her iPad have a *Find my iPhone* and a *Find my iPad* facility on them. It is a GPS tracking app which they can both use to track her iPad or his iPhone should they mislay them or should they be stolen. She likes that. He likes it because it is uncomplicated and he is a bit of a Luddite when it comes to computers.[151]

---

[151] "Luddite", *Wikipedia*. https://en.wikipedia.org/wiki/Luddite These days, the term "Luddite" is often used to describe someone who is opposed or resistant to new technologies.

The following five photos sum up much of the relationship between them at this point. They also demonstrate why Keith adores her. She knows this, appreciates it, and often returns the affection with cuddles and kisses that she initiates. Nevertheless, she has come to understand him and has his measure. She knows his feelings for her and is sometimes cheeky and impish as she plays up to him. She is a little vain at times and likes posing for him to photograph her. She takes him for granted and increasingly belittles him until one day soon she has a sudden complete reversal in her negative attitude towards him.

There is a hint of self-centred spoilt brat in her. Sometimes she walks over him. When combined with her impulsive courage there are be problems these are soon to come to a head. In the next chapter this will be the underlying cause a serious life-threatening near disaster for her. Keith is perhaps too much of a softie playmate rather than a parent. However, shortly after her sixth birthday, he quickly switches from playmate to protective parent and this saves her life. He puts his life on the line for her. She realises this learns a fundamental lesson about him and that she values his bonded love for her. It is a turning point in her life as she switches to unshakeable loyalty towards him.

In this photo she has persuaded him to have a game of football with him on the back lawn but in the rain. He doesn't want to but gives in to her. They have fun.

When she is like this, a phrase runs through his mind: "She melts me." (*iStockphoto*. Posed by model.)

In the Bunya Mountains rain forest Eppie is crossing a creek using a fallen tree trunk. She loves challenges like this. (Note: she is barefooted.) Keith loves her courage and toughness.

She is a beautiful child in both looks and in her very independent personality as well as being clearly very intelligent. He believes his caring and parenting might be a small factor in that but deep inside he feels that the person that she is has been largely inherited. It's in her genes. So, he often wonders what her biological parents were like as people, their relationships with others, and what their interests were. He then wonders if and when he gets Eppie's birth certificate, will the Police look for her birth mother. Will he be able to arrange a meeting between Eppie and her? How would it go? Will she like Eppie? Will Eppie like her? He thinks more of Eppie and his adoration of her. He is for ever amazed that such a lovely person came into his life by chance. Or, sometimes the romantic in him wonders whether perhaps it was divine intervention?

A photo which Keith took of Eppie in Tenterfield three months before her fourth birthday. It is cold and he has dressed her for the weather. He adores her. She knows this and is willingly posing for him.

Eppie, shortly before her sixth birthday. There is a cocky and enigmatic cheekiness in this photo. She loves him but, as a developing girl, she is getting restless and impatient with him. She has his measure, tends to manipulate him, and even denigrates him at times. She is increasingly a difficult child. (These photos by *iStockphoto*. Posed by the same model)

Growing vanity of youth

We've seen what Eppie at age six. If we go back a few years, we see her personality just beginning to rebel. This culminates in near violent death for her shortly after her sixth birthday. Earlier, after she has turned three, they are in Canning Town to buy groceries. After loading the groceries into the car they go to a chemist shop. While Keith is waiting to be served, some rather cute little bead bracelets catch Eppie's fancy. She picks one down off the display rack. After he has been served, Eppie tells him she wants it. But, he is not in to buying her anything she wants whenever she wants it. "We'll think about it next time we're in town."

But, she starts demanding: "I want it!"

Keith: "Come we're going." He holds her hand as he leads her out of the shop.

A classic look of defiance. (*iStockphoto*. Posed by model.)

Once outside on the footpath, she shouts: "I'm not going! I want it!" She stomps her feet and shouts again. "I'm not going! I want it!"

People watch the commotion. Adults smile as they witness a typical toddler tantrum.

Keith holds his ground. Without a word, he holds her hand and gently but firmly pulls her as he starts walking towards the car. Still protesting loudly she allows him to lead her away. As he is getting his keys out of his pocket and unlocking the car, she stands waiting, very grumpy with arms folded across her chest in a classic gesture of defiance. He lifts her into the car and tries to buckle her up but she arches her back and won't let him. He waits and pretends to check the groceries already packed in the car. Seeing that he is not responding to her tantrum, she settles down. He buckles her up and off they go. He puts on a CD of some of her favourite *Playschool* songs.

He has seen it all before with his previous kids and knows there may be more of this behaviour to come. However, he doesn't realise that this is a very clever kid. As time passes her defiance sometimes morphs into manipulation of him, exploiting his softness and adoration of her.

He tends to dress her in practical clothes for everyday use like shorts and T-shirts. One day when she is still four they briefly visit an op-shop in Graniteville. They are on their way to a car sprint racing show near Toowoomba. She suddenly wants him to buy her a second-hand red dress that she has seen. He buys it for her as it costs only two dollars. Then, she sees some silver coloured girls shoes. She wants them even though they are too big for her. But, they cost only a dollar. So, he buys them. Once in the car and about to leave for the car

show, she wants to change into her new clothes. "I want to look pretty in a nice dress."

Keith: "But, you're pretty anyway."

She starts getting undressed in the back of the car. So, he helps change her. The dress does look nice on her but the silver shoes are way too big.

At the car show, she is thirsty. Their car with cool water in it is in the carpark. She wants a can of cool fizzy drink. So, he buys her a can. She loves walking along in her new "pretty" dress and holding the cool drink. She's not used to fizzy drinks, doesn't really like it, and doesn't drink it but, keeping her distance from him, she thinks she is "cool" walking independently in her new dress, fancy silver shoes, and fizzy drink. He thinks this stirring of an independent streak in her is sweet.

The ever so 'cool' Eppie at the car show, pretending to be independent and not connected with Keith. This is the pink dress and the far too big silver shoes.

Six months after her fifth birthday, they are in the Grand Central mall in Toowoomba. She wants a black dress she has seen in a shop window. She is insistent. "It's so cool."

He doesn't say so but he thinks it is too mature looking for a little girl of five. He resists and she puts on a tantrum, stomping her feet and being a nuisance. He gives in. But, she is sulky for the rest of the day. Back at home early next morning, she wants to wear it. He helps her put it on. When she looks in the mirror, he agrees with her that she looks lovely in it. But, before lunch, she is still cross with him. So, she picks up one of her dollies and goes for a walk down the drive. After a few minutes, he is concerned and walks down to the drive entrance. He sees her walking along the side of the road.

Eppie walking along the road in her new 'cool' black dress with one of her dollies. She is oblivious to the dangers for a little girl alone on a lonely country road. (*Getty Images.* Posed by model.)

He makes a sudden but very rare switch from being a friendly playmate to being a parent. He runs after her, picks her up, and carries her squealing and kicking out her legs all the way back to the house. In the sitting room he stands her up in front of him and holds her firmly at her upper arms as he sits on the couch in front of her. He tells her in no uncertain and very strong terms about the danger she put herself in. She hasn't really seen him like this before and is stunned and silent. He is not angry but forceful. "You are a very pretty little girl and you're dressed in a very pretty way, too! You are gorgeous! A man driving past might have seen you all alone by yourself. He would see a pretty little girl all by herself. And, she's wearing a sexy looking dress. Like a fox, he would think: 'What a tasty little girl. And, she's all by herself. There's no other cars. So, nobody can see me picking her up.' He would have thought: 'This is my lucky day'. He would have grabbed you and taken you to his house, taken your clothes off, and done horrible things to you. Remember we talked about a little girl called Kylie after we saw something on the TV news. A man gave her a lift in his car. He didn't take her where she wanted. No, he drove her to his house. After doing horrible things to her vulva, he killed her by squeezing her throat so she couldn't breathe. Do you remember what happened to that girl Kylie?"[152]

Eppie is quiet apart from a meek "Yes."

One of the presents he gave her for Christmas when she turned five was a little girl's make-up set which he bought her in Graniteville. She sometimes indulges herself by using it. She is growing up. He shows her how to use it but with an emphasis on moderation and subtlety.

(*Inmagine.* Posed by model.)

In mid-September, two months before she turns six, they travel to Toowoomba for the annual Carnival of Flowers. During the Grand Parade along the main streets in the centre of town, there are many beautiful and clever floats. Eppie is enthralled by them. However, just at the start of the Parade a Police car drives along the streets making sure everybody has moved out of the way to the footpath. Stubborn Eppie is slow to move. Keith asks her to come back to the footpath with him. She ignores him. The Policeman driving the car points at her and shouts at

her quite loudly using the car's loudspeaker: "Move back to the footpath!" Eppie gives him the finger and doesn't move. The Policeman ignores her and drives on. Once the car has passed, she saunters back to Keith standing on the footpath. "I just don't like somebody giving me orders like that. He could have said: 'Would you please move back to the footpath.'" Keith smiles but reminds her that it might not be a good idea to attract attention to herself.

Eppie and the Police car.

---

152 See: "Murder of Kylie Maybury" in *Wikipedia* at https://en.wikipedia.org/wiki/Murder_of_Kylie_Maybury (Note that back in 1978 Kylie's grandfather and uncle were suspects and they both committed suicide in jail. Over thirty years later and with DNA profiling unknown at the time of her murder, the real killer was caught and jailed for life. Having himself been falsely accused, convicted of rape, and jailed, Keith is acutely aware of what happened to those two innocent men.)

She says: "Okay. But, he could have been polite and not such a loud bossy boots."

We see Eppie as a growing little girl who sometimes makes life a little difficult for him. Although now still only five but approaching six, she is also beginning to head towards being a "tweenie". With some prepubescent interests just beginning, these have been stimulated by her use of the internet through her iPad. She doesn't have any *Facebook, Tik Tok,* or *Instagram* account yet, mainly because she and Keith have discussed how these could lead to her discovery and her fear of the dreaded foster care. However, every Saturday morning she watches *Rage* on ABC Television.[153]

Two of the posters on her wall: (*Left*) Taylor Swift. (*Wikimedia/ CreativeCommons*) (*Right*) Spice Girl Geri Halliwell. (*Wikimedia/GeriHalliwell*)

She has been using her iPad to view performances of popular female singers that she likes such as Dami Im, Taylor Swift, Mylie Cyrus, Adele, and the Spice Girls. She has downloaded and printed posters of some and put them up on her bedroom wall. She and Keith have discussed them and it is clear to him that one of the things that impresses her about these idols is: "They look so pretty and so sexy. I want to be cool and hot like them when I grow up. Not like you. You're so old."

He is disappointed but doesn't respond.

She is increasingly going on about wanting to wear 'cool' sexy clothes like female stars and idols. One morning, he has dressed her in her favourite 'pinkified' dress and spent ages on her hair. She tells him: "I want short sexy outfits like Taylor Swift. This one isn't cool." She is surly and sour.

Eppie doesn't like her 'pinkified' dress any more. She says: "It's not sexy." (*Shutterstock.* Posed by model.)

---

153 See: "Rage" (TV program), *Wikipedia*: https://en.wikipedia.org/wiki/Rage_(TV_program)

He loves her so much. But, despite his efforts to please her, she is increasingly and overtly negative. He doesn't know what to do now that she has recently turned six.

She goes on more about wanting to wear cool sexy clothes like the stars. Keith is finding her exasperating. So, he gets her to watch a *YouTube* clip of Shirley Temple. He asks her to sit on the couch next to him and look at a few things on his computer. "You know that song *On the Good Ship Lollipop*? It was sung by Shirley Temple."

Eppie: "Yes, I know."

Keith: "Well, I'd like to show you a little more about her. She's dead now and died aged 85, a little older than me. As an adult, she became a famous diplomat. But when she was your age she was famous for being very cute and pretty especially in movies. She also used like to wear short dresses. I have no problems with that for her or for you. That's what she liked and what you like."

ShirleyTemple.
(*Alamy* Images.)

Using his computer, he shows her some photos of Shirley Temple in her short dresses.

Keith: "I think she looks lovely. You also like short dresses?"

Eppie: "Yes."

Keith: "Okay, now I want to show you something where Shirley is singing that famous song of hers *On the Good Ship Lollipop*. It's on *YouTube*."

They watch a video clip of 6-year-old Shirley Temple in 1934 singing *On the Good Ship Lollipop* as she walks down the aisle of a DC-2 airliner. They watch her reaction as men subtly start groping her. He pauses the *YouTube* clip at the crucial moment about halfway through to watch the men's hands. "Notice how Shirley was trying to pull her short skirt down several times to stop it riding up and showing he *broekies*. She was instinctively trying to protect her modesty".[154]

---

[154] To view Shirley Temple singing *On the Good Ship Lollipop* among a group of ogling men as she strolls down the aisle of a DC-2 airliner, see https://www.youtube.com/watch?v=WLLSqpYyPD8. About halfway through at almost exactly 2 minutes, see how she pulls her short dress down to stop it riding up. Watch the men's hands.

See what novelist Graham Greene had to say about Shirley: "Her admirers – middle-aged men and clergymen – respond to her dubious coquetry, to the sight of her well-shaped and desirable little body, packed with enormous vitality, only because the safety curtain of story and dialogue drops between their intelligence and their desire". (*Wikipedia*, https:// en.wikipedia.org/wiki/Shirley_Temple)

Eppie: "Why?"

Keith: "She was a good actress and only six years old at the time. But, did you see how in the middle of all that singing there were those creepy men hanging around her."

Eppie: "Yes, I saw that."

Keith: "Those men in that movie all seemed to want to put their hands on her thighs and perhaps then move them elsewhere on her body, didn't they?"

Eppie: "Where to?"

Keith: "To the crotch of her *broekies*. They wanted to touch where her vulva is. But, she was lucky. She had a protective mother who was always present during filming and everywhere little Shirley went. "

Eppie is silent, taking in what she has just been shown.

He adds: "In that clip it is almost as if there was a little six-year-old girl in a short sexy skirt all alone in a plane and surrounded by paedophiles eager to get their hands on her thighs and even her vulva. The people who made movies with her starring in them played upon that. It made them big money. I don't think that movie would be acceptable today. You know what a paedophile is?"

Eppie: "A man who wants to have sex with a little kid."

Unfortunately for Keith, while that *YouTube* clip of Shirley Temple does have a cautionary effect on Eppie, she still thinks he is too old and doesn't appreciate modern 'cool' sexy things. She tells him so: "You're just too old. You need to keep up with the times."

Later, they are walking along a forest trail in the Bunya Mountains National Park. She strides on ahead of him. She is too fast for him. Eventually, she stops and stands with her hands on her hips waiting for him. In a disparaging tone: "Come on! You're so slow."

On another occasion, she berates him: "Oh Mumma. You're such an old fuddy-duddy!"

Increasingly, Keith is feeling disappointed about himself and his relationship with her.

She persists in wanting a new more sexy dress. Eventually, he gives in. Shortly before her sixth birthday, they drive to Toowoomba and the Grand Central Mall there. They walk around the many shops. She loves the exciting bustle of the place. In one of the specialist children's shops where they also sell dance and ballet clothes, she decides there is an outfit she really likes. It's actually in the dance wear section. With a white open neck T-shirt and a light blue skirt with little bobbles at the hem, she tries it on. "It's just what I want. I must have it! It's like Shirley Temple."

Keith: "Isn't it a bit short? A person can almost see your *broekies*."

Eppie: "I love it! It's sexy. It's cool."

Not wanting to displease Eppie, he buys it. She doesn't change back into the 'adult style' black dress she was wearing when they drove to Toowoomba. In the mall she tries to show herself off in her new dress, putting on airs and graces as she occasionally spins around. Some people notice her. He also notices occasional grown up men's eyes taking a glancing interest in her.

Back at home, she wears the new very short outfit all day next day and the next day. He actually compliments her several times because he genuinely thinks she looks lovely in it. At one stage, he sees her in her new 'sexy' skirt standing on a chair looking out of the dining room window while it is raining outside. He thinks

Two days later at home in her new dress. (*Depositphotos.* Posed by model.)

she she is like a little baby bird looking out of the nest at the outside world. Not enough feathers to fly yet, she is so eager to escape from the nest into the exciting world of shops, beautiful dresses, and showing herself off to the public. With her little immature matchstick legs and pretty face, he is entranced by her.

As Eppie's sixth birthday approaches she wants some special *broekies* she has seen on the internet. She showed him. He told her: "We can get new *broekies* at K-Mart or Big W."

No, she is adamant she wants these. "They're so cool and pretty."

Finally, he gives in and lets her order a pair using his VISA card. They arrive in the mail in time for her birthday. The pants are extremely skimpy and held up with bows at her hips.

He tells her: "But, they're really a pair of bikini swimming tog bottoms."

Ignoring him: "I'm going just to wear the *broekies*, not the top. So cool like that."

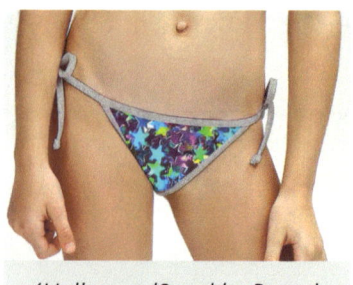

(*HollywoodSparkle*. Posed by model.)

She loves them and tries them on, getting him to tie the bows at her hips. She chose the smallest size. She admires herself in the mirror. "Cool! Sexy! Don't like the bra top. I love the *broekies* with those stars. They say there's something sparkly in there."

She senses Kieth is not impressed but he doesn't say so. Reluctantly he takes photos of her posing. He is upset that she pushes him to do so. "Please only wear them at home. They're so brief. Very alluring. I worry about you wearing them."

Eppie: "Yes. That's why I like them, they're exciting. I feel cool wearing them. I just love them as my secret sexy *broekies* not just swimming togs. You're such an old fuddy-duddy."

He worries about her fixation with sex. He wonders: 'She's only six. As *broekies*, they're way too erotic for a little girl. She's far too young. Has her internet access got out of hand? Or, am I being too prudish? I suppose she's a normal little girl with developing sexuality.'

For parents of little girls with internet access, this is a common dilemma.[155]

He is beginning to see his parenting and now his efforts to keep her on side coming to nought. He is running out of options. She is so difficult. What can he do? He feels from her criticisms of him that he must be too old and going to seed. Sometimes at night, this grown man cries himself to sleep. Who can he turn to? A psychologist would have to report him and he is so sceptical about psychology anyway. And, it would be foster care for her. "I love her so much. It would be an absolute disaster." He is, as they say, caught between a rock and a hard place.

---

[155] Thomas, C., "Should you really dress little girls in leopard-skin bikinis, Liz? Actress accused of sexualising youngsters with bikini range", *Daily Mail*, London, 17 September 2012. https://www.dailymail.co.uk/news/ article-2204284/Liz-Hurley-accused-sexualising-youngsters-bikini-range.html Many news outlets ran with this controversy. What is more disturbing to some is the 'come on' sexualised expression on the little girl's face as she models Liz Hurley's leopard skin pattern bikini. In this novel, Eppie puts on similar sexualised looks as she models her new panties for Keith. That is what concerns him, quite apart from the panties.

Also: Varma-White, K., "Gwyneth Paltrow's kid bikinis stir debate: Are they appropriate for girls?", *Today*, 24 April 2013. https://www.today.com/parents/gwyneth-paltrows-kid-bikinis-stir-debate-are-they-appropriate-girls-6c9575906

Two weeks after her sixth birthday, she is in a huff with him. "I want to live in town. I don't like these chooks anymore. And, I'm bored with this bush and those big rocks. They're not cool. You're not cool. You're old and slow and crinkly. You're a loser. You don't even know how to use your phone. I have to show you! Now, I want to wear cool town clothes every day."

Pouting for the camera, her face is looking overly made up for a little six-year-old, especially with so much lipstick, blusher, eye-lid sparkles, and some eye shadow. They make her look pasty-faced and tarted-up. Keith did this under pressure from her. She kept wanting more of every make-up item. But, he also did it just for a bit of fun for her. (*Shutterstock.* Posed by model.)

Her very short skirt outfit is in the washing basket waiting to be washed. She is quite bossy: "You should have washed it."

Keith: "I couldn't. You were wearing it."

In a peevish way, she takes one of her older but slightly less pinkified pretty dresses, and shoes and socks out of her wardrobe. She wants him to help her "look nice".

As an overbearing and imperious six-year-old, he is desperate to please his increasingly difficult little girl. He recently read an article in an old TIME magazine about a six-year old not dressing the way her mother wanted her to.[156] So, he decides to work with her. Using the kids make-up set he bought for her fifth birthday, he puts make-up on her. He adds some blusher to her cheeks. She keeps wanting more of each item. She looks at herself in the mirror. She is pleased with what she sees but doesn't thank him. He thinks: 'Actually, she's over-made up, quite tarted-up. It's okay in private at home. And, I've had fun and she liked me doing it. But, I'd never go shopping with her like this.'

Keith putting glitter on her eyeshadow. (*iStockphoto.* Posed by model.)

He changes her into that less 'pinkified' dress although she insists on wearing her new sexy *broekies*. She gets him to do up

---

[156] Schrobsdorff, S, "The daughter dress code: you only get to make the rules for a little while". *TIME*, New York, 02 November 2015. https://time.com/4082953/the-daughter-dress-code-you-only-get-to-make-the-rules-for-a-little-while/

the laces at her hips. It is all fun. He takes out his iPhone photographs her face. She pouts and puts on airs and graces.

Still pouting. Keith doesn't believe she'll really run away. She doesn't either. He still sees her as sweet. A serious mistake on his part. (*Shutterstock*, posed by model)

He feels dressing her up like this is a safe and enjoyable thing for her to do at home. And, she clearly enjoys it. He also feels it is helping their relationship.

While he makes some sandwiches for their lunch, he sees her pack her iPad and two of her fairy books into a little suitcase or port.[157] She takes her sandwiches, wraps them, and puts them and an apple in the port. Then, in an off hand affected way: "I'm going to Toowoomba." She grabs her teddy bear, walks out of the house with the little port, and sets off down the long driveway.

Because she has walked off before and went on the road, he tells her: "Don't go on the road. Some baddie might pick you up. Remember what happened to that Kylie girl."

She thinks: 'No baddies got me when I walked along the road in my black dress.'

He sees her as sweet and believes she'll be back soon. A serious mistake by him. She walks off down the drive. He doesn't believe she's really going to Toowoomba. She doesn't either. It's all pretend. She has walked off in a huff before. What happened to Kylie was far away in Melbourne. She'll eat her lunch by herself next to the gate where she can sit on one of the rocks.

The rocks are to the right of the open gate. But, in her grumpy mood, she decides to walk along the roadside. And, she deliberately left the gate open.

At the gate she doesn't sit on a rock to eat her lunch. It's too warm to sit in the late November sun, especially as she has forgotten her hat. This makes her more grumpy. She

---

[157] 'port': a North Queensland word to describe a small suitcase which children use to take their books and lunch to school. Probably derived from "portmanteau".

opens the gate and crosses the road to where there is more shade. Spitefully, she deliberately leaves the gate open.

There is no traffic. Then, a grey car approaches from the east. She decides to be rebellious and daring. At times, in the car with Keith, they've seen people hitch-hiking. He told her what they were doing, telling her about some of the risks.

In her bad mood, she defiantly puts out her arm. The little grey car drives by with a youngish man driving. After passing her, it stops a hundred metres further up the road. It waits. After a minute or so, it reverses back to her and stops near her.

Curious, she stands and watches.

Unfortunately, the examples of raped and murdered little girls that they have discussed previously have tended to be seen by her as sad cases that happened somewhere else and wouldn't happen to her, not in the protected world she has been living in.

Keith waits a while. He strides down the drive but can't see her. Then, in the distance he sees her standing at the side of the road about two hundred metres away from their gate. Is she actually hitch-hiking? In the past, he has pointed out to her people hitch-hiking at the roadside.

He catches a glimpse of Eppie in the distance hitch hiking. (*Shutterstock.* Posed by model.)

A Subaru Forester has stopped and the driver has put her into the front passenger seat.

In the distance, he sees a car pull over at the side of the road. Its a Subaru Forester. It stops next to her. The driver, a man in his forties, gets out and opens the front passenger door. He is saying something to Eppie. He lifts her, her port, and teddybear into front passenger side of the car. Without doing up her seatbelt, he closes the door.

Keith picks up some gravel at the edge of the bitumen and throws it at the car. He shouts as loud as he can as he sprints towards the car.

The man hears the gravel hit his car, sees Keith, changes his mind, rushes back to the passenger side, opens the door, and violently pulls Eppie out. She is thrown onto the gravel at the side of the road. He tosses her port and teddybear out and slams the door. He quickly jumps back into the front. Revving the engine and wheel-spinning in the gravel at the side of the road, he takes off at full tilt towards Kinross,. Eppie is left lying on the ground.

Keith rushes up to her. He lifts her up and brushes dust off her dress. He notices there is some gravel rash on her right knee.

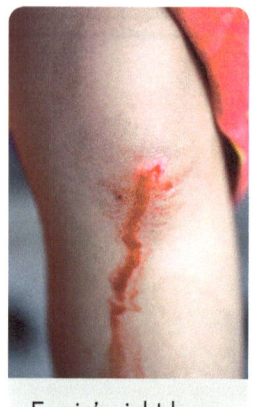

Eppie's right knee. (*Shutterstock.* Posed by model.)

Shocked, she is silent at first.

In view of what has just happened, he switches from being a friend and playmate to being a parent. This is a rare thing for him.

He picks her up, suitcase and teddy bear included, and forcefully carries her all the way back up to the house. She kicks out and squeals. He takes her into the bathroom, gently pads her gravel rash with a damp cloth and makes sure there are no tiny stones or gravel left there before putting two large band-aids on her leg. It's sore for her but he is very gentle.

He takes her into the sitting room. He stands her up in front of him and holds her firmly at her upper arms as he sits on the couch in front of her. He tells her in no uncertain and very strong terms about the danger she put herself in. She is stunned and silent. "You are a very pretty little girl and I've dressed you in a very pretty way, too! You are gorgeous! That man in that car man saw you all alone by yourself. He saw a pretty little girl all by herself. He would have thought: 'What a very tasty little girl. And, she's all by herself. There's no other cars. So, nobody can see me picking her up.' So, he stopped and was offering you a lift. Did he offer you a lift?"

Eppie, very timidly: "Yes."

Keith: "What did he say?"

Silence.

Then, Eppie, meekly: "He said he's going to Toowoomba. 'Hop in. I'll give you a lolly.' "

Keith: "I saw him, a man in his forties, not a cool teenager. He wanted to take you away in his car. Then, when he saw me running up to you and shouting, he pulled you out and quickly raced off. He was guilty alright! You saw how he took off so fast. If he had driven off with you, he would probably have taken you to a place hidden in the bush. He would take your clothes off and make you lie down in the grass. Then, he would start doing really horrible and painful things to your vulva like touching her in a sexy but rough way. And, do you know what he would do next? He would take his pants down and start forcing his big grown up man's penis inside your tiny little girl's vagina. He would fuck you. It would be so sore for you because you are not big enough. It would rip you open and you would scream in pain. Your little girl's vagina would split and tear so that it joined up with your anus, your bottom hole. You've seen my penis when I was in the shower and you came in one day. So, you know a grown man's penis is big. But, mine was floppy. When a man is sexually aroused, it gets hard and stiff and strong and pointy and long. So, you'd be screaming in pain. He would push and push his penis deep inside you. You'd be screaming even more. When he's finished, he'd squeeze you hard at your throat so you couldn't breathe. And, you would die. He would dump your dead body in the bush and cover it with branches and leaves so nobody could find you. And, because you'd be dead you couldn't dob him in to the police. Dingoes would eat some of you. Crows and maggots would eat the last bits of your meat. One day, somebody might find your bones in the bush. Remember how we've seen kangaroo bones in the bush."

Keith pauses. She is starring at him, wide eyed and worried.

He continues: "Now, what I have told you is true. When I was in jail I saw men there who had done that sort of thing to little girls just like you. Those men were spending many years in prison for what they did. They were ordinary quite nice looking men and even friendly like that man who wanted to get you in his car. But, they

Eppie, suitably admonished by her parent. (*iStockphoto*, Posed by model.)

were evil men inside who had done horrible things to little girls just like you before killing them. Now, those little girls are dead! They can never wake up! Their life has gone. Those men killed those girls after they raped them because they didn't want them to dob them in."

Eppie is silent.

Keith: "So, you see why I grabbed you and carried you back up to the house. I love you like anything. I don't want to let some horrible man do that to you! … Okay?"

He pauses for her to answer. But, she doesn't. She is upset and embarrassed.

Keith: "Remember we talked about a little girl called Kylie after we saw something on the TV news. A man gave her a lift in his car. He didn't take her where she wanted. No, he drove her to his house where he took her clothes off. After doing horrible things to her vulva, he had sex with her. Yes, he put his grown man's penis deep into her little vagina. She didn't want sex. She wasn't old enough for it. She was six like you. His big man's penis ripped her open. She was tiny and way too young. It hurt her like anything. But, he didn't want her to dob him in. So, he squeezed her throat so she couldn't breathe. She died. He dumped her body in a street gutter. Do you remember that?"[158]

Eppie very weakly answers: "Yes."

Keith then shows her something he has just seen on the internet. A five-year-old girl was raped and died from her injuries in Kansas, USA. She is impressed because these US reports even show photos of the little girl shortly before she was killed. (Something which would never happen in the Australian press.) So, its easier for her to relate to the news item.[159] She is impressed with these news items, especially this American one.

She is stunned not just at what Keith has been telling her but by the controlled stern way he has just talked to her. She is silent and her eyes are wide open and staring at him. She has never before seen her loving, kind, and gentle parent like this. She bursts into tears.

---

158 See: "Murder of Kylie Maybury" in *Wikipedia* at https://en.wikipedia.org/wiki/Murder_of_Kylie_Maybury (Note that back in 1978 Kylie's grandfather and uncle were suspects and they both committed suicide in jail. Over thirty years later and with DNA profiling unknown at the time of her murder, the real killer was caught and jailed for life. Having himself been falsely accused, convicted of rape, and jailed, Keith is acutely aware of what happened to those two innocent men.)

159 Reilly, P. "5-year-old Kansas girl raped, murdered after mom kicked her out of the house." *New York Post*, 05 October 2023. https://nypost.com/2023/10/05/5-year-old-girl-raped-murdered-after-mom-kicked-her-out-of-the-house/

"I'm so sorry, Mamma. I'm so sorry."

He gives her a long hug. She calms down a bit. Now he realises that he just has to maintain her self-esteem. He can't pull her down like this and leave her down. He picks her up and sits her on his lap and cuddles her for several minutes.

Feeling remorseful for coming down so hard on Eppie, he tells her: "It's still morning. So, if it's okay by you, I'd like you to hop in the car and I'll drive you into Toowoomba, to the Grand Central shopping mall. That's where there are so many specialist children's clothing shops are. We'll buy you a new pretty dress. And, you can choose the one you would like. Okay? Yes, you choose it. But, please, I love you so, so much. You must promise me that you'll never ever try to hitch-hike like that again. It's so dangerous. Okay?"

Even though she knows a trip to Grand Central in Toowoomba is a major journey of two hours, she agrees with a timid but smiling "Okay, I promise".

As they drive, he talks to her about another danger about running away like that. "If a bad man didn't pick you up, somebody might take you to the Police saying they found a lost little girl walking along the road. The Police would take you straight to the Child Safety ladies and they would put you in foster care. You know how bad things happen to little girls and boys in foster care, too. Not always, but sometimes. Remember we talked about what happened to Tiahleigh Palmer in foster care. The foster care man killed her and dumped her body in the creek." [160]

Yes, she remembers that. They had seen much about it for weeks on the TV News, too.

Keth: "So, I never ever want to see you go into foster care. So, there's no way I would let you be taken into foster care. I would fight to stop them. I have to protect you from the foster care ladies. You see, I really, really love you."

At first, she is quiet. She holds his hand. He hugs her.

Then, she surprises him when she asks: "Are they witches?"

He smiles: "That's a way to describe them. I think that's how they behave, like in *Hansel and Gretel*. They don't eat children but they do capture lots of them. And, some of those kids cry and cry because they've been taken from their parents."

---

[160] See: "Murder of Tiahleigh Palmer" in *Wikipedia* at https://en.wikipedia.org/wiki/Murder_of_Tiahleigh_Palmer

She is silent again. (She knows the *Hansel and Gretel* fairy tale by the brothers Grimm.)

Keith: "Now, remember why we are on a journey this afternoon? We're on our way to Toowoomba to buy you a really nice dress and I want you to choose it yourself. That's why. And, you can take as long as you like. And, it really must be your choice." Keith is feeling somewhat guilty about all this. But, he realises that he had to do it. He is now setting about building up her shattered self-esteem.

They spend ages in shops in the Grand Central mall in Toowoomba. There are classy specialist children's clothing shops like 'Cotton on Kids' and 'Love Henry' but they also focus on the big rather exclusive 'Myer' department store which has a specialist section for children's clothes. And, there are the more ordinary 'SportsGirl', 'Best and Less', 'Big W', 'K-Mart', and 'Target', all with good selections of children's clothing. She is enthusiastic about trying them on and loves doing this dress buying together with him and asking him what he thinks as she tries on the dresses. Her self-esteem is being repaired much to Keith's delight.

Keith smiles. She is almost desperate to grow up.

She tries on many frilly 'pinkified' dresses. He is there to help her change. He takes photos of her in some dresses as she poses in the fitting booths. She looks at the photos of herself. That helps her choose. She loves the attention and the indulgence. He is aware of what has been termed "the pinkification of girls"[161] but, not only does he think she looks gorgeous in 'pinkified' clothes but he can't see any harm in letting her indulge especially as she spends a lot of her time almost as a tomboy in shorts and T-shirt climbing rocks and looking after chooks. Yet, she already has some 'pinkified' clothes like the dress which she astutely chose to wear when she tried to hitch-hike. She instinctively knew what would attract. Her natural developing sexual awareness is what many do not accept from little girls of her age. Although having had daughters before and accepting Eppie's behaviour as normal for little girls, Keith failed to realise and accept Eppie's veneration of pop stars as normal for <u>his</u> five to six-year-old. He has a tendency to see her in shorts, climbing trees, and looking after chooks. He sees her behaviour in terms of a dichotomy. A typical father's response.

---

[161] Henley, J. "The power of pink." *The Guardian*, London, 12 December 2009. <u>http://www.guardian.co.uk/ theguardian/2009/dec/12/pinkstinks-the-power-of-pink</u>

She takes her time as she tries on several more dresses with frills and even lace and sequins on them. Most seem to be intended as little girls' party dresses or bridesmaids dresses. Keith takes photos of her in some of the dresses. She is also loving the attention that he is paying her.

Then, she tries on a white dress with some flowers on it. This takes Keith a little by surprise. He thought she would prefer a frilly party style dress. By comparison, it is almost plain but still pretty on her.

She turns and looks at him. She can read his mind. "Please, please can I have this one? I can tell that you like it. So, let's have it."

Feeling remorseful about trying to hitch-hike, she is desperate to please him.

He buys it for her.

Her attempt at hitch-hiking has had a sobering

With a beguiling and persuasive smile, Eppie implores him to buy this dress. It's not really her taste but she wants to please him. (iStockphoto. Posed by model.)

effect on her, especially the way her Mumma came down hard on her. She is a now subdued little girl. For the time being, she is not the cheeky vivacious little girl she was in the last chapter. She is fearful deep down and craves the security and love Keith provides. She is pleased that her new dress is one that he likes.

On the way home she hardly says a word. She is deep in thought. Then, she suddenly asks him to stop. It is early summer and her sharp little girl's eyes spotted something. She has seen some domestic flowers among the weeds at an abandoned house. He turns around and goes back.

She asks: "Please watch over me while I go into that yard. I want to pick some flowers."

A little surprised, he does as she asked. He has become used to her assertively getting her own way. Having seen her attempts to please him, he now realises that he has been remiss in not seeing her behaviour about clothes and pop-stars as part of a normal natural growing up process. His reluctance to accept this lead her to running away and hitch-hiking. He is now blaming himself. He watches her walking carefully into the overgrown garden, avoiding big thistles and other weeds. He thinks: 'Oh God, I love her like anything.'

Eppie knows his body language and can read his eyes - the product of spending her whole life so close to him. She knows how to please him. That is why she chose that dress and why she is picking flowers for him. There is nothing devious about her. She needs his love and loves him

The abandoned house with overgrown garden.

(*iStockphoto*. Posed by model.)

She spends a while picking flowers. When she has found enough, he watches her walking out through the overgrown garden, slowly and carefully making her way through the tall weeds and thistles. Once out, she walks around the back of the car to the driver's door.

Looking up at Keith with an almost bland expression, she passes a small bunch of flowers up to him: "These are for you. Thank you for being my Mumma."

Keith is stunned and brought down to earth by this little girl he loves so much. This is a wake up call for him. He takes the flowers from her, puts them carefully on the car dashboard and gets out of the car. He picks her up and gives her a massive hug. She nuzzles into him.

CHAPTER 9

Horror

Even though Eppie was not abducted, it was a close thing. So, Keith decides that he must redouble efforts to reconnect with her. She has become too critical of him and he has not been understanding enough of her. He must try much harder. And, she now knows that the two dangers for her are another abduction and her being taken into foster care.

Several weeks later, Eppie is on better or improving terms with Keith. They've had trips away to Byron Bay and to Mooloolaba on the Sunshine Coast, as well as usual trips to the closer Girraween National Park. They've been busy and enjoyed each other's company. Keith is being successful in re-engaging with her.

Early in January it is the school holidays. With her birthday in mid-November, Eppie is now six, and she spends an afternoon at a friend's house. It is the school holidays. A little girl who is now in Grade 2 at Graniteville State School, Melanie Shaw, and who knows Eppie from Playgroup has asked her Mum if Eppie can come over to play for the afternoon. The girl's mother is the same woman, Belinda Shaw, who at Playgroup asked Keith about her name and *Silas Marner*. She is single and an activist with several environmental and social causes. Eppie is slow to reconnect. But the older Melanie is kind and welcoming. So, soon the two girls have a good time on the trampoline, playing imaginary games with Melanie's dolls and using each other's iPads. Over afternoon drinks and fruit, the persistent mother starts subtly probing Eppie for information. She even asks why she hasn't started school yet because her daughter is now in Grade 2 and she is only nine months older than Eppie. She asks if Keith is her grandfather or her father.

"No, he's my Mumma. Every kid needs a Mumma. He's always been my Mumma."
She then asks if he was once a teacher in Townsville.

Canny little Eppie is not keen on this inquisitive questioning and is offended. With her hands on her hips, finally she tells Belinda assertively: "I'm not saying."

Back at home, Eppie is still irked by the questioning and tells Keith about it. He is surprised and proud of her forthright strong reaction. Yet, he is worried all over again. They discuss it. They are both worried. However, as before nothing happens. At least, not yet.

Two days later, with the warm weather, they decide to travel to Brisbane just to see the sights and to go to the wonderful South Bank park artificial beach again. They go to the South Bank Parklands where there are shallow water pools and artificial beaches with lovely white sand. They came here one morning before when Eppie was three. It is a wonderful play area for families and gets quite crowded especially on public holidays. They leave the VW campervan parked in the street at Dutton Park station, a suburban railway station only

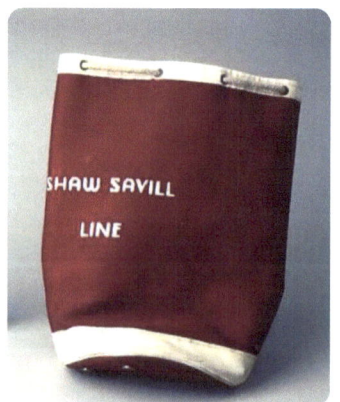

two stops away from South Bank station and catch the train the rest of the way to the South Bank because there is no free parking near the South Bank and it'll be packed, too.

They change into their swimming togs in the campervan and catch the train. She is wearing a T-shirt over her swimming togs and Keith keeps his shirt on. They wear a hat each and carry matching small beach towels with prominent stripes on them. It is only a ten minute journey but this short suburban train trip is still an exciting experience for Eppie. They then walk down to the artificial beach. Keith has put drinks and fruit bars in his favourite old Shaw Savill duffel bag which he has had since 1960. That was when his family immigrated to Australia by sea on the *Southern Cross*.

The South Bank Park

There are lots of people at the South Bank, mainly families with young kids paddling in the shallow water. While many have claimed shady spots, they find a small spot in a sandy cove with just a little shade next to some low densely packed palm trees. Eppie is excited and quickly puts her thongs, hat, and towel on the sand next to the old Shaw Savill bag. After taking her T-shirt off, Eppie runs into the cool water. Other little kids are splashing and having a good time. Like Eppie, Keith had already changed into his swimming togs in the privacy of their campervan when they parked it at the Dutton Park railway station and continued wearing his blue shirt. So, they didn't have to use public changing rooms which Keith was afraid of because he would have to take his little girl into the men's changing room and thus attract attention. He carefully puts his iPhone, the car keys, and his wallet into the old duffel bag and covers the bag with one of their two towels. He'll try to keep an eye on them. He's a bit worried. Theft of all those things in the bag would be a disaster. An elderly lady sitting watching the little boy that she is with tells him: "It's okay. I'll watch your bag for you."

Keith thanks her.

Eppie calls out to him to join her in the cooling water. "Come on, Mumma! It's so cool!" She doesn't use that modern meaning of the word 'cool'. He can see that he is being cheeky and will splash him as he walks in. It's fun. He looks at her and thinks she is so petite and beautiful. And, so full of life. A truly happy kid. He adores her.

Still wearing his hat, he starts undoing his shirt buttons to take his shirt off as she starts walking out of the water towards him. She wants to grab his hand and lead him into the water.

Suddenly they hear: "Bam! … Bam! Bam! … Bam! Bam! Bam! Bam! … Bam! Bam!'

It's gunfire. There are screams. Lots of screams. People are running out of the water as fast as they can. Eppie looks over towards the gunfire. She can see a young woman standing and shooting at people. She sees people being hit.

Keith can't see this yet. There are low palm trees and bushes in the way.

Eppie runs to Keith. She quickly puts her T-shirt over her swimming togs.

More gunfire: "Bam! Bam! … Bam! Bam! Bam!"

It's from just behind those rocks, low palms, and bushes and it's coming closer.

Now, Keith sees two people just nearby running but shot in the back. They fall into the water. "Bam! Bam! Bam!"

Eppie grabs his hand.

In an instant Keith switches from playmate to parent.

His maternal protective instincts come into play and determine what he does.

His mind races through the options. No time to run. Can they hide in behind the little clump of palms? No, there's not enough cover. And, other people are hiding there and can be seen. He has to do something to save his Eppie. What can he do?

Will he lie over her to protect her from the bullets? Through the bushes, he can just make out the shooter approaching, walking slowly, stopping frequently to fire the assault rifle at people, carefully picking them off.

More running people are hit.

Eppie is standing, frozen, and watching.

He tells her: "Lie down! Quick!"

She immediately lies down in the sand. Keith covers her with a beach towel.

Several metres away somebody is lying uninjured in the sand. He seems to be feigning death. It doesn't work. The shooter pumps him with bullets. The man remains still.

The elderly woman who was watching over Keith's duffel bag rushes over to the water about four or five metres away. She tries to protect her little toddler, holding him and turning her own back to the shooter. Both are shot and fall into the water, presumably dead.

Now, Keith sees the shooter emerging slowly around the corner from behind the dense clump of palms and some rocks. The shooter is a mid-twenties woman. He now has a clear view of her. She is silent. Holding a semi-automatic assault rifle, she starts shooting some more: "Bam! Bam! Bam! … Bam! Bam!"

In fact, it is a version of the Russian AK-47 Kalashnikov.

The shooting stops for several seconds. Standing still with gun lowered for a moment, she removes the now empty 30-round magazine, drops it to the sand and quickly loads another magazine. She slowly surveys the scene of carnage she has just created.

In those few fleeting seconds, so much flashes through Keith's mind. He realises the woman will notice him in a second or two. He's a sitting duck, trapped in an alcove edged with tightly packed rocks, palms, and bushes. Eppie is lying down in the sand but not well covered. How can they escape? They can't. He mustn't just wait to be shot. Running will draw the woman's attention and both will be pumped full of bullets. Lying over Eppie won't protect her. He's just seen that woman and her toddler killed. She was trying to protect the child. Standing next to Eppie, his mind flashes through the situation: 'She'll still be hit! Me, too! Both of us. No escape. We're sitting ducks. Got to do something. Can't do nothing. Time has run out. Oh no!'

There is now no issue of fight or flight. And, freezing is out of the question. No, he must simply protect his baby at all costs, even if it means losing his own life in the process. Eppie's survival is paramount. This is his biological, subconscious, and instinctive primal imperative.

In a sudden flash of insight, he bends down and with both hands together scoops up a large amount of dry sand. As he does so, the woman sees him looking up at her. That's when he briefly sees her steely determined eyes and realises the fury in her face. His hat flies off his head as he rushes full tilt four metres towards her as she is raising her gun.

This is what Keith sees as he starts rushing headlong towards the shooter. (*iStockphoto*. Posed by model.)

She points the gun at Keith. But, an instant before the she pulls the trigger, Keith has thrown that dry sand right into the her face. Because he is running, it's a stroke of luck that he didn't miss. But, unable to stop, Keith crashes into her.

For a couple of vital seconds, the shooter can't see properly. The gun goes off in rapid fire: "Bam! Bam! Bam! Bam! Bam!"

But, all the shots are into the sand and the water just missing Keith. He hears the bullets whizzing past. Both the woman and Keith fall into the water. There is much splashing.

Despite his age and being driven to protect his child, Keith is able to get up quickly as the shooter scrabbles around trying to retrieve her gun and get up from the water. The Kalashnikov will function even though wet.

While she is getting up, Keith turns to rush towards Eppie.

This is when he has a very fleeting glimpse of several Policemen in dark battle dress uniform racing past him towards the shooter. They are not shouting. They are silent. Then, there are more but different sounding even more rapid gunshots: "Paap! Paap! Paap! … Paap! Paap! Paap! … Paap! Paap! Paap!" This sound is the Queensland Police Special Emergency Response Team's (SERT) Remington R4 carbine .223 semi-automatic assault rifle.

A terrified Eppie is still lying on the sand. Peeping from under the towel, she has seen it all.

He grabs her arms and pulls her up. As he does so, he turns and sees the shooter lying motionless face down in the shallow water. Two policemen fire two or three more rounds at her.

People are running *en masse* from the scene. Some are sobbing and screaming.

With Eppie now standing next to him, Keith quickly picks up one of their towels and the Shaw Savill duffel bag. He gets his thongs on but there isn't time for Eppie to put her thongs on. They have fancy straps with plastic flowers on them. They leave her thongs, her hat, his hat, and a towel behind as, dragging her along, he starts running as fast as he can. This time, still charged with adrenaline and despite his age, he is faster than she is. He is wet and sandy. So is she.

As they sprint away through the park gardens towards the railway station, Keith looks briefly at her. She is terrified. (*Adobe*. Posed by model)

All this is happening incredibly quickly. They run along with heaps of other people up the long path to the South Bank railway station.

At the platform, a train is about to leave. It is packed with distraught people. He squeezes himself and Eppie on board just as the doors are closing.

The southbound train leaves the station. It is full of largely silent and shocked people. Many are sobbing quietly. He picks up Eppie and holds her on his hip. She is still light enough for him to do this and he is still fired up. She is in shock. Her eyes are wide and staring. Her lips are quivering and she is shaking. Her arms are open and her hands are flailing about. He holds her close to him. She snuggles up and starts whimpering. He says nothing to her. He is panting and, finally, beginning to feel weak. His heart is racing and he is aware of his neck arteries thumping. The train is jam packed and he can't sit down.

A kind woman with some kids helps him stand up, supporting him. She tells him: "I saw what you did, mate. God, you saved us! We were next! … You're a bloody hero!"

The minutes seem to flash by.

The train arrives at Dutton Park station at the back of the Princess Alexandra Hospital. Keith squeezes past other passengers and gets out carrying Eppie, a towel, and the Shaw Savill bag. He is feeling even more weak. They almost fall out of the train. He slowly stumbles with his load up a long pedestrian ramp to Kent Street next to the station where he parked the VW campervan just a few metres away. Other people are also hurrying up the ramp and push past him.

Opening up the duffel bag, takes out his keys, unlocks the campervan and climbs in with Eppie. He leaves the side sliding door open because, parked in the sun, it is hot in the van. He collapses onto the back seat. He is holding a terrified Eppie. He puts her on the seat next to him. He opens some windows. He sits down again and holds Eppie close once more. They spend ages just sitting there in silence, sometimes panting. He is feeling very weak. His neck is still thumping.

After a few minutes, he is able to get up and pump some cool water into cups for them to drink. Then, he opens the fridge and gets out some cold fruit juice Poppers for each of them.

They slowly calm down but still do not talk. Keith is too traumatised to talk and so is she. It was horrible what they went through and it was so unexpected. They were having a happy time.

He is now feeling quite weak again. It's been almost too much for his elderly body.

Finally, summoning up his weakening strength, he lifts Eppie up off the back seat and straps her into her booster seat in the front. He goes around to the driver's side. He starts driving through dense traffic to leave Brisbane for the long journey home. The car's air-conditioning is a blessed relief. Eppie crashes asleep.

After three hours, he realises he has become too dog tired. He tends to drift to the edge of the road as he consciously tries to force his eyes to stay open. It is getting dark. At the top of the Cunningham's Gap through the high escarpment, he pulls into a rest area. He opens out the rear bed, puts a sheet on it, and puts a sleepy Eppie to bed. He has another drink of water and lies down next to her. Within seconds he has crashed asleep, too.

They are woken up by the hot early morning sun streaming through the windows. He has to move the car to a shady spot. Both go to the toilet outside among some bushes.

Back in the car he has decided not to debrief Eppie. He'll let her talk if and when she wants to. Of course, he is also traumatised and is reluctant to talk. In the meantime, in silence, he makes breakfast. It's Weet-Bix.

As they eat, Eppie breaks the silence, slowly and with nervous breaks: "Mumma, I saw … I saw. Yes, … I saw … ."

Keith: "What did you see?"

Eppie: "It was a lady. … You threw sand … in her face. She tried to shoot you. … She and you bumped into … each other. You fell into the water. … I thought she shot you. … I thought you were killed."

Keith: "She just missed, only just."

Eppie: "When you got up, I had some happiness. … I saw Police running. She was getting up. They shot her lots … lots of times. She fell … fell … back into the water. She wriggled … just a little bit. They shot her more. … That was … well … then, you grabbed me. I saw that lady was lying in the … the water. … We … you and me … we ran really, so fast … to the train. There was lots of other people running. …Everybody … was running."

Keith: "So, you watched it all?"

Eppie: "Yes. …Yes. … I was so scared. … Oh, Mumma, that lady was so mean … real mean, like a fox … not saying anything … just shooting … shooting and killing people!"

Keith: "Oh!"

They are silent for a moment.

Eppie: "I woke up before you this morning. … I lay in bed just thinking. Yes, I was thinking when I woke up this morning. … I saw that lady shooting people dead. … She was so mean, horrible! …. So mean. … They fell down and some blood came out. Blood squirted out from that old lady's neck. … I was so scared. I saw dead people … and little kids were dead, too. … And, some people weren't dead … but they were hurting and crying … crying because … because it was very sore for them. … And, blood was coming out of them, too. … I just ran and ran with you."

Keith gives Eppie a long, long hug.

His little girl has witnessed a truly shocking event. Blood and death have a big impact on her. So, during the next few days and weeks he must not shirk from talking it over with her but only if she feels comfortable enough to want to talk. He will not press her.[162] He doesn't want Post Traumatic Stress Disorder for her.[163] Can he avoid it? But, what she saw must not be covered up.

Eventually, in the next days and weeks, they talk about what they saw, even try to analyse the event but it is always at her initiative. That's the way he wants it. He doesn't want her to re-live the event. Sensibly, because he is also traumatised, he is allowing discussion of what happened to be a shared discussion but when they want it. He won't let it become a contrived debriefing.

They drive home through Graniteville and on to their house in silence.

At home, they feed the chooks and sit on the verandah quietly looking at the view. They talk about other things, not what happened at the South Bank. However, he hugs and kisses her lots.

---

[162] He is also traumatised and reluctant to discuss what happened.
[163] For PTSD see *Wikipedia*: https://en.wikipedia.org/wiki/Post-traumatic_stress_disorder

Then, in the afternoon, he can't find Eppie. He searches the house calling out her name: "Eppie, Eppie … Eppie. Where are you."

He goes outside and calls her but doesn't find her. And, she is not at the cubby house among the granite boulders.

(*Dreamstime.* Posed by model).

Concerned, he goes back inside still calling her.

He hears a squeaky voice: "Mamma."

He looks in the laundry. He finds her hiding in an empty storage space under one of the draws.

She is crying and shaking. He picks her up and carries her into the living room and sits on the couch with her on his lap. He holds her really close for ages in silence just slowly rocking from side to side. Then, still hugging her, he talks to her slowly and calmly, re-assuring her yet again that the bad woman is dead. "The Police shot her."

Eppie: "But, she could still come back."

Now, he gets up and, holding her hand, he walks her throughout the house in order to convince her that there is no baddie with a gun. He does the same walking through the garden. He tells her: "The Bargens will sort her out if she dares to show up here."[164]

Later, they drive into Graniteville for some grocery items. On the way they talk more about the South Bank park event. Keith tells her he wonders how the newspapers have reported it. So, in Graniteville he buys the main tabloid Brisbane newspaper, the *Daily Times*. The front page and the next two are dominated by the South Bank shooting and the deaths of fourteen people and possibly more as some are 'critical on life support' in hospitals. Many of the victims are men and boys. The paper does point this out but it stresses the terror of it all. It makes mention of the shooter being a young woman believed to belong to 'a little known fringe feminist group calling itself the Granddaughters of Bilitis'.[165]

---

[164] These are the granite boulders in their back yard that Eppie calls 'Bargans'. In her imaginary games, they sometimes come alive and do things to protect the environment like rolling down the hill and crushing bulldozers.

[165] See also: "Daughters of Bilitis", *Wikipedia*. https://en.wikipedia.org/wiki/Daughters_of_Bilitis

On page 2, there is a blurry photo which has been enlarged. A still from a CCTV camera, it shows Keith from behind rushing at the woman as he throws sand at her. Then, in big print, it says "Who is this hero?" The newspaper elaborates:

South Bank Terror - Who is this hero?

After the shooter was finally taken out by Police, an elderly man was seen running away with a little girl. He was the man who bravely tackled the armed offender who was silent throughout as she randomly took out multiple lives with her assault rifle. He put a stop to the vile carnage just before Police got there. That saved many more lives. The man and the little girl, like so many, were likely terrified and just wanted to get away. A woman on the next train out of South Bank station has reported that she spoke briefly to the elderly man. He was carrying the terrified little girl and an old duffel bag. Then, she lost track of them in the packed train. Who is this elderly hero? What he did saved so many lives.

Queensland Police have not yet identified the man. From CCTV images seen so far, he carried a distinctive old British Shaw Savill shipping line travel bag and a towel with coloured stripes on it.

Eppie is looking at the newspaper with Keith. "That's us, hey?"

Keith: "Yes."

Eppie: "Should we tell them it was us?"

Keith: "No, we mustn't."

Eppie: "Why not?"

Keith: "We mustn't tell. If we did, the Child Safety Department will know about you and me. They will investigate and come knocking straight away. We just have to keep it a big secret. We must tell nobody. I would hate it if the Department found out. I didn't let that woman shoot you and I won't let those Child Safety ladies get you. That's my promise to you. I really mean it. But, if they find out … well, there'll be big problems. So, please keep it a secret. Tell nobody."

Eppie: "Yes, I promise, Mumma."

Keith: "Thank you, Eppie. I know you won't. It's our special secret."

Keith decides that they should watch at least some of the 1959 movie *The Diary of Ann Frank*.[166] He saw it when he was teenager. He explains the background to her about

---

[166] To watch the 1959 film. https://www.youtube.com/watch?v=WtHGKj1xyxQ

why Ann's family were hiding. There are two sections he wants her to notice. When the family first starts hiding, they hear the siren of a Gestapo police car. They are hushed as it approaches: "Dee-Dah Dee-Dah Dee-Dah".[167] But, fortunately the police car passes by. The family is relieved. Then, one day they hear the siren again but this time it stops right outside the building where they are hiding. They have been betrayed and the Gestapo arrive to take them away to Bergen-Belsen concentration camp. Eppie and Keith talk more about a betrayal and the Child Safety 'witches' coming.

In the early evening news they see those same questions being asked on the TV news about who the mystery old man was. And so, what Eppie and Keith got up to at the Brisbane South Bank park remains a secret, at least for a while. Eppie is very good and tells no one. At six years old, she is now genuinely scared of the real possibility of being taken from her Mumma.

There is something else which has been on Eppie's mind since the South Bank. Three weeks later, she surprises Keith. Quite out of the blue, she takes him by the hand and sits him down on the couch and sits next him: "Mumma, I've got something to say to you."

Keith: "Oh, what's that?"

Eppie: "I'm very sorry. You know how sometimes you've forgotten why you went into your bedroom and then forgot what you went in there for. I laughed at you and said you're a silly old man. I was joking but I'm really sorry. I once laughed at you because you didn't know how to use my iPad. I'm so sorry for that. One time in the kitchen you were a little upset because you let a saucepan of milk boil over and I said that you've passed your use-by date and you should have let me do it. I'm really sorry for that."

She squeezes his hand. He can see she has tears in her eyes.

"Sometimes … sometimes, when we've been walking along National Park trails and you couldn't keep up, I teased you because you're old. Mamma, what you did at the South Bank has shown me how wrong I've been. I saw young men running for their lives. But, not you. You took on that lady all by yourself, all on you own, just you and only a scoop of sand against her with a Kala … Kalashnikov. And, you won! … You saved my life and lots

---

[167] To hear a modern German police siren similar to the 1940s one. https://www.youtube.com/watch?v=w_Q6HsYBdQ0

of other lives. Nobody helped you. So, there is no way that you're past your use-by date. … Please forgive me. I promise I'll never again pick on you for being old. You also saved me from myself when you stopped me being picked up by that man when I was hitch hiking. And Mumma, at the very beginning of my life … well, I wouldn't be alive and so happy today if you hadn't picked me up and then cared for me and loved me like you did and still do. You do so much for me like teaching me to read and all those things and saving me, too. And, you cuddle me and hug me as well. You really love me. You are just the best!!!!" She wipes her eyes with a hankie and gives him a massive hug and kiss.

He so admires his intelligent little six-year-old. "Eppie, I love you like anything. In those incidents I just had to do what I did. I had no choice. I couldn't have left you in the bush at Bolivia Hill. I couldn't have handed you over to Child Safety. I had to care for you. And, I just had to stop that man taking you in his car. At the South Bank, I had no choice. I just had to do what I did."

Eppie: "Yes, I know all that. But, so much of what you've done for me has been because you are old. Young men wouldn't have done all what you've done. At Bolivia Hill a younger bloke have would would have left a yukky baby alone in the bush or he would handed me over to the Child Safety witches at the Tenterfield hospital 'coz I was too much of a problem for him. And, at the South Bank young men just shot through. I saw them. They were looking after themselves. They ran as fast as they could. I saw. I know what you are like."

Keith: "Well, thank you dear. Thank you."

Now, he hugs her.

CHAPTER 10

After the South Bank

The trauma of what happened at the South Bank is not swept under the carpet. Keith is aware of what stress does to people and the lasting effects. So, he now wants to calm Eppie's life.

Yet, one night she woke up screaming in terror. Keith had to bring her into his bed for the rest of the night. It was a wake-up call for him. Her PTSD was not over. He had to work more on her anxiety and fear. So, they often discuss the event. He feels discussing it is an integral part of preventing or minimising PTSD. He discusses it only when she initiates the conversation. It is clear to him that talking over it it is her way of seeking reassurance about the protective bond she sees in him. This process lasts for well over a month.

(*Left*) Eppie woke up one night in terror. Keith had to bring her to his bed for the rest of the night. For the next week she insisted on sleeping with him.
(*Right*) Eppie likes the seriousness of their conversations about what happened at The South Bank. Here she holds his hand as they talk.
(Both photos *iStockphoto*. Posed by same model.)

He encourages her to talk about what happened.[168]

During the next weeks the issue of "Who is that hero old man with the little girl?" comes up again in the papers. Sometimes, when it's on the television news, Eppie smiles and tells Keith: "That's our secret!"

Apart from the reality that revealing the secret could be disastrous for her because it would lead to foster care, Eppie also finds keeping that "big secret" quite exciting. Keith realises this and sees it as a kind of buffer against PTSD developing. So, he always makes a point of discussing something of what happened at the South Bank park whenever she mentions it or when there is something about it on the television news. And, she often initiates discussion about it. He feels that although it must be secret, what happened must never be covered up or pasted over. Rather like his finding her abandoned in the bush, Eppie must always be aware of the reality of what happened. He feels or hopes that is the best way to minimise any post traumatic stress issues in relation to the terror she experienced at the South Bank park. Indeed, within three weeks they discuss whether the Police should have shot and killed the woman. However, Keith knows nothing about the psychological aspects of PTSD. In fact, he is sceptical about psychology, something he inherited from his friend Fiona.

Eppie says: "They shot and shot and shot her. I saw what they did. She was already dead in the water. So, why did they have to do that?"

---

[168] See: Hendriksen, E., "5 Reasons to Talk About Trauma". *Psychology Today*, 27 March 2019. https://www.psychologytoday.com/au/blog/how-be-yourself/201903/5-reasons-talk-about-trauma

Also, Maddox, L., "Is it always good to talk? How to help survivors of trauma." *The Guardian*, London, 24 July 2017. https://www.theguardian.com/science/sifting-the-evidence/2017/jul/24/is-it-always-good-to-talk-how-to-help-survivors-of-trauma "Even the best talking intervention will only be properly accessible if other more basic physical needs are met." Keith provided Eppie's basic physical needs and was already able to connect with her emotional needs. We all react differently to trauma. Thus, Keith is being sensible about how he parents her at this time.

For recovery from serious personal trauma, perhaps the best authority is Herman, J. (1997), *Trauma and Recovery: The Aftermath of Violence – From Domestic Abuse to Political Terror*. New York: Basic Books. Judith Herman's three stages of recovery form Part 2 of her book are "Safety, Remembrance and Mourning/Reconnection". Eppie already has the safety, security and supporting love of Keith who was there with her when the event happened. Nevertheless, he does later go through some of the second stage conditions which Herman sets out, for example, he provides her with opportunities for introspection and analysis (as in Herman's "Remembrance"). Keith knows nothing about all this and is driven by what he feels is common sense.

Keith: "I don't really know. I suspect that they were all charged up with adrenaline and just let themselves go."

Eppie: "What's adrenaline?"

Keith: "It's a hormone or like a thing that our body squirts into our bloodstream in an emergency. It gives us a sudden boost of power to either fight or run away. I think it's the hormone which made me run at that shooter and throw sand in her face. It gives us the emergency power for what they call the 'fight-or-flight response'.[169] It's a survival thing. And, in our case I knew that there was no hope for us if I just lay down in the sand and pretended to be dead. She would have pumped us anyway. I saw her doing that to others."

After some silence, Eppie: "Well, why did those Police do that? They didn't have to fight or run away. They already shot her. I saw. She was lying in the water. Her face was in the water. I don't know if she was dead but she was already stuffed."

Keith: "Good point."

Eppie: "Yeah, I saw them do that."

Keith: "I didn't. But yes, I agree. In fact, we were the ones who were faced with the 'fight or flight' dilemma. They had powerful guns and there was a lot of them and just one shooter. She was what they call a 'lone wolf' terrorist, just on her own against all of them."

Eppie: "Yes."

Keith: "I think, and this is just my thoughts ... well, I think they are so highly trained with practicing for this kind of thing repeatedly over and over so that when its real and not just training, their adrenaline is so used to being pumped into their system that they just get all super aggressive and rush in. I think their pent up adrenaline made them pump her with more bullets even when she was face down in the water and probably dead." [170]

Silence between them for a moment.

---

169 See: "Adrenaline" in *Wikipedia* at https://en.wikipedia.org/wiki/Adrenaline
170 See: "Bonnie and Clyde" in *Wikipedia* at https://en.wikipedia.org/wiki/Bonnie_and_Clyde Bank robbers Bonnie and Clyde were eventually tracked down and ambushed by Police who then shot them at nearly point blank range in their car with over 130 rounds well after they were clearly dead. It was a kind of extrajudicial killing because Bonnie and Clyde had no chance to react and shoot back or defend themselves. In an ideal world they should have been arrested and put on trial. But, the Police were all energised or hyped up for the kill.

Keith: "Actually, I think I'm lucky that the Police didn't shoot me, too. They could have mistaken me for the person doing the shooting or with being an accomplice. Or, perhaps I could have got a stray bullet in me. They were so fired up or enthusiastic and 'gung ho'." [171]

Eppie: "Guns are not good."

Collin: "You're so right! Guns kill even by mistake. And, when a person is shot dead they can't get up and start living again. Guns are not pretend. They kill. And, that's final."

Even though she is only six-years-old, this is the kind of analytical conversation they had several times. As usual, Keith treats her respectfully virtually as an adult. Dealing with the issue by opening up her thoughts in this way enabled Eppie to be increasingly rational about what happened and helped prevent a deep trauma from setting in. And, it needs to be said, too, that the same could be applied to Keith. Discussion helped him. He was also motivated by what he saw as a parental duty for him to be strong and not succumb to the effect of the trauma merely for Eppie's sake.

One day she asks him: "That shooting lady at the South Bank, you know, she was doing what bad men do. And, she was lady. Why?"

"Well, ladies can do bad things too."

Eppie is silent in thought.

Then: "I reckon she was very angry about men. You know, like me."

Keith: "Maybe. Think of it this way. In the newspapers and TV news, it's men doing this sort of bad thing like killing people. That's what we read and see all the time. So, we expect men to do these things. And so, men do these bad things. It's the same when a

---

[171] See: "Lindt Cafe siege" in *Wikipedia* at https://en.wikipedia.org/wiki/Lindt_Cafe_siege A dramatic 2014 hostage situation at a Sydney café in the centre of the city came to an end when, after the hostage taker killed a hostage, the Police stormed the café. As the storming began, the hostage taker was shot and killed by a sniper just as police were about to enter the café. The sniper said: "I watched the (gun's) laser ... from the centre of his chest go to his head and his head exploded and he fell". Yet, already dead, he was shot a further 22 times by two other Police officers. Moreover, one of the hostages was killed and three others were wounded accidentally by stray Police bullets. So, bearing in mind this real life siege at the Lindt café, Keith was lucky not to have been wounded or even killed. Some might say that he should not have got involved. Well, in fact, as he pointed out he had no choice in the matter. He had no idea that the Police were minutes away and if he had delayed, like lying down in the sand, he would have been "pumped" with the lone offender's bullets. He had seen that happen to others. And, he was driven to defend his child.

newborn baby is found dumped all alone in the bush, everybody does not expect an old man to pick her up, care for her, cuddle her, and love her. That would be what people expect a woman to do."

Eppie understands the analogy straight away. She smiles. "That's why you are an old man and my Mumma. And, I don't think many people would understand that."

Keith: "Yes, exactly! Actually, many would think there's something wrong with me because I don't conform to their expectations. Am I a nutter or even a paedophile?"

"But, I know what you are really like: the best Mumma I could ever have."

A month after the South Bank shooting, Eppie and Keith are in the middle of having a late breakfast. They have already been active with the chooks and guinea fowls, letting them out and collecting eggs. A car arrives at their front driveway gate. They watch it on Collin's computer through the CCTV camera they set up previously. They see two young men climb over the gate and walk up the drive. Looking through the living room door, Eppie can see the two men walking up towards the house.

Keith: "I think they might be Police in plain clothes, you know detectives. It's an unmarked car. They are smartly dressed."

As the pair of policemen approach, two chooks walk in front of them. They are not afraid of humans.

Looking from the front door. (*Getty Images*. Posed by model.)

Eppie immediately takes off and races out the back door and off into the bush. She hides in their secluded cubby house area between two big granite boulders.

Keith goes outside and meets the men at the top of the driveway. They tell him they are from Queensland Police headquarters at Roma Street in Brisbane. They show him their Police identity badges.

He politely invites these young men in their twenties and thirties onto the front verandah. He offers them a seat each.

Detective Sergeant Bruce Wilson gives him his business card and introduces his younger offsider who remains silent throughout. Detective Wilson tells Keith: "The Deputy Commissioner has asked us to conduct some enquiries about the shooting at the South Bank Park in Brisbane last month. We understand that you were present?"

Motivated to be honest and not get caught up in any web of lies and half truths, he gives a simple answer: "Yes."

Detective Wilson: "Would you be able to tell us some of what you saw."

But, Keith sidesteps the question and asks: "How did you know I was there?"

Detective Wilson: "During our enquiries we have examined a number of CCTV camera recordings at railway stations along the southbound line from the South Bank station. One of them has images of a person we believe is you disembarking from the first train after the shooting and walking from the station. It also shows you approaching and then getting into a white VW camper van with registration '398 WGY' which was parked near the station in Kent Street at the back of the PA Hospital. You were carrying a little child and a distinctive old shoulder bag with the words 'Shaw Savill Line' printed on it."

Suddenly defensive, Keith responds: "I'm not at all connected to that woman who did all that shooting! I've never in my life seen her before!"

Detective Wilson: "Please don't worry. We are not suggesting that by any means. We are merely trying to locate the man who so bravely and single handedly took on that shooter. We believe it may have been you."

A much relieved Keith is silent for a moment.

Keith: "Yes, it was me. … I just had to do something. We were trapped in a little sandy cove surrounded by palms and rocks. I didn't want us to die. We couldn't run. Yes … well, we were trapped … nowhere to run.… well, we were trapped like the Rats of Tobruk … nowhere to run."[172]

Detective Wilson: "You've probably read in the press and media that the man who took down that offender during this attack is generally unknown to the public."

That last comment about Tobruk is over the heads of these two young Policemen.

Keith: "So, why do you want to know?"

---

[172] For an explanation of the phrase "rats of Tobruk" see *Wikipedia* at https://en.wikipedia.org/wiki/The_Rats_of_Tobruk

Detective Wilson: "Two reasons: the Deputy Commissioner is required to complete a report. The other reason: he has suggested that your name could be put forward for an award for outstanding bravery if it can be confirmed that it was you."

Keith: "Of course, as you've worked out, it was me. I appreciate your need to wrap this up. I understand. But, I do not want any award or any kind of publicity."

Detective Wilson: "Why not?"

Keith: "Well, I'm a private person. That's why I live here."

Detective Wilson: "Your response to that armed offender was heroic. She had just reloaded the gun with a fresh 30 round magazine. You likely saved countless more lives minutes before the SERT arrived on the scene.[173]"

Keith: "Probably."

Detective Wilson avoids disagreement: "May I also ask who was the female child that you were with. You certainly saved her life, too."

Unusually for Keith, he answers with a lie: "A friend's daughter. I was merely motivated to defend the child who was with me. She was my responsibility. I had the care of her that afternoon for fun at the South Bank and I just had to do it. That's not heroic. I could not have lived with myself if somehow I had survived and that child had died."

Detective Wilson: "Is that not heroic?"

Keith: "It isn't. I was doing my duty and we were trapped. That's not heroic. It was merely a matter of survival."

Detective Wilson: "I'm surprised at that take about what you did."

Keith: "Well, it's the truth. So, I emphatically do not want my name revealed to the press, the media, and the public. What I did is private."

Detective Wilson: "Are you sure?"

Keith: "Absolutely."

Detective Wilson: "I think we'll have to accept that. It's your choice."

Keith: "Yes."

---

[173] "Special Emergency Response Team" or SERT. *Wikipedia.* https://en.wikipedia.org/wiki/Special_Emergency_Response_Team_(Queensland)

Detective Wilson: "Our records show that you are living at this residence as the sole occupant. So, I would now like to ask you more about the child who was with you and who you say you had a responsibility to defend. Is she a relative and could we talk to her parents or parent?"

Keith pauses for ages. He is suddenly a little worried. He doesn't want to get caught in a web of lies that he creates. How should he respond? Finally: "Well, you could say she is a relative. However, I want to protect her identity. To tell you the truth, she has an unusual and troubled background. As I said, I had taken her to the South Bank for some fun time. So, I cannot give you information about her parents. You'll just have to accept that this little girl was there and that I defended her. As you will understand, I know her, had responsibility for her, and so, well, I put my life on the line for her. As I said, I had to do something to protect her and I did. I had no choice. You will just have to accept that."

Detective Wilson: "I suppose you were responsible. Did you take her home afterwards?"

Keith: "Of course. Straight home. She was very upset … she needed safety, just like all the other people who were there … and me too. I was very stressed out. All the people on the train were, too. People were crying and shaking. The little girl, too. I'm nearly eighty and physically I became very weak. Somebody on the train helped me stand up. So, please, no publicity at all."

Detective Wilson: "Are you sure?"

Keith: "I am adamant about all this. I want no publicity about me or about her. And, I would like an assurance from the Police that our privacy will be guaranteed. This is very important for her, her family, and for me."

There is silence for moment.

Keith continues: "If you go back to Brisbane and look up your Police records on me, you will find that I was jailed for allegedly raping a fourteen-year-old girl. I didn't do it but I suffered much antagonism from the public and the press before and after I was jailed. I was beaten up in jail and then, finally after nearly two years my conviction was quashed on appeal and the so-called victim was then convicted of perjury. You can now see why I don't like publicity. Many still want to believe I did it even though the girl made it all up. So, I don't want people and the press saying I'm not a hero because I raped a teenager. And, some will ask why I was alone with a little child, a rapist alone with a little girl. They love to have a villain. I just don't want to be the focus of attention for public speculation and nor do I want it for her."

Detective Wilson, feeling a need to reassure Keith about his legal status: "I'm sorry to hear that. Before coming here we did check our records about you. What you say is correct. Look, I now understand why you don't want publicity. So, rest assured, nothing will be released by the Police Department regarding your or the child's identity without both your and her parents' consent. There are principles and regulations outlined for us in both the *Police Service Administration Act of 1990* and the *Information Privacy Act of 2009*. Those two *Acts* determine how we collect and store information about individuals. You have told us that you don't want publicity. I understand why. The public can assume things too easily. There was no publicity given about the teenager's perjury conviction because of child protection legislation. So, they could assume that your conviction was overturned on a legal technicality. We will respect your wish. And, the child with you is a minor. We have to respect that. I will advise my commanding officer about your wish for no publicity."

Keith: "Thank you. I'm pleased with that reassurance."

Detective Wilson: "No worries. I think the Deputy Commissioner will be pleased that we have found you but, like us, will maintain your privacy. I would expect you to receive a letter from him in coming days. It will confirm your heroic rôle at the South Bank that afternoon and reassure you about maintaining your and the child's privacy." He smiles. "I expect that I will have to draft the letter." [174]

Keith smiles, too.

The 'official' formal interview has wrapped up and small-talk continues about the lovely secluded bush property Keith lives in. They even talk about how it occasionally snows here. Both Policemen clearly admire the place. Keith even tells them: "Sometimes, as I'm living alone, I have nobody else to share this beautiful place with, only my chooks. But, they keep me company."

---

[174] Keith receives the letter a week later.

During the entire time the Policemen were there they remained on the front verandah with Keith. If they had gone inside they would have seen things connected with Eppie like some of her toys and books, her iPad, and the breakfast things still on the table including the two half eaten bowls of Weet-Bix. They had not finished eating when the Police arrived at the gate and Eppie took off in a hurry.

So, the Police detectives leave with good grace.

Keith is immensely relieved and momentarily prays desperately that his charade has worked: 'Dear God, please make sure that I've tricked them. Just before they left, I told a lie about living alone and only having chooks for company. Please don't let that backfire on me. Amen.'

Yet, Keith realised early on during initial contact with these Policemen that right from the start they had a positive attitude towards him. And so, he successfully played on that. He has experience of police negativity. It was also fortunate that they had seen the chooks. He knows that if they had come on a criminal matter and he was a 'person of interest', their demeanour would have been subtly hostile and things may well have turned out very differently.

He walks up to the cubby house and finds a worried Eppie. He sits down with her and tells her in detail who the men were, what was said and discussed, and that they have guaranteed privacy. She accepts what he tells her. She has absolute trust in him. They walk back to the house to finish their breakfast each with a fresh bowl of Weet-Bix.

After breakfast, Keith e-mails Fiona in Yarrabah about what happened at the South Bank and then today with the Roma Street Police visit.

Her response by e-mail next day gives Keith and Eppie much hope.

CHAPTER 11

Birth Certificate

That night Keith emails Fiona about a birth certificate. Here is Fiona's return email:

Dear Keith and Eppie,

Well done at the South Bank! Both of you! I saw it on the news but had no idea it was you. I am stunned! And, because of that, I think it provides you with an excellent chance in a Court case. So, I agree that now is the opportune time to go to Court. Basically, you are going to Court to obtain a birth certificate for Eppie and hopefully also for your custody of her. So, please think about it. Tomorrow morning I will send you an email with guidance about how to go about it.
Again, congratulations!
Love to you both.

Her return email then includes a list of things to do and people to see:

1. See solicitor Paula Wellings at Turner Lawyers in Toowoomba. She has a history of successfully standing up against the Child Safety Department. Some in the Department fear her. Explain your own history to her and then how you came to have Eppie in your possession. Tell her your first priority is a birth certificate. That's a simple process. This will allow you to have her registered with Medicare and for her to have catch-up vaccinations. Of course, she can't go to school without a birth certificate. Next, you need to explain why you want formal custody of Eppie. You can inform her of your care of her during the last six years, detailing how she came into your possession and listing all Eppie's skills. Despite your age, you have demonstrated that you are capable of

parenting her. That recent near rape is important. Paula Wellings is not likely to be cheap.

2. Have Eppie medically examined to show her fitness and the fact she has not been sexually abused. You need a sympathetic doctor and you will have to pay for it.

3. You need a social assessment report from a recognised psychologist, preferably somebody accredited by the Family Court. Myra McSwan is such a person I can recommend. She is also based in Toowoomba. She is Aboriginal. You need to contact and engage her soon as she is likely to have a lot of cases to work through. These reports are normal in Family Court and Children's Court custody cases. She is very experienced and has a good name. Again, you will have to pay for her report.

4. Have yourself medically examined. In this regard, I would love it if you would consent to me taking over Eppie as her custodian and guardian should you become too ill to care for her. I would gladly submit myself to questioning by the Court. I would hope that my background in teaching and years with the Child Safety Department would carry some weight as well as my contact with her.

5. Finally, we have to have a Police report. This is not a big deal. They merely report on any criminal activity you have been involved in. I recommend an Inspector Halloran at the Toowoomba police. He is not an aggressive man. Paula would get the report.

    With all these five items in place you would be ready to go to Court with Paula Wellings' support. Hopefully, all this could be done before the start of school in late January.

The process of going to court takes a long time. This is frustrating for both Eppie and Keith. It also means that Eppie will not be able to start school at the beginning of the school year. It is now late January. She will have to wait until July when she is six and a half.

Keith sits down with her and goes through the list with her. She asks many questions but finds it all a little worrying because of the element of uncertainty is exacerbated by her near rape. Together, they compile for her a USB stick of photos and descriptions documenting Eppie's life from when he found her to the present. This is for Myra McSwan as background for the social assessment report. It is about her and he thinks it is only right that she should influence it.

Keith also arranges to see a Dr Sylvia Morton in Toowoomba. She moved from Townsville recently. He knew her as a sympathetic doctor for girl students in trouble while at Fulham State High, especially with regard to sexual issues like going on the pill and abortions. He stresses the non-Medicare nature of this appointment and that it is to assess a girl for Court purposes.

At first, Keith talks to her about Eppie and what the report is for. He tells her about finding Eppie at Bolivia Hill, parenting her on his own, and then the South Bank horror. He tells her he will not allow Eppie to be interrogated for two reasons: she is a foundling and would be removed into 'care' and he does not want to re-traumatise her. He also asks if she can examine Eppie to prove she has not been sexually abused especially by penetration.

He then leaves Eppie with Dr Morton so that he can't be seen as having any influence over the medical report. Eppie comes through the medical with flying colours. While Keith is not present, Dr Morton and Eppie have good discussion. She is very impressed with Eppie's weight, fitness, general health, and especially her intelligence and says so in her report.

Dr Morton explains what a hymen is and adds: "With the type of hymen you have it is almost a forgone conclusion that you to have not been penetrated." She shows her a diagram in a book: "A normal and common hymen for a little girl like you is crescent shaped like a new moon or sometimes like a half moon. Your's is not so common but is still normal. It's called 'septate'. There is a band of membrane across the vaginal opening. So, you can see it is certain nobody's fingers or penis have gone inside. You are small. So, it would have been painful and you might have bled quite a lot."

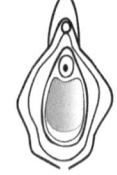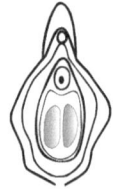

(*Left*) crescent hymen.
(*Right*) septate hymen.
(*Wikipedia*)

She tells her she should mention the hymen in her report "if that's alright by you?"

Eppie: "Yes please. I want to show that my Mumma has not sexually abused me."

She is very impressed with Eppie. Towards the end of her report, she adds: "For her age, this child is very sagacious and level-headed. Although only six-years-old, she is approaching Gillick competence."[175]

Overall, her medical report about Eppie's health means that Keith's not handing her over to authorities after he found her at Bolivia Hill did not place her "at unacceptable risk of harm". She thrived with him. He feels vindicated.

However, Eppie asks him not to mention the near abduction by that man to other people. "Dr Morton was okay. I liked her. But, you see I'm embarrassed about it. I was so stupid and everybody would know about me being stupid."

Keith: "Not to worry. I promise I won't."

Thank you.

Keith: "I'm also embarrassed for letting you walk off like that. I failed as a parent."

Eppie: "No you didn't. I was so difficult for you. Then, even being so hurtful in what I said to you, you came after me and saved me. Mumma, I wouldn't be here without you."

They hug.

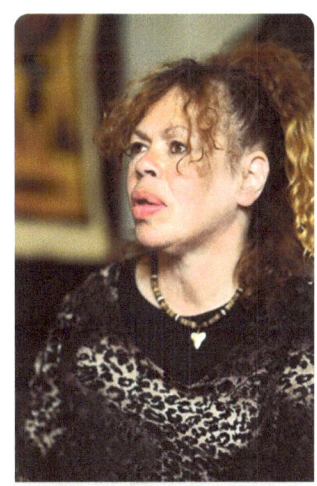

Psychologist Myra McSwan spends a day with Keith and Eppie separately. Eppie spends time with her first. After spending a couple of hours with Eppie, Myra McSwan asked Keith to come inside from the garden. She asked him to sit down. Eppie was already sitting on the couch with her head slightly bowed. With a sheepish worried look, she apologised to him quietly: "I'm so sorry, Mamma. Please forgive me. I said we have a secret."

With a very serious and slightly angry countenance, Myra McSwan spoke to him: "Mr Todd, as part of my assessment, I asked Eppie if there are any big secrets she should tell me. After much nervousness on Eppie's part, she has told me that there is

Myra McSwan is not impressed.
(*iStockphoto*. Posed by model.)

---

[175] A term used in medical law when a minor child may be able to consent to his or her own medical treatment. It is based on a British House of Lords case *Gillick v West Norfolk and Wisbech Area Health Authority (1985) 3 AI ER 402*. The decision defined conditions which would enable a doctor to decide that the child is 'Gillick competent'. https:// en.wikipedia.org/wiki/Gillick_competence

a big secret between you two but she will not say what it is. This does not bode well. Are you able to come clean?"

Keith stands up and sits on the couch next Eppie with his arm around her. "Dear Eppie. I understand you. You are worried that all this investigation of you and me and our relationship as parent and child is going to be torn apart. You are very honest. So, I think I must tell Myra what the secret is."

He gives her a massive hug.

Still sitting next to Eppie as Myra looks a little angry, Keith tells his worried little girl: "When a parent has been sexually abusing his child, he will often impress upon her that the sexual relationship between them must be kept a strong secret. He will tell her that if anyone finds out he will go to jail and she will be sent to foster care. He may even threaten to bash her if she tells anyone. Social workers like Myra are well aware of this. And, I think she is suspicious about this secret between us. I think she believes you are hiding sexual abuse from her because I have been threatening you. Well, I'm going to explain a few things. I have to."

Now, he tells Myra about Eppie's disenchantment with him being too old, wanting to be like teen idols, wanting sexy dresses like the Spice Girls and Taylor Swift, and how all that lead to her running away down the drive and accepting a lift. He shows her a photo on his computer of Eppie's bloody knee and how it got like that. "The other thing is that both Eppie and me are embarrassed about what happened when that man tried to take her. She thinks she is stupid for falling into a trap. I'm embarrassed for failing as a parent by letting her wander off like that."

"No, Mumma. I made a big mistake letting that man put me in his car." She turns to Myra: "My Mumma saved me by shouting and running to the car. The man was guilty and so he threw me out of his car onto the ground. So, I know I was wrong about my Mumma being too old. I've said sorry to him"

Keith: "Yes, she's been quite contrite. She has apologised and given me flowers."

Next, Keith tells her about what happened at the South Bank. He adds: "Police have agreed to keep what happened at the South Bank confidential. I don't want Child Safety to trace us. We are frightened that the Child Safety Department would put Eppie into foster care."

Eppie: "I love him so much. He saved my life. Please, he's not past his use by date."

Understanding what Keith has been saying, Eppie tells Myra: "So, you see, it's our secret because if the Safety witches find out about what happened, they would know about me and my Mumma and they would take me away into foster care. They don't know what he did. He saved my life at the South Bank. And, he stopped that shooting lady. But, the police then shot her. They didn't need to. Those Safety 'witches'[176] don't know that my Mumma is just <u>not</u> too old."

He shows Myra the letter he got from the Police Deputy Commissioner.

Her response is quick: "Oh, Eppie and Keith. I am so sorry. Now, I understand your secrecy. It's wise of you. Yes, Eppie, they would immediately take you into care. Yet, I'm sure you are so proud to have him as a parent you can call 'Mumma'. I know it is likely that he saved your life and so many other people's lives. I saw it on the TV news. And Keith, I'm in full admiration of what you did. You did what a very committed parent would do. Your child needed you desperately, you rose to the occasion, and risked your own life in the process." Her choice of words is clear. She is endorsing his rôle as Eppie's 'parent'.

All are smiles now.

Myra adds: "I think I'll mention this in my report for the Court so that the Magistrate knows. This report is for the Court. As yet, the Child Safety Department is not involved in this case. And, I know the Police report on you, Keith, will not find anything about Eppie and it will find nothing adverse about you. As you know, proceedings of the Children's Court are absolutely confidential. Breeching that confidentiality can attract a prison term. Nobody in the Court would dob you in. My recommendation will be for both custody and guardianship."

Keith thanks her.

To Keith and Myra's surprise, Eppie says to Myra: "I want to show you something."

---

[176] She rather cheekily used the word 'witches'.

She goes to the display cabinet in the room and takes out her 'lucky jewel box', opens it, and shows Myra the contents, explaining the significance of many items. "There's Tiger's Eye, Malachite, cowrie shells, New Zealand Greenstone, and coins. This Rhodesian tickie[177] is special for me because it is from where my Mumma comes from in Africa. And, here is my first tooth that came out last week."

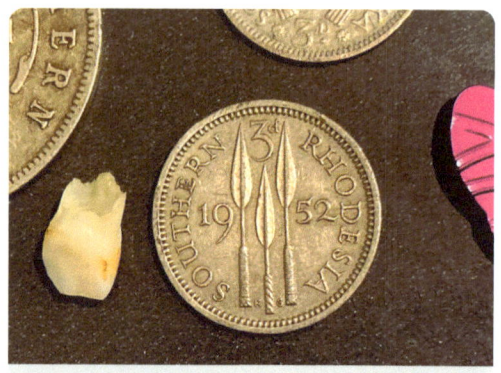

(*Left*) The 'tickie' next to Eppie's tooth.

(*Right*) Eppie's lucky jewel box opened up for Myra.

Myra is visibly touched by Eppie's showing her these personal special little girl's treasures. "That's a fantastic collection. Look after them. They're very special for you."

Three days later, her social assessment report is really quite glowing. She is especially impressed with Eppie's worldliness and Keith's care and protection of her since her birth.

When they see lawyer Paula Wellings, she tells them that Myra's report is especially important because she is a well-known and widely respected consultant for courts. Then, she tells them that she has received the report from Inspector Halloran. Now, the process for obtaining a late birth certificate is really quite simple. "The Court needs evidence of the birth, the time, date and place. Then, because it occurred in New South Wales the Court here in Queensland will virtually instruct the registrar of births, deaths and marriages in Sydney to issue a birth certificate and forward it to the Court here in Toowoomba. Eppie will then have a birth certificate. It's as simple as that."

---

[177] A thrupenny coin or 'tickie' was used in Northern Rhodesia where Keith came from. (Northern Rhodesia didn't have coins or notes of its own. So, Southern Rhodesia currency was used.)

Keith is amazed and says so.

Paula adds: "But, that birth certificate will have no parents listed on it. There will simply be the word 'Unknown' in the boxes for parent details. There will be nothing to link you to her. But, we will ask the Magistrate to make an interim ruling on your custody and guardianship of her until such time as the New South Wales Police have completed a search for the birth mother. But, to obtain that interim custody and guardianship it would be advantageous if we went to Court armed with the medical report on Eppie, Myra's social assessment report, and a Police report on you, Keith. What would also be helpful would be the presence at the Court hearing of your friend Fiona Morris in Yarrabah. As a teacher and former child safety officer she would be excellent to back up your case for interim custody, especially as she has said she would be willing to take over Eppie should you become incapable."

Keith is very pleased. Eppie has been listening quietly and is also happy.

Paula continues: "So, now we need a hearing date at the Canning Town Magistrates Court. If Fiona Morris could make herself available for that date it would be very useful. Then, we'll go ahead. She then shows Keith and Eppie the relevant section of the NSW *Births, Deaths and Marriages Act of 1995*. "Here, at section 13(2) it says any Court in Australia can order the NSW Registrar to register a birth. So, we have to get the Canning Town Magistrate to make that Order."

That is what happens. Paula Wellings arranged for Inspector Halloran to attend the hearing. The Magistrate asks almost no questions of him. His report on Keith showed his conviction, his acquittal, and the payment of compensation. However, he now knows the full story of Keith's finding Eppie at Bolivia Hill.

The Court hearing before Magistrate Heather Austin is in late March just after Easter when the school holidays have begun. This is convenient because Fiona comes to stay with Eppie and Keith for a week. Eppie gets on very well with her and they even talk much about foster care. They take Fiona on sightseeing trips around the Granite Belt.

The Magistrate, Heather Austin, was impressed with the evidence produced from Keith's iPhone, an affidavit which Keith supplied about finding Eppie, as well as the medical and police reports. And, there is an affidavit from Keith about what happened at the South

Bank. Then, there was Fiona's presence at the Court. The Magistrate questioned Keith on some details of his discovery of Eppie at Bolivia Hill.

She also asked questions of Fiona, mainly about her time as a Child Safety Officer and how that affects her views on Keith's parenting of Eppie. Of course, she gave very positive responses.

The Magistrate asked the Registrar to contact the Child Safety Department to find out if they had any record of an 'Eppie Todd DOB 15/11/2018'.[178] She adjourned the hearing until next morning. It was a worrying night for Keith and Eppie. However, a faxed response came in time for the resumed hearing in the morning:

> The child 'Eppie Todd DOB 15/11/2018' is unknown to the Department. To date there have been no notifications or matters of concern about a child of that name. [In confidence.]

Keith and Eppie are relieved.

At the resumed hearing, the Magistrate referred to a Family Court Order about a very different type of case where custody and guardianship of a child was granted to a non-biological parent.[179] She uses this case as a precedent to back up her decision because Keith has established that, through his actions, he became a person "concerned with the care, welfare and development of the child." She cites the case and says: "As the judge in that recent 'non-parent' case said: 'It is not parenthood which is crucial to the best interests of the child, but <u>parenting</u>'." Magistrate Heather Austin adds: "It is abundantly clear that Keith Todd has been the child's 'primary carer'.[180] All her life he has been her parent, well, in fact, her only carer since her birth over six years ago. And, I might add, the parenting involved has by all accounts been exemplary."

---

[178] It is dated the 15 November because, although Keith found her during the morning of the 16th, she had already been abandoned when Keith arrived at the bush clearing late on the evening of the 15th.

[179] Pavey, A. "Judge rules for stepdad over grandmother in child custody battle". *Courier Mail*, Brisbane, 12 November 2013. https://www.couriermail.com.au/news/queensland/judge-rules-for-stepdad-over-grandmother-in-child-custody-battle/news-story/4921e4f694b4a497efbef63ce7c76cbb

See also: https://waterslawyers.com.au/im-not-the-childs-parent-can-i-still-apply-for-custody/

[180] Fadzai Mamvura, "What is a primary carer in Family Law?" *Corney & Lind Lawyers*, 15 October 2020. https://www.corneyandlind.com.au/family-law/what-is-a-primary-carer-in-family-law/

She then moved on to Keith: "Do you know the difference between adoption and a Permanent Care Order or PCO?[181] The first, adoption, is quite strict and rigorous and permanent. The second is more open and flexible."

"Yes, your Honour. I've thought about them and discussed them with Eppie. We feel we need to leave Eppie's situation more open, just in case her unknown mother is found. We would prefer neither of them. One of the issues is that both Eppie and me simply do do trust the Child Safety Department."

The Judge: "Yes, I read in the *Social Assessment Report* that Eppie calls officers of the Department 'witches' and that is related to the Hansel and Gretel story."

She then makes her judgement. "I will now come to the judgement of this Court. I am making these orders simple and uncomplicated. In a way, they are unique. I cannot find any precedent where a foundling has been cared for so well by the person who found her and where the bond between the is so profound. However, there is guidance in the *Act* in this issue. Section 11 states: "A **parent** of a child is the child's mother, father or someone else (other than the chief executive) having or exercising parental responsibility for the child."[182] In this regard, as Mr Todd has been *in loco parentis* all the six years of her life, I now refer to section 5A of the *Child Protection Act* which requires this Court to ensure that 'the safety, wellbeing and best interests of a child, both through childhood and for the rest of the child's life, are paramount'. That is the guiding principle which this Children's Court is compelled to implement. I quote further from that section 5 of the *Act*: 'All other principles stated in this *Act* are subject to the principle stated in section 5A.'[183] From evidence produced in Court, in particular the *Social Assessment Report* and the *Medical Report* which I have read, not just the recommendations, it is clear that Mr Todd has placed the safety, welfare, and best interests of this child over and above his own needs. That was a especially so during the recent incident at the South Bank. Moreover, those best interests have been paramount over

---

[181] *Types of Childrens Court Orders*, 25 October 2018. https://www.qld.gov.au/community/caring-child/foster-kinship-care/information-for-carers/rights-and-responsibilities/legal-matters/types-of-childrens-court-orders#PCO

[182] The *Child Protection Act* of 01 February 2024 at section 11(1).

[183] Section 5A of the Queensland *Child Protection Act* as of 01 February 2024.

the more than six years of the child's life. This Court will now formalise Mr Todd's rôle as the child Eppie's carer and *de facto* parent as this is in her best interests."

She made a formal Order granting custody and guardianship to Keith using the overarching section 5A and sections 59(7A) and 59(7B).

She paused and then added: "I might also point out that, in the absence of any known biological parent or relative, in terms of the Queensland *Child Protection Act* at section 11(1), the decision of this Court makes Keith Todd legally Eppie's parent. She is now no longer parentless. I have added a non-binding recommendation that the NSW Police try to locate the birth mother. There is no deadline for this but a Court should review the situation in three years time.".

Of course, Eppie and Keith are very happy with the outcome. (*Getty Images*. Posed by models.)

Fiona, Keith, and Eppie celebrate their success by going out to dinner at the top Cunningham Hotel in Canning Town before Fiona flies home next day from Toowoomba airport. It is a happy occasion.

Eppie sums it up telling them: "I feel I'm a real person now … not a sneaky one."

During the dinner, Fiona raises an issue which Keith has thought about often before but never discussed with Eppie. She asks him: "I'm not being judgemental or anything like that, but as a non-biological parent of a child, have you ever seen yourself as a foster carer?"

Keith: "No, I haven't. There are several differences between me and foster carers. Eppie was never taken from a parent and given to me to care for. There was never any assessment of me as a possible foster carer. I've never been paid to care for her. When I found a newborn baby, I was motivated only to save the baby. But, because I was out of the mobile phone coverage area, I was unable to contact triple zero. I had to sort out the baby myself. That is when mother nature took over and bonded us, you know, all that oxytocin and those those pheromones. I became her mother especially when I gave her that first cuddle and she instinctively snuggled into my chest. And, when I first fed her some formula milk, I squirted it into her mouth from my mouth and she got microbes from me. So, I think the hormonal and chemical bonding between us right at the very beginning was there. When I look back on it, what I did was what bonded us like female mother-baby bonding. And, I did not deliberately set out to bond with a baby. In fact, I tried to phone the police but couldn't. We were out of range. I decided to hand her in at the Tenterfield Hospital but the bonding had already started. That was when I had undone my shirt buttons and held that very cold grubby little baby at my chest. So, I just couldn't. That unintentional bonding which occurred was more than a foster carer could achieve even if given a newborn baby to care for under section 22 of the *Child Protection Act*.[184] So, mother nature or Oxytocin determined that I just couldn't hand her over."

Fiona: "Well said. And, you've done an excellent job, too."

Eppie gets up, steps over to Keith and tells him: "I'm so happy. Remember you said even though bad things happen, good things happen, too."

She hugged him.

Now, Fiona adds something else: "Keith, what you have done has been a remarkable display of resilience in defying societal expectations: an old man has shattered basic norms as he successfully single-handedly cared for and nurtured a brand new baby and now a little girl. You have wrecked notions that not only old age but also male gender are inimical to motherhood."

"Thank you Fiona. I'm sure Eppie understands what you've said, despite the big words."

Eppie: "Yes, I do. Mumma you couldn't be a better Mumma."

They take Fiona to the Wellcamp (Toowoomba) airport next day for her to fly home.

The NSW birth certificate arrives in the mail four weeks later after the trial. Keith arranges with Centrelink for Eppie to be added to his Medicare card and then for her

---

[184] Keith is referring to section 22 of the Queensland *Child Protection Act* of 01 February 2024 which empowers the Department of Child Safety to remove a baby at birth from its birth mother. When this happens, the baby is given to a foster carer. It is invariably devastating for the birth mother. In each Australian state there is child protection legislation which permits the state government department responsible for child welfare and safety to remove babies at birth. It happens often and in Queensland on average once a week. It is a form of state sanctioned violence which is traumatic for both the birth mother and her infant.

to have catch-up vaccinations. This takes a further month. At CentreLink, the place of birth on Eppie's birth certificate, Bolivia NSW 2372, initially caused an issue. The woman interviewing them said: "You'll have to produce her visa so that we can assess her eligibility for Medicare coverage". This quickly ended in laughter when Keith explained that this 'Bolivia' is a sparsely populated grazing district 35 km south of Tenterfield in NSW not in South America.

Keith is happy she seems to be overcoming her post-traumatic stress. In fact, she has been hiding some her deeper emotions from him. It's not out of malice but to please him and reassure him by demonstrating that she is moving on and happy as a result of his care and love for her. But, what she can't hide are the recurring nightmares she still sometimes has, nightmares where Keith is woken up by her screams and has to carry her into his bed to calm her down while cuddling her back to sleep. This has worried him a little for he realises that these nightmares or classic flashbacks are symptoms of Post Traumatic Stress Disorder. What she saw at the South Bank has affected her deeply. So, he has been reading up on PTSD and one of the guides he finds very useful is a book by Harvard psychiatrist Judith Herman.[185] He realises that he has already been been guiding her through the 'Safety' which Judith Herman refers to as the first stage of recovery where Eppie feels secure and safe in her familiar environment with her loving parent. It's working. He also realises, too, that he has already been discussing the how and why of the perpetrator's actions.

However, in a later email to Keith, Fiona adds something else: "While you two have had a wonderful court victory, to some extent what happened at the South Bank and how you saved Eppie was an important factor in influencing the Magistrate. If that had not happened, it would have been more of an uphill battle. Though, I still think you would have won."

Keth replies: "Our relationship was on a serious down hill slide. She was becoming so difficult and rebellious. That was the reason she hitch-hiked and got in that man's car.

---

[185] Herman, J. (1997), *Trauma and Recovery: The Aftermath of Violence-From Domestic Abuse to Political Terror*. New York: Basic Books. Herman's book is about guided recovery from serious trauma. She is a professor of clinical psychiatry at Harvard University.

After I was able to prevent that abduction, she not only developed a completely different and wonderful relationship with me.[186] The South Bank trauma reinforced that."

Fiona: "There are so many pitfalls and traps in parenting. You are human and you've done your very best for a baby you found abandoned. You put her first in your life. You have benefitted her enormously. Don't forget, too, that at the South Bank you put your life on the line for her. You were no match for a Kalashnikov. And, importantly, she knows it."

---

[186] Woolard, A., "Experiencing trauma can change some people's outlook on life – sometimes for the better." *The Conversation*, Melbourne, 06 April 2023. https://theconversation.com/experiencing-trauma-can-change-some-peoples-outlook-on-life-sometimes-for-the-better-199088?

CHAPTER 12

Eppie taken into 'care'.

It is now the beginning of winter and too late for Eppie to start school immediately. So, she has to wait until after the school holidays in the last week of April. At the start of those holidays, at Eppie's request, arrangements are made for her to spend a day with her friend Melanie Shaw who she knew from when both attended Playgroup. Eppie feels she would like to talk to Melanie about school. Melanie is already in Year 3. She has a good time with Melanie.

Back at home while Eppie and Keith are talking about the day at Melanie's, she mentions that Melanie's mother asked her about Keith. But this time Belinda Shaw asked Eppie if her Dad was once a high school teacher. It was done in a casual seemingly innocent way. When Eppie said yes, Belinda asked if he had teaching at a school in Townsville. Eppie became weary, clammed up, and only said: "I don't know."

Belinda got the message and asked no more. In fact, she then did some research of her own.

Both Eppie and Keith have suspicions about 'nosey Parker' Belinda Shaw.

Two weeks later, Eppie is very happy about going to school.

Kinross State School school is small with only 70 students. Originally built with classrooms for up to 120 pupils, numbers of enrolments have been declining slowly over the years. Keith is pleased that it is a small school. He feels it will enable Eppie to integrate into society better. He wonders how Eppie will fit in. He doesn't want her held back.

She is demure and quiet during the interview with the Principal, Mrs McGregor. Keith provides her with information about Eppie such as her birth certificate, his finding her at

Bolivia Hill, his caring for her since birth, how he has encouraged her to be self-reliant, and fit and healthy. He tells her of Eppie's responsibilities with the vegetables and with the chooks on their property. He tells her she has visited national parks and knows a bit about forests. And, she has travelled on camping trips even out west to Cunnamulla. But, she has had little contact with other children. He warns her Eppie can be outspoken at times with her opinion. She could be a bit 'bolshy' at times.[187] Mrs McGregor mentally double takes at Keith's use of that old-fashioned term.

He tells her she reads books and uses her iPad to access the internet. Then, Eppie proudly demonstrates her reading ability when Mrs McGregor randomly picks a child's chapter book off the shelf behind her. It is a friendly interview. It is decided that Eppie will skip the Prep Year. She starts in late April when she is six and a half, which is a little late. Legally, she was supposed to start school before her sixth birthday. She has been placed in a composite Year 1 and Year 2 class of only 10 children, mainly because she is well beyond Prep age and she can read and write quite well and is computer literate.[188]

Still in her dressing gown, she is crying. (*Bigstockphoto*. Posed by model.)

She emerges from the interview happy, bouncy and excited about going to school. He thinks her enthusiasm is sweet. However, on the first day of the new school term Eppie tells Keith: "I want to go to school but I don't want to. I'm scared."

Keith: "You've endured horrible things. This is going to be a breeze for you. And, I know parents of new kids are allowed in the classroom for part of the first lesson. So, I'll be there with you at the start of your first day."

Keith helps her get dressed into her uniform.

---

187 'bolshy': term for a stirrer or a trouble maker derived from the rôle Bolsheviks played in the Russian Revolution.

188 Baker, J., "A gift of time: Children who start school later fare better, study finds". *Sydney Morning Herald*, 09 April 2019. https://www.smh.com.au/education/a-gift-of-time-children-who-start-school-later-fare-better-study-finds-20190408-p51bw1.html The University of NSW study found those who started later were more resilient, competitive, trusting, and far more self-confident than those who had started earlier. [Despite her initial shyness, this certainly shows with Eppie.]

Kinross State School.

The photo Keith took of Eppie in her school uniform at home before he drove her to school for her first day. Self conscious, she is holding up a flower. Shy and anxious, she didn't want to be photographed on arrival at the school. She is the only new kid starting in April. (*Austockphoto*. Posed by model.)

He spends around thirty minutes in the classroom with her.

While there, he realises what a very little kid she is. She is the smallest in the class and she is so slim. Something flashes through his mind about the attempted rape six months ago: 'She is so little and so sweet. Why would somebody want to capture, rape, and even then murder such a tiny exquisitely beautiful child? I just don't understand.'

Half an hour later, it's about time for him to leave. Eppie looks around at the kids in the classroom. She is anxious all of a sudden and gets very clingy with him. Holding onto his leg with both arms, she won't let go. She looks up at him. She's crying. This scene lasts for ten minutes or so.[189] He picks her up and cuddles her. Eventually, he carries her to a low work table and is able to put her down onto an empty chair. There are felt tip pens and papers

---

[189] Among young children 'separation anxiety' is normal and developmentally healthy. "Separation anxiety in babies and children - 6 months to 8 years". *Raising Children.* Australian Government, Canberra, 31 December 2022. https://raisingchildren.net.au/babies/behaviour/common-concerns/separation-anxiety Given Eppie's isolation during six years and her near rape, her anxiety is understandable even though she is six-years-old. See this classic painting from 1948: https://www.art.com/products/p53766589900-sa-i6111889/george-hughes-separation-anxiety-september-11-1948.htm

and other kids sitting at the table are drawing. He whispers to her: "Please do a drawing of me and give it to me when I pick you up this afternoon."

Eppie, sniffing: "Yes, okay."

He kisses her on her forehead. She turns, grabs his face and kisses him on his mouth. "I love you, Mumma. *Chabwino*."

As he walks out, her teacher sees him with tears in his eyes.

Sensibly and with Keith's advice, Eppie doesn't flaunt her skills. She just sits quiet. She is happy meeting kids her own age and likes the little and big lunch breaks where she talks to other kids, both boys and girls. She loves games kids play like 'Duck,

This is the drawing Eppie did for Keith when he picks her up in the afternoon. Her teacher is surprised at the maturity of it and told Keith she took ages to do it. With the classic flat-top savanna acacia tree, the style is African which she has inherited from Keith. She and Kieth often to draw together.

duck, goose' and even that old favourite 'What's the time, Mr Wolf'. When Keith met her to take her home at 3:00 p.m. on that first day, she ran to him and almost jumped on him. He picked her up and they exchanged hugs and kisses. "Mumma, I didn't say anything in class all day. I just listened. I liked talking to other kids during little lunch and big lunch." She added: "It was a little strange because they are not interested in the things I'm interested in. They talked about the Broncos and the Lions.[190] I listened. But, they did like Taylor Swift."

She is so worldly wise that sometimes she finds it hard to connect with other kids.

The Year 2 teacher, Mrs Crowther, introduces Keith to the Wushka reading program.[191] For homework she has to read selected short texts. She flies through them. She is just not challenged.

A week after starting school, quiet and demure Eppie accidentally let her skills known to her teacher. While looking on the shelves at the back of the classroom, she exclaimed to

---

[190] Two Brisbane-based rugby league teams.

[191] The Wushka reading program is used widely in Queensland primary schools. "Digital Reading Program for Beginning to Fluent Readers", *Wushka*. https://wushka.com.au/

the teacher when she saw *Charlotte's Web*.[192] "We've got this at home!" She opened it at her favourite part, Chapter XIX 'The Egg Sack', and started reading it to the teacher. When she realised other kids in the class were listening, she stopped and sat down at her table with the book. When Keith arrived to collect Eppie at the end of the day, the teacher told him: "I was stunned. I just listened as she read two pages without pausing and got every word right. Did you teach her to read?"

"Yes, she was four when she learned to read. She learned not with phonics but through word recognition. It started slowly and then escalated exponentially. The more she reads the more proficient she is. Being able to read has opened the world to her. It's empowered her. She knows such a lot now. I'm proud of her."

Mrs Crowther: "I'm not sure what I can do for her. Her reading proficiency is way, way above Year 2 level. I might get her to quietly mentor some kids with their reading."

At home, she and Keith discuss the school. "I like being with kids. I know I don't fit in well but I'm glad I'm not so innocent as them."

Apart from her reading ability and experience in life, there is another problem for her.

Having spent so many years not in contact with other children, to other kids she sounds snooty and up herself. To hear a little of what Eppie's accent is like, listen to that the five-year-old British girl who berates British Prime Minister Theresa May.[193] It's not exactly the same for it is tinged with Keith's mild central African accent. She has acquired her mixed accent during her secluded life with Keith's accent which is in some ways similar to the late Ian Smith's.[194] (Although, he would not share the same politics.) Stubbornly, she deliberately resists modifying her accent. And, she won't use in vogue words like 'cool', 'sick', 'youse', 'kinda', and 'deadly'. She sticks to words like *'broekies'*, *'voetsak'*, *'pasop'*, *'totsiens'*, and *'agh sis'*. She has picked up from him a few Chinyanja words she likes such as *'ngombe'* (cow), *'bwana'* (boss), *'zikomo'* (thank you), and *'chabwino'* (good bye). She deliberately remains an outsider.

---

[192] White, E.B., (2006), *Charlotte's Web*, Puffin/Penguin, Melbourne. First published in USA 1952.
[193] https://www.youtube.com/watch?v=xncfOR1X9n4
[194] https://www.youtube.com/watch?app=desktop&v=pdK1i0q0LAc Arriving in Australia as fifteen-year-old, the author was teased for his similar accent. He quickly learned to moderate it.

Nevertheless, Keith is worried especially when she complains: "Some can't even read. And, they know so little about the real world. Maybe I should be with the Grade 3 to 4 class?"

On a Monday in late May, her fourth week at school, disaster! Shortly after big lunch the Principal comes to the class and asks if Eppie can come with her to the school office. There, at the office, are three Child Safety Officers or CSOs and a Policeman.

Told that the three women are Child Safety Officers, Eppie is suddenly worried, she won't talk and resists being taken to a car waiting outside. She holds onto the leg of the Principal's desk. They struggle to prise her fingers off it. Chairs are knocked over. Papers are scattered across the floor. She is carried out struggling, shouting, and resisting strongly as the Policeman and the CSOs violently force into the back of a government car. She shouts that she wants her Mumma to come. Then, one Policeman holds her down as he forcibly puts the seat belt on her, giving her a whack on her arm as she wriggles and shouts. He tells her: "Keep still you little mongrel!" The child safety lock on the door on her side is activated. One of the CSOs sits next to her in the back.

Eppie continues screaming as she is driven away.

At 3:00 p.m. Keith arrives at the school to pick her up. He can't see Eppie.

The Principal, Mrs McGregor, walks up to him and asks him to come to the office. There are another two Child Safety Officers. A CSO gives her card to him. She is a Senior CSO. The school's secretary leaves the room. Without any further introduction and in front of Mrs McGregor, the Senior CSO tells him formally that under sections 38 and 39 of the *Child Protection Act*, the child Eppie has been "taken into the care of the Department on a three day Court Assessment Order and removed to a place of safety". She adds: "The Order has been filed with the Children's Court in Toowoomba together with the Department's grounds for taking out the Order, namely that she is in urgent need of protection. In terms of section 14 of the *Child Protection Act*, the child has been placed into the protective care of the Director of the Department of Child Safety and taken to a place of safety."[195]

Keith is stunned. But, sensibly, he clams up. He says absolutely nothing.

The Senior CSO asks him: "Do you have any questions?"

Again, Keith says nothing. He simply clams up.

The Senior CSO thanks the Principal. Then, with with the other CSO and the Policeman, she walks out.

Keith asks the Principal, Mrs McGregor: "When did they take Eppie?"

She tells him: "Just after big lunch." Then she adds: "Mr Todd, officers from the Child Safety Department have advised me you are suspected of having abducted Eppie and sequestered her isolated in the bush. They added that you are a convicted child sex offender and were jailed for raping a 14-year-old girl. That is why Eppie has been taken into care and removed to a place of safety. So, on their advice, I must now ask you to leave this school immediately. As principal, I must not accept the presence of a serious child sex offender on these premises. Please leave."

Keith: "You have not been told the true facts … ".

She interrupts him: "Mr Todd please leave. If you don't I will have to call for Police assistance. So, here are Eppie's things. Now, please leave."

She gives him a plastic bag with some of Eppie's exercise books and other materials in it.

Stunned, Keith takes the bag and walks out to his car.

He intends to drive to Toowoomba to see his solicitor, Paula Wellings. But, before doing so, he phones her. She'll ring him back in a few minutes. She does that. She has phoned the Child Safety Department's Regional Office in Toowoomba. "They've told me Eppie has been removed into foster care under a 3 day Temporary Court Assessment Order approved by a magistrate. This is the routine way they begin to remove children 'into care'. Usually, this

---

[195] Section 14 of the *Child Protection Act* states: "If the chief executive becomes aware (whether because of notification given to the chief executive or otherwise) of alleged harm or alleged risk of harm to a child and reasonably suspects the child is in need of protection, the chief executive must immediately take other action the chief executive considers appropriate." That action was deemed by Departmental officers to be her removal into the 'protection' of foster care.

Order is then extended to a 28 Day Assessment Order followed by a two-year Order and then a Long Term Order and possibly adoption. However, with your consent, we will contest the validity of the Order because of March's Court Order which conferred custodial and guardianship responsibilities on you as her 'parent'."

Keith: "But, the Canning Town magistrate accepted that she could continue to live with me."

Paula Wellings: "That is correct. It was a temporary ruling valid for three years while Police investigate and try to locate Eppie's birth mother. And, we are only a couple of months into that three-year period."

Keith: "Yes, I know that. But, why have the Child Safety people ignored the Canning Town magistrate's ruling?"

Paula Wellings: "I'm sorry, I don't know. We'll have to find out more in the next days. The Department will have to present material in the form of affidavits outlining their reasons for taking her into care. They will have to do so at least 24 hours before the hearing in Canning Town."

Frustrated, not with the lawyer, but about the turn of events, Keith drives home slowly. The house is empty and he feels very, very, down.[196]

He is absolutely shattered and thinks: 'Having a child removed by officious and supercilious government officials when you have done your beloved child no harm, only good is devastating. This is especially so as you have devoted yourself to her loving care for more than six years and did so under quite trying conditions. We are indelibly bonded by circumstances and by nature.'

He feels gutted. Profound feelings of loss well up inside him. These combine with a deep and growing anger as well as another growing sense that it is his duty to rescue her. But, what can he do? He knows the power of bureaucracy. His friend Fiona has explained that to him before.

---

[196] The author's eldest daughter had her daughter removed into foster care by child protection authorities. Officious and sanctimonious Departmental officers offered her no support and left her with the impression that she was being blamed for being a bad mother. Several days after the Department's intervention and in the depths of despair, she committed suicide.

At home, he has dark sinister thoughts about violent actions he could take. Of course, he knows these would get him nowhere and make getting Eppie back even harder, especially if he ends up in jail. Distraught, Keith turns to music on the CD-player. He plays an old favourite of his: Wagner's *Tannhauser Overture*.[197] For him it represents ultimate triumph over desolate despair.

Meanwhile, Eppie has been taken to an experienced foster carer who has fostered children for more than twenty years. She and her husband live on a semi-rural acreage property fifteen kilometres south of Toowoomba near the New England Highway a kilometre along the turn-off road to Cambooya. The property has two horses, chickens, and play equipment for 'in care' children. They also have a Toyota mini-bus which they use to deliver children each day to schools locally and in the Toowoomba area. They currently have seven kids 'in care' including Eppie, four girls and three boys. Their ages range from four to fourteen. The foster carers also have two of their own children aged

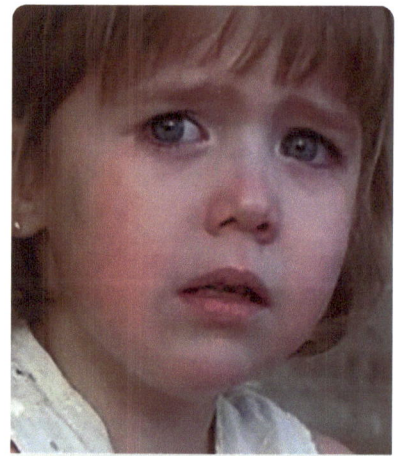

A very distraught Eppie is silent and refuses to talk or perhaps she can't. Her entire world has crashed. (iStockphoto, Posed by model.)

fifteen and eighteen, both boys. It is a well organised rather commercial foster care centre. Occasionally, a troublesome child is housed in an on-site 'donga' if they need isolation.[198] The foster carer husband and wife are experienced at handling kids removed into 'care'. They have received awards for their devotion to children deemed 'unable to live at home'.

The foster carers and their two sons live in their separate a larger older house on the property. For her first night, Eppie is placed in a room in the separate girls' house, with two other girls aged 10 and 11. They are expected to talk to her and try to comfort and reassure

---

197 You may listen to it at: https://www.youtube.com/watch?v=SRmCEGHt-Qk Very sad and yet triumphant.
198 Terzon, E. "Origin of the word donga a bit of a mystery". *ABC News*, Darwin. 23 September 2016. https://www.abc.net.au/news/2016-09-23/origin-of-word-donga-ongoing-mystery-to-linguists/7871488 Often used at building sites and caravan parks. Sometimes known as a 'portakabin' in Britain. (For photos see, the end of this chapter.)

her. She sits on a bed moved temporarily into the room for her. She refuses to talk to anyone. Out of concern for her, these other girls try to talk to her but she is extremely upset, in fact devastated. She just looks at them without saying anything when they talk to her. Her pain is written all over her face.

In the evening, while trying to talk to Eppie, the girls told her: "The foster Mum's got a wooden spoon. An' she uses it on little kids like you.[199] Hurts like buggery. So, make sure ya always do like she tells ya. Never answer her back."

At dinner time in the main older house Eppie eats some food. After dinner, she is given some clothes to wear: long pants, underwear, some socks, a nightie, and her school shoes. The rest of her school uniform is to be washed and dried.

She has a restless night. She cries herself to sleep. The other girls hear her but can't console her. They even complain among themselves about her continual sniffing. Next morning, they told the foster carer about this.

Before dawn, she wakes up and her mind begins working full bore. She makes up her mind to fight what is happening to her. Like so many distressed children, Eppie is facing the terrible upheaval of foster care. But, she is stubborn and doesn't give in. She resists. Metaphorically, she is not alone even though at the moment she is physically. She knows Keith will fight for her.

After breakfast on Tuesday, she is driven into Toowoomba to the Police Station in the centre of town. There is a special supposedly child friendly interview room with comfy chairs, Disney pictures on the walls, and some cuddly toys. There is also a TV set and a DVD player. The room is monitored through one-way glass by a video camera. It's a room where children

---

[199] "William's foster dad lied to crime commission", *In Queensland*, Brisbane, 07 November 2023. https://inqld.com.au/news/2023/11/07/missing-williams-foster-dad-lied-to-crime-commission-hearing-told/ The foster father lied to the NSW Crime Commission to protect his wife from allegations she used to kick and also hit foster children with a wooden spoon. Yet, secret Police surveillance showed she had done so. Violence against foster children by foster carers is not uncommon. (Similar non physical punishments meted out to children in foster care also happen like forcing children to eat dry Weet-Bix cereal for breakfast and lunch and being made to sit outside in the cold weather (revealed to the author by a child in foster care.)

are encouraged in an ICARE[200] interview to disclose about sexual abuse sometimes with the use of anatomically explicit toys.

An actual 'ICARE' interview room at the Toowoomba Police Station. Note the one-way glass and the video camera just visible behind it. During a supposed child-friendly interview, the light in the adjoining room behind the glass is turned off and the camera can't be seen.

Here, Eppie is given a fairly standard 'ICARE' interview by a specially trained woman who is a Police Child Protection Unit officer. She is not in uniform. Still traumatised, she is extremely stubborn and uncooperative. The woman puts on a friendly facade but Eppie sees straight through it. After trying to sweet talk Eppie, she asks straight out: "This man Keith, is he your father?"

Eppie's slightly defiant immediate response is: "He's my Mumma!"

Although she has read a very limited Departmental background briefing about Keith and Eppie, the woman pretends to be a little confused: "I don't understand. He's a man."

Eppie: "Yes. But, he's still my Mumma and he has been ever since I was a teensy-weensie new-born baby. He loves me and I love him."

Side-stepping the issue by trying to compliment Eppie saying how pretty she is and what a nice outfit she is wearing, Eppie responds: "I don't like it."

She then questions Eppie more about Keith: "Is he your father?"

"He's my Mumma."

Then, with Eppie's silence, the woman changes tack and, straight to the point, asks: "Dearie, does Keith ever touch your privates?"

Eppie: "Do you mean my vulva? That's the proper word for it."

The woman: "Yes, er … you're right."

---

[200] ICARE is the standard "**I**nterviewing **C**hildren **A**nd **R**ecording **E**vidence" set of procedures used in Queensland by the Police Child Protection and Investigation Unit. Specialist Police are trained in these interview procedures to be sensitively supportive of child victims but at the same time avoiding suggestion or leading questions which could result in evidence being thrown out of Court.

Eppie: "So, do you mean does he fiddle with my vulva?"

The woman: "Yes, dearie. Does he touch you down there?"

Eppie: "When I was a baby he used to change my nappy and and wash me. When I started Play Group he had to pick a threadworm out of my vulva with a toothpick. Then, we both had to take Combantrin tablets. Listen, he's never fiddled with me in a sexy way! I know the difference!"

Stunned, the woman persists: "Does he do things that you don't like with your … er … vulva? Does he hurt you at your vulva?"

Eppie: "I told you, he doesn't molest me? He doesn't use me for sex. You're only interviewing me like this because you want pin things on him so you can keep me in foster care and send him to jail. You're a witch! And, I've had enough of this discussion. It's over."

She clams up and says nothing more. Eppie is now stubbornly silent.

(*iStockphoto*, Posed by model.)

Astounded at this little girl's knowledge, stubbornness, and imperious attitude and accent, the woman tries to engage with her some more. But, Eppie just stares straight at her, refusing to respond. After continued silence from Eppie, the ICARE interview is aborted and Eppie is taken back to the foster care house by two Child Safety Officers.

After Eppie had been returned to the foster care house, she was taken to a doctor for a medical examination. This is routine for children recently removed into 'care'.

The doctor was been briefed by Department of Child Safety officers about Eppie's situation, of course, from their perspective. At first, she was pleasant and calm with Eppie. Smiling: "You're here for a standard check-up. We're going to see how healthy you are."

Eppie says nothing. The doctor asks Eppie to take off her shirt and trousers. She does so begrudgingly with the doctor's help. After weighing and measuring her and checking her temperature, the doctor asks her to take her underpants down and sit on an examination bed.

Eppie refuses. "You're not going to check my vulva and look inside my vagina!"

Taken aback by this little girl's forthright refusal: "This is just a routine check-up."

Eppie: "I've already been given a check-up by another doctor. The doctor looked in my vagina. I've not been sexually abused. There's a hymen there. And, it's septate. Now, you're not going to look inside me! That's private!"

She immediately sits on a chair with her knees bent and refusing to remove her *broekies*.

The doctor is a regular GP or general practitioner, neither a Child Safety Officer nor a paediatrician. She is not trained or experienced enough to deal with an upset foster child. She has been hired and briefed over the phone by the Department for an urgent appraisal of Eppie. However, she soon becomes frustrated with this child. Foolishly, she again tells Eppie bluntly to take her underpants down. But, she steadfastly refuses.

Not understanding what Eppie is on about, the doctor quickly gives up on this difficult child. She phones for Eppie to be collected. An upset and crying Eppie is taken back to the foster care house by two CSOs. She is feeling very, very alone.

The doctor emails her brief report to the Department:

> This is an excessively mature child especially on sexual matters with a knowledge well beyond that expected of a child of her age. This may warrant further forensic psychological investigation regarding her relationship with the man who I understand she has been living with alone. There could be more of a sinister nature to uncover.[201] If a foster carer gains her trust and confidence, she may disclose. This might give the Department to opportunity to have him charged. She is rather agitated and obstinate. So, I also suspect autism which may have been exploited by the male person she has been living with and may have resulted in the inappropriate sexual abuse relationship she probably has had with him.[202] I suspect her loyalty to him is part of an accommodation

---

[201] Typically, the aim here was forensic: a fishing expedition to nail the parent for sexual abuse of the child. It was not primarily focussed on the best interests and welfare of the child which is the paramount requirement of the *Child Protection Act* (section 5A). Rather, it was focussed on nailing a man they believe has been sexually abusing the child. The child's interests were secondary.

[202] This type of unprofessional diagnosis of autism is too readily accepted by the Department of Child Safety as validation for controlling an upset or difficult child. It is rare for a GP to have the training in psychiatry to be able to competently diagnose autism. Like so many children removed into 'care', Eppie is simply upset at her removal from her parent, an entirely natural reaction but used as an excuse for sedation. Diagnosis of autism is controversial because it is regarded as a 'spectrum' disorder with many seemingly diverse facets. Thus, it is too readily diagnosed by some not really qualified to make a diagnosis. "Autism Spectrum". *Wikipedia.* https://en.wikipedia.org/wiki/Autism_spectrum

syndrome.[203] I recommend that to ascertain proof of sexual abuse she should be medically examined under sedation.

She is a difficult child with a mind of her own. Keeping her in an isolated situation until the medication I have prescribed has a calming effect would seem to be the way to go for a few days. To calm her and render her more compliant with the foster care situation, I have attached a prescription for 100mg *Chlorpromazine* anti-psychotic tablets. She should be given one tablet each day about an hour before dinner. The tablets are less effective on a full stomach.[204]

The prescribed medication is delivered by car to the foster carer in the afternoon.

As an experienced foster carer, she takes note of the doctor's analysis of Eppie as a 'difficult child' and doesn't want to have to deal with sulkiness, tantrums, or violence. So, she hopes this medication will render the child more compliant and easier to manage. Until then, she is keen to have Eppie isolated and well-dosed up. So, Eppie is placed in the 'donga' at the back of the main house. The foster carer is aware that it is current practice for the Queensland Police [205] as well as child protection departments across the country to isolate children who have a history of serious control problems. Isolation is seen as an opportunity to provide 'therapy' and remove the child from danger to others as well as themselves. However, this is only done in quite extreme cases like the much abused and very angry foetal

---

[203] Summit, R.C., "Child sexual abuse accommodation syndrome", *Child Abuse and Neglect*, Vol. 7, 177-193, 1983. https://web.archive.org/web/20140222221321/http://www.abusewatch.net/Child%20Sexual%20Abuse%20Accommodation%20Syndrome.pdf

Summit describes how he believes sexually abused children respond to ongoing sexual abuse. Children "learn to accept the situation and to survive. There is no way out, no place to run. The healthy, normal emotionally resilient child will learn to accommodate to the reality of continuing sexual abuse."

This theoretical 'syndrome' is often used to explain a child's loyalty to a parent. It assumes sexual abuse and is sometimes used to attach sexual abuse to a parent when the child's loyalty seems to be hampering investigation. It does not take into account genuine reasons for a child's loyalty to her/his parent like simple love, bonding, and attachment. As we shall see in the next chapter, some in the Department believe that loyal Eppie ran away so that she could protect her abusing parent by demonstrating loyalty and even continue to be sexually abused by him. Accommodation Syndrome is dated but is still a common belief among staff in the Department.

[204] See "Chlorpromazine", *Wikipedia*. https://en.wikipedia.org/wiki/Chlorpromazine It is made clear on the packet that the tablets should be taken regularly only once a day well before a meal.

[205] See this example of Queensland Police isolating a 13-year-old girl they regard as 'difficult' to manage. With force, she is locked in a cold windowless cell with nothing in it but bare walls. When her arm is caught in the door, she is taken to hospital in handcuffs and leg chains. "Screaming, freezing, struggling to breathe", *The Guardian*, Brisbane, 18 July 2024 https://www.theguardian.com/australia-news/article/2024/jul/17/queensland-youth-crime-watch-house-footage-police-treatment-ntwnfb?

alcohol spectrum 10-year-old girl at Aurukun in North Queensland back in 2007.[206] Eppie's case is nothing remotely like the Aurukun girl's situation. The foster carer is just super cautious. With the doctor's comment about her being 'difficult' and using the word 'isolated', she is worried that Eppie might become a 'problem handful' child like the Aurukun girl. The last thing her foster caring business needs is a 'truculent unruly' child who she now believes to be highly sexualised and autistic, a scenario which could get worse.[207]

The foster carer's practice depends upon several important factors for its continued operation. One of those factors is the children in her custody accepting the foster care arrangement.

The prescribed medication, *Chlorpromazine,* is the type of medication which Fiona once warned Eppie about: "when some kids were very upset at being taken away from their parents, you know, crying and even screaming, the foster carer would give them a tablet to quieten them. It made them all dopey and dreamy."[208]

---

[206] Margan, D., "Department's 'flawed culture' led to Aurukun rape." *ABC News*, Brisbane, 20 December 2007. https://www.abc.net.au/news/2007-12-20/departments-flawed-culture-led-to-aurukun-rape/2600226 Worth reading. About Child Safety Officers: "They struck me as people with no morals, no ethics and they are only there for careers and not for a concern about the people who they are taxpayer-funded to serve." The girl was first raped at age of four and by six she had already contracted gonorrhoea from multiple sexual assaults.

[207] For excellent short background: "Aurukun rape victim in hiding." *Courier Mail*, Brisbane, 11 January 2008. https://www.couriermail.com.au/news/queensland/aurukun-rape-victim-in-hiding/news-story/0dfe7504bb8f 9a60723f326e6410ffa5 With what we see happens to Eppie in Chapter 13, she could end up rather like this little Aurukun girl: a "highly sexualised girl" continually touting for sex – the only way she can get attention – and repeatedly sexually abused by males of all ages. This is what the foster carer fears. Although, Eppie is a very intelligent and stubborn little girl she is only six and could succumb to what she is coerced into doing.

[208] Prescription of this medication for a child like Eppie is very inappropriate but common. It is often described as "Off-label" because of its use outside its intended purpose which is to treat schizophrenia and other psychoses like paranoia, mania, anxiety, agitation, and dangerously impulsive behaviour. "Doctors are treating foster children's behavioral problems with the same powerful drugs given to people with schizophrenia and severe bipolar disorder. We simply don't have evidence to support this kind of use, especially in young children." Gavett, G., "The Medicated Foster Child", *Frontline*, Public Broadcasting System, Arlington, Virginia, USA. https://www.pbs.org/wgbh/frontline/article/the-medicated-foster-child/

Flahive, P., "Federal judge finds Texas use of psychotropic drugs on foster children 'appalling'." *Texas Public Radio*, San Antonio, USA. 12 April 2023. https://www.tpr.org/government-politics/2023-04-12/federal-judge-finds-texas-use-of-psychotropic-drugs-on-foster-children-appalling On the use of psychotropic drugs in the Texas foster care system, the Judge told the Family and Protective Services Commissioner: "These children are being repeatedly raped in your care. They're being drugged in your care if they complain."

Berry, P. "Infants drugged to their eyeballs: inquiry", *Brisbane Times*, 20 August 2012. https://www.brisbanetimes.com.au/national/queensland/infants-drugged-to-their-eyeballs-inquiry-20120820-24hug.html Foster children as young as 12 months are being "drugged to their eyeballs" in Queensland to control their behaviour, an inquiry has been told.

Eppie "Before dinner, the foster care witch gave me a glass of water: 'Swallow this pill. It'll make you feel better.'. She made me swallow it. Then, every evening after that before dinner she sent her son, Jason, to give me a pill. When he gave it to me he always thought I swallowed it. But, I always pushed it with my tongue to the side of my cheek and pretended to swallow."

(*Above*) Eppie has been placed 'in care' along the Eton Vale - Cambooya Connection Road about a kilometre from the New England Highway. The larger house in the foreground is where the foster carers and their two teenage sons live and where the kids in foster care come for meals. The smaller white-roofed houses to the right are where foster children aged six to fifteen are housed: three boys on the right and four girls on the left. Eppie spent her first night in the girls' house. These two smaller houses have security screens on the windows apparently to protect the children from intruders (but probably also to prevent escape). The main family house does not have security screens. After the medical examination and until she is calmed with medication and is accepting of foster care, she is placed in a 'donga' next to trees just visible behind the main house.

Until the medication begins to take effect in several days, the experienced foster carer is isolating Eppie by locking her in the on-site 'donga' until she becomes compliant. Isolation in this case would theoretically not have the approval of the Department but from past experience with problem children, she wants this difficult child rendered manageable before she gets out of hand. From the doctor's report and now worried about this child, she feels isolation until the medication makes her docile in about a week or so is the way to go. She feels she can't be criticised because she is following the doctor's medical advice. [209]

This is the one bedroom 'donga' in which Eppie was locked. It has windows, a bed, shower and toilet as well as air-conditioning. Like the two smaller houses on the site, the windows have security screens. But, locked from the outside, it cannot be unlocked from the inside.

[209] Branley, A. & Scott, S. "Anti-psychotic medication overprescribed to Australian children, experts say." *ABC News*, Sydney, 16 November 2014. https://www.abc.net.au/news/2014-11-16/anti-psychotics-over-prescribed-australian-children-experts-say/5892822 Scroll down to where this article discusses "'Chemical restraint' in foster care" and "Children in foster care are being inappropriately overmedicated".

CHAPTER 13

Three Day
Assessment Hearing

The Department is accustomed to Children's Court hearings going their way and undoubtedly expects this case will, too. They have seemingly unlimited power in terms of funds and even legal expertise. The cards are stacked in their favour. Most child protection cases involve low income parents who don't fully understand what is going on or who are angry and hostile towards the system but unable to afford good legal representation. If they get a Legal Aid solicitor, and often they can't, that lawyer is either inexperienced or overloaded. So, the Department's officers are confident this 3-Day Assessment hearing will be a quick open and shut case.

Paula Wellings told him "the Children's Court three-day assessment hearing will be on Friday at the Magistrates Court in Canning Town from 10:30 after Eppie has been 'in care' for four nights. The Magistrate scheduled for the case is the same one who only in March granted you custody of Eppie for three years. It gives us a fighting chance."

She continues: "I can also tell you that Eppie was placed in foster care with a family at a small semi-rural property fifteen kilometres south of Toowoomba. However, I am aware that at that particular foster care home there has been an allegation of sexual abuse. The Department did nothing. For legal reasons, I cannot go into detail but I am concerned to get Eppie out of there as soon as possible. If you do some research and find the place, please don't go there or try to see her. It could lead to a Police arrest."

Keith: "Okay, I won't. I want Eppie returned as soon as possible."

While checking the Department's papers before the hearing, Paula Wellings emails Keith a copy of an affidavit written by the foster care 'mother'. In it she says two things. "We keep a close eye on her and give her all the caring attention she craves. And, I can say she loves it. The other children are very supportive of her. She has quickly settled into our household."

Paula: "That's bullshit. Typical foster carer's spin. So, just ignore it. Magistrates are used to that and see through it. Now, this is other thing she claims. She reads a passage from the affidavit.

> During the child's first night here after she was taken into care, the other two girls in the large shared bedroom were kept awake by her masturbating as she grunted and groaned. They tried to stop her by telling her to be quiet as they wanted to sleep. I believe masturbating is something the man she was living with has taught her. The two other girls complained to me about it next morning.

Keith: "I am shocked by that. I've seen my other daughters masturbating, not just fiddling with their vulva when they were a bit older, more towards puberty, not as young as Eppie. To this day they don't know I saw them. Eppie has sometimes had her fingers at her vulva. That's never troubled me. I've always known little girls, and boys, are sexual beings but with their overt sexuality just emerging. It's normal even for babies. Once when I was tickling her when she was about four, she pulled her pants down. She had a smiling naughty look on her face. She said; 'Look at my vulva.' I said: 'Why?' She replied 'I'd like you to.' I smiled back and told her in a supportive loving way that her vulva is private and I don't need to look at her. I even said: 'If you're feeling sexy, that's fine but you shouldn't involve me because I'm a grown up man. And, we've talked about how sex with an adult would really damage a little kid like you. Remember those girls in South Africa. She accepted that. I kissed her and she pulled up her pants. That's the nearest we've ever come to interacting sexually. I know she accepts what I said. And, of course she knows about sex with an adult mainly because we talked about it a lot afterwards especially how it would seriously damage her and the man would likely kill her afterwards. We've discussed examples we've seen on the internet like Cherish Perrywinkle in America and Kylie Maybury in Melbourne and others."[210]

Paula: "Yes, I understand. In cases where an issue of child sex abuse has been raised or even suspected, the Department will go to great lengths to highlight or even fabricate evidence. What they've said about Eppie masturbating is a tactic used many times in the Childrens Court and particularly in the Family Court where a mother is battling for custody. Family Court judges then have to refer the child to specialist counsellors for investigation. Allegations of sexual abuse are notoriously hard to counter. Like an aggrieved mother, the Department gets involved in similar tactics and for similar reasons. That's why they have concocted the story about her masturbating and keeping other girls awake. They want possession of a child and sexual abuse allegations are a classic weapon which is very hard to counter."

Keith: "I can't imagine Eppie masturbating during her first night in foster care. Feeling sexy would just not be on. More likely, her emotions would be a mix of anger and fear. And, I can imagine her crying and sniffing all night."[211]

Paula: "Agreed. Well, I think for the moment, because it is such a fraught area, in Court I will not initiate the issue. If they look like losing, they might well bring up the issue. But, if they do so, I'll really get into them. I have had experience with this sort of thing and I know this particular Magistrate has, too."

On the Thursday evening before the Court hearing, Keith had another call from his lawyer.

Paula Wellings: "I can tell you that this evening Eppie absconded. She wasn't missed until around 6.30 p.m. The Police are on the look out for her but they haven't found her yet. Only a few minutes ago they decided an Amber Alert should be issued. They were reluctant

---

[210] These are two cases which were in the news and which Keith and Eppie discussed several times. "Murder of Cherish Perrywinkle", *Wikipedia*, https://en.wikipedia.org/wiki/Murder_of_Cherish_Perrywinkle and "Murder of Kylie Maybury", *Wikipedia*, https://en.wikipedia.org/wiki/Murder_of_Kylie_Maybury

[211] Weeks later, Keith discusses Eppie's first night in foster care with her. He mentions the affidavit about masturbation. Her response is one of anger. She is adamant that she was "shit scared and just not feeling sexy. That would have been the very last thing on my mind." He tells her Paula Wellings explained that it was a typical tactic used by the Department of Child Safety to muddy the waters. She said it was perjury but very hard to contest. Eppie's response: "I always reckoned they're witches." (He had to explain 'perjury' to Eppie.)

at first because of privacy provisions in the *Child Protection Act*.[212] However, the Amber Alert won't reveal that she is in the 'care' of the Department. Now, they have requested that I ask you if you could supply a suitable recent photo of Eppie which will be used in an Amber Alert. So, please email me a photo."

He immediately emails Paula one of his favourite photos.

Just before 9.00 p.m. the Amber Alert is issued on local radio, television and Facebook. Keith sees it.

MISSING: 6-year-old girl Eppie.
Police have grave fears for her safety.
She may be in the company of an elderly male person who is known to her.
Small stature 102cm, slim build, light brown hair.
Wearing floral dress and thongs.
Last seen at 6:30 p.m. at Etonvale 15km south of Toowoomba.
If she has been seen since then, phone '000' urgently.

(*iStockphoto*. Posed by model.)

Next morning, the Friday of the Court hearing, Keith has another phone call from Paula Wellings. She updates him on what has happened: "Getting on towards midnight she was taken into custody by a routine Police patrol at Graniteville. Somebody saw a little girl out late at night alone in the town in the rain. They flagged down a passing Police car. She ran but the Police caught her. It was only when she was brought to the Graniteville Police Station that local Police suspected she might be the missing foster care child from Toowoomba. She was photographed and the Police Child Protection Unit in Toowoomba was emailed. They

---

[212] The Queensland *Child Protection Act* at section 189 prohibits publication of information leading to identification of children in the care of the Department. This aspect of the law has presented problems for Police when searching for a missing child if the child was subject to protection orders. They could not immediately seek public help with an Amber Alert published in the press or media. This caused public outcry: Remeikis, A., "Tiahleigh Palmer: Death sparks sweeping changes to missing children response". *Brisbane Times*, 11 July 2016. https://www.brisbanetimes.com.au/national/queensland/tiahleigh-palmer-death-sparks-sweeping-changes-to-missing-children-response-20160711-gq35am.html As a result, Police have been given the authority to decide whether an Amber Alert or media release needs to be issued if they have concern for the child's safety.

confirmed that she was the missing child. I've been told she has not been harmed. The Police took her all the way back to the foster carer's house. Have you seen the Amber Alert?"

Keith: "Yes, I have. I found it offensive. It implies that I am likely to harm her."

Paula: "They've taken it down."

Keith: "Good. But, how on earth did she get to be found far away at Graniteville?"

Paula Wellings: "I asked about that. They don't know and the Police are baffled. She will not talk. You are a suspect or 'a person of interest', as they say, but you didn't know where she had been placed in foster care. She had no phone and no way of contacting you. Nevertheless, officers from the Police Child Protection Unit will visit you this morning and they'll want to see your phone. You see, she may have made it to a public phone booth and phoned you from there. Remember, calls from Telstra public phone booths are free now. Does she know about this?"

Keith: "Yes, she does. And, she knows my number. But, she hasn't phoned me."

Paula: "Okay. Don't delete anything on your phone. Tell them your password and let them go through it. Make sure you co-operate with them."

Keith: "Okay, I will. But, was she really found at Graniteville?"

Paula Wellings: "Yes, incredible. It's about 150 kilometres from Toowoomba."

Keith: "She must have been heading home. You see, she knows she is not allowed to hitch-hike under any circumstances. I know she wouldn't try it because she knows about other little girls who accepted a lift and were raped and murdered. We've done internet searches about it. She'd be too scared to do it now."

Two female Child Protection Unit officers in 'power suits' arrived at Keith's house in an unmarked car at 8:30. They drove straight up to the house because he had opened the gate. He invited them onto the front verandah. With bland inscrutable expressions, they flashed their ID badges. They said nothing about Eppie's escape and her having been found. After entering his password they went straight into his phone and found no evidence of any contact he might have had with Eppie. They also checked his deleted messages. There was no deleted recent contact with Eppie. They warned him he would face criminal charges if he tried to contact Eppie.

He texted Paula Wellings and told her the Police had come and gone. He had co-operated with them and they found nothing incriminating on his phone.

She reminds him not to be late for the Court hearing.

She adds: "And incidentally, the foster care mother will be in attendance in Court. The Department has advised that they may need her to give evidence. So, whether she will be called upon to give evidence is not clear to me. It's not usual at a three-day hearing but I suspect they may want her there if they try to have a 28-day Assessment Order extended into a Long Term Order. They would want that if they assume Eppie has no parent and you have abducted her. They will allege that you have been sexually abusing her. A common ploy in Family Court custody battles."

Keith: "Gosh."

A pre-hearing conference between Keith and the Department starts on schedule at 10:30 a.m. on Friday. There is Keith and his solicitor, Paula Wellings, and two Child Safety Officers or CSOs and the Court Registrar. Keith and Paula Wellings are already seated when the two Departmental officers arrive. The air in that room is suddenly filled with

The two CSOs. Karen Wells in the dark suit is the Senior CSO.
(*Left: iStockphoto*. Posed by model. *Above: Inmagine*. Posed by model.)

disdain and hostility so thick it could be cut with a knife. Keith has never met them before but Paula Wellings has. She scribbles on a notepad for Keith: 'Karen Wells, in the dark jacket is the Senior CSO. She'll be aggressive.'

After the Registrar's introductions, Senior CSO, Karen Wells, leads the discussion with a confrontational statement: "So, Mr Todd you've had a six-year-old child living isolated and alone with you! Given your age and single status, the Department has been compelled to remove her. You also have a criminal record for sexually abusing 14-year-old girl. It was a full penis rape. So, this child, Eppie, is in need of protection. Our mandate under the *Child Protection Act* is to afford protection for vulnerable children. We make no apologies for protecting a child from an elderly single man with a record like your's. By all accounts, you've kept a child prisoner on your bush property."[213]

Paula Wellings steps in: "Ms Wells, I believe you are seriously misinformed about my client's background. The child has spent all her life living alone with him healthy and happy in a safe and protected environment. And, she attended Playgroup. She is devoted to him in a loving relationship. That's correct, isn't it Keith?" Her cue for Keith to speak.

Keith: "Since her birth, Eppie has lived a very happy and fulfilling life on my secluded property in the granite hills near Kinross. I have … "

The Senior CSO Wells butts in: "I don't believe you. You allege that you have kept her isolated all these years! Listen to me: she is not your wife![214] She is a small child, not a mate for an old man! Thankfully, she is now in a safe place.[215] But, to date her behaviour is quite

---

[213] This belligerent attitude by Child Safety Officers is not unusual. Levy, A. and Lavelle, L., "Complaint filed against child protection department, with class actions to follow across Australia." *ABC News*, Brisbane, 31 January 2024. https://www.abc.net.au/news/2024-01-31/class-action-lawsuit-racial-discrimination-stolen-generation/103291808?
 The author's eldest daughter took her own life as a result of the bombastic blaming attitude of the Department after her daughter had been removed and placed into foster care.

[214] This was once a comment made by a Senior CSO to a single parent father during a scheduled 'family meeting' in a Department of Child Safety office.

[215] This often used term "in a safe place" is a classic bureaucratic euphemism for foster care. Yet, foster care is inherently NOT safe for children removed into "care" (another common euphemism). "Child Protection Australia 2020-2021". *Australian Institute of Health and Welfare*, Canberra, Child Welfare Series No 76, 19 September 2023. https://www.aihw.gov.au/reports/child-protection/child-protection-australia-2021-22/contents/safety-of-children-in-care/how-many-children-were-abused-in-care This section of the Report is based on "best estimates". **How many children were abused in care? Answer: about 1,200, about 52% of girls abused, and about 19% of girls sexually abused.**
 While in foster care Eppie was NOT "in a safe place". Her safety was seriously compromised by the foster carer's 18-year-old son in the same way that 12-year-old Tiahleigh Palmer was raped by the foster carer's 19-year-old son. Note: Tiahleigh was then murdered by her foster father. https://en.wikipedia.org/wiki/Murder_of_Tiahleigh_Palmer
 McNamara, N., "Religious leader jailed", *Toowoomba Chronicle*, 04 November 2023, page 3. https://ground.news/article/former-toowoomba-religious-figure-found-guilty-of-raping-foster-child (Paywall) A former Toowoomba religious figure was found guilty of raping and maintaining a sexual relationship with his 11-year-old foster daughter. He was jailed for eight years. This item reveals that the girl was regularly raped by her foster carer in her bedroom during two years. (Often full penis penetration.) Isolated from family support, the girl was an easy target for him. No mention is made of the fact that she was removed from her family by the Department of Child Safety and placed into a likely more dangerous situation. Typically, the press do not take the Department to task over its vicarious liability in that it failed to protect the child. The Department is untouchable. Note: she was only able to go to the Police after she turned eighteen and was therefore no longer a ward of the state.

challenging for carers. Interviews with her revealed that she is a child who has likely been exploited sexually. We believe she absconded last night to be back in the abuse you have trained her for."

Keith is stunned and deeply offended. He responds quietly: "Since I found newborn baby Eppie abandoned in the bush at Bolivia Hill, I have lovingly cared for her and nurtured her as a daughter, certainly not as a mate or a sex object."

CSO Wells: "So, groomed by you since her birth! She has been stubborn and difficult for her foster carer, professing loyalty to you, a classic case of 'accommodation syndrome'."

Keith: "I know what that means. Have you met Eppie?"

"I have not but based on the expert opinions of Police child protection officers and the experienced medical practitioner, it is clear that she is in need of protection. With her advanced knowledge of sexual matters and on the basis of the medical practitioner's report, we believe she has been coached by you to conceal and deny sexual abuse."[216]

He turns to Paula Wellings: "I'm not going to stand for this. I'm walking out."

Expecting Paula to urge him to stay, instead she whispers to him: "I agree."

Both of them walk out. She takes him to a café in the nearby shopping mall so that he can calm down. She tells him: "I believe she is motivated by misandry. Between you and me, it's believed among some of us in this industry that as a child she had an abusive father. Don't ever repeat this. You didn't hear it from me."

Keith: "Wow! That's sad."

Paula: "That kind of prejudice and aggression is rife in the Department. It's okay for Julia Gillard to get up in Parliament and accuse Tony Abbott of misogyny but she was riding a popular wave of female rejection of male power which I believe still exists.[217] Yet, there is no current outcry against misandry and many women would deny that it exists. Some would say misandry is a figment of a misogynist's imagination. That is predominant thinking in

---

216 In a legal sense, 'coached' means give (someone) instructions as to what to do or say in a particular situation. For example, 'he had improperly coached a witness to testify more credibly'. (*Oxford English Dictionary*.)

217 "Misogyny Speech", *Wikipedia*. https://en.wikipedia.org/wiki/Misogyny_Speech

parts of the Department. After protests, there has been a recent statement by the Department on anti-father bias. But, it's a feel good token gesture."[218]

Keith: "Well, I suppose that Wells woman has never been able to move on."

Paula: "Possibly. But, when it comes to child sexual abuse, much depends on how parents react, you know, how they support the child afterwards."

Keith: "Like that American girl Elizabeth Smart."[219]

Paula: "Exactly. She's a shining example of recovery with family support."

He is quietly pleased to hear this last remark.

Paula continues: "With her experience in the child protection business and given the usual power differential between Departmental officers and hapless parents, she expects to have a total advantage. I don't believe she or anyone in the Department has read the *Social Assessment Report* from March's court case. We'll leave it to the Magistrate to set the record straight after lunch. She did read it. Karen Wells doesn't seem to know the full story. I'm sorry to say this to you but that outburst from her was typical of comments I've heard from her in private group discussions within the Department. So, when I walked out with you, something I wouldn't normally do, I feel that when we go into the Court she is going to fall flat on her face."

Nearly two hours later and after lunch, he is composed as they enter the Court room for the hearing. Technically, it is a three-day temporary assessment hearing which would normally extend the foster care for 28 days.

When Magistrate (referred to nowdays as a Judge) Heather Austin enters the Court room, all stand up and bow. It is clear from her scowl that she is not in a happy mood. The Registrar must have briefed her.

The Magistrate addresses the Court: "This hearing will consider an application from the Department of Child Safety in respect of a six-year-old child Eppie for a two-year

---

[218] "Gender bias in Child Protection: Working with Fathers", *Child Safety Practice Manual,* 07 January 2021. https://cspm.csyw.qld.gov.au/practice-kits/care-arrangements/working-across-difference-in-care-arrangements-1/seeing-and-understanding/gender-bias-in-child-protection A token gesture full of platitudes about valuing fathers.

[219] Smart, E., *My Story* (2013), Sydney: PanMacmillan. At the age of 14 she was abducted, held captive for nine months, and endured daily rapes before finally being rescued. https://en.wikipedia.org/wiki/Elizabeth_Smart

custody order in favour of the Department's CEO." She turns to Senior Child Safety Officer, Karen Wells: "Ms Wells, would you please present the Department's case for applying for the usual 28-day Court Assessment Order to be extended for a two-years."

Karen Wells stands up: "Your Honour, Mr Todd has had the six-year-old child, Eppie, living alone with him. Given his age and single status, the Department has been compelled to remove her. Mr Todd was convicted for raping of a fourteen-year-old girl. So, the Department is of the view that this child, Eppie, is in need of protection. Our mandate under the *Child Protection Act* is to afford protection for vulnerable children. We make no apologies for protecting children. In this case we are protecting a child from an elderly single man with a criminal background of serious child sex abuse and keeping her in the bush isolated from the community. Unfortunately, the child has to date been unwilling to co-operate with our counsellors. In particular, the medical practitioner reported an advanced knowledge of matters sexual, knowledge unacceptable in a child of her apparent age. She has recommended a forensic psychological examination of the relationship between the child and Mr Todd. I will quote from her report which the Court has:

> An excessively mature child especially on sexual matters with a knowledge well beyond that expected of a child of her age. This may warrant further forensic psychological investigation regarding her relationship with her father who I understand she has been living with alone with. There could be more of a sinister nature to uncover. If a foster carer gains her trust and confidence, she may disclose.

We hope to have her co-operation in the near future as she builds up trust with the foster carer who, I might say, has over twenty years experience as a foster carer especially of victims of sexual abuse. Unfortunately, we have yet to ascertain her true identity. When we establish her identity, we will seek parental permission for a DNA test. If that is not possible, we will apply for a court order. Regardless of the outcome, the Department is steadfastly opposed to her having any further connection with Mr Todd. It is unacceptable that a child of her age should be residing alone with a male person of Mr Todd's age and with a criminal background of serious sexual offending against a child. She is now in a safe place protected from a predatory paedophile."

The Magistrate asks Paula Wellings for a comment.

She responds: "No comment, Your Honour."

She does not try to counter what Karen Wells has said. She leaves this to the Judge who knows the full story of Eppie.

Karen Wells stands up again: "Your Honour, when we arrived at the child's school to take her to a place of safety, she immediately started calling for her mother. If I recall rightly, she was distressed and shouted: 'I want my Mumma! Please get my Mumma! … Mumma, please save me!' Your Honour, we suspect there has been an abduction involving this child. The aim of the Department's intervention in this case is to stabilise this child so that we would hopefully return her to her mother."

Paula Wellings stands and responds briefly: "Your Honour, I believe my colleague does not know who the person the child calls out 'Mumma' to is. That is the name she chose as a toddler for my client Keith Todd because he has been her only mother figure all her life since her birth."

Magistrate Heather Austin: "Thank you. I am aware of that from March's *Social Assessment Report*. Now, Ms Wells, are you aware that this Court dealt with the custody and guardianship of this child in March?"

Karen Wells: "I'm not aware of that, your Honour."

Magistrate: "You should have been aware of that case before the Department's officers stepped in and peremptorily removed this child from her custodial parent and guardian. In March, after considering affidavits, a thorough medical report, a Police report, a lengthy detailed *Social Assessment Report*, and even a short response from the Department itself, this Court determined that it was in the child's best interests that Keith Todd be recognised as Eppie Todd's custodial parent and guardian. Those Orders were made in terms of Section 5A of the *Child Protection Act*. Didn't anyone in the Department think to ask Police under section 142C of that *Act* for information about Mr Todd? The Police check would have told you that Keith Todd has no criminal history."

Karen Wells: "Your Honour. We did ask the Police. The Police check was negative. They advised that he has no criminal history record as such. But, press reports at the time of Mr

Todd's conviction indicate that he was given a nine year sentence for raping a 14-year-old girl. Your Honour, the Judge in that case said:

> Our society will not tolerate the type of attack which you inflicted upon one of its most vulnerable citizens particularly with the aggravation involved. Therefore, you are to receive a long sentence not only as a means of ensuring your correction but also to protect other children from you.

With that in mind, the Department's removal of child Eppie to a place of safety is in accordance with that Supreme Court Judge's summing up. Your Honour, we did ask but the Police check was negative. However, we received a notification from a very reliable source. That source is an experienced former Child Safety Officer who has had suspicions about the relationship between Mr Todd and the child Eppie. From that we determined that something was amiss with the Police report. With the former CSO's notification, we could not accept the Police report at face value. Our mandate is to protect vulnerable children. So, we had to investigate. I repeat, our reliable source is an experienced former Child Safety Officer who I am not legally permitted to name. So, we took it seriously. That's when we discovered press reports which showed that Mr Todd had been convicted of raping a 14-year-old girl. Moreover, the child Eppie has refused to co-operate with the doctor especially with regard to a medical examination of her genitalia. This told us that perhaps the child was protecting Mr Todd, indicating a likely classic case where coaching to hide that sexual abuse had taken place. In fact the doctor suggested that Accommodation Syndrome was at play here." [220]

After a brief silence, the Magistrate addressed Senior CSO Karen Wells: "May I suggest that you read both the *Social Assessment Report* and the doctor's *Medical Report* from this Court's hearing in March. The *Social Assessment Report* also covered Mr Todd's conviction for rape. It would have told you that his conviction was quashed on appeal and he was paid compensation for wrongful conviction. His criminal record was expunged by Supreme Court

---

[220] Summit, R. C., "Child Sexual Abuse Accommodation Syndrome", 1983, *NCJRS Virtual Library*, US Department of Justice, Washington, USA. https://www.ojp.gov/ncjrs/virtual-library/abstracts/child-sexual-abuse-accommodation-syndrome#:~ Note: Neither the American Psychiatric Association nor the American Psychological Association has recognised this syndrome and these days it is largely discredited.

Order. Possibly a reason why you are not aware of Mr Todd's successful appeal is due to the confidentiality provisions of Part 6 of the *Child Protection Act* which mean that his exoneration and the conviction for perjury by the person who made the original claim of rape against him cannot be published in the press. I urge the Department to ensure that its records are up to date. I will say no more on this matter. Now, taking into account the information currently before this Court, I see no new or additional evidence which would require that this Court revoke that decision of last March." She then read read out today's Court Orders for this case:

> In relation to the child Eppie Todd, the Department of Child Safety's application for a 28-day Assessment Custody Order in favour of the Chief Executive is denied. The Department's three-day Assessment Order is terminated and the said child is to be returned to the custody of Keith Todd with immediate effect. I am satisfied that these Orders adequately provide for the child's protection which is unlikely to be ensured by a further protection order from this Court on either more or less intrusive terms.

Magistrate Austin adds: "The emotional distress and harm caused to this child and to her custodial guardian by the Department's unnecessary intervention in her life is a matter for concern. I am aware that last night she absconded from the foster care placement. I saw the Amber Alert. I am also aware from the *Social Assessment Report* tendered to the Court in March that there was an attempted rape of her in November and she was saved from probable death by the timely intervention of Mr Todd. So, I can imagine the distress that removal into foster care must have caused her. I have no doubt that it prompted her to abscond. Yet, appropriate record keeping and careful background research would have provided the Department with details of last March's case before this Court. It would have avoided the waste of this busy Court's time. So, I repeat: the child Eppie Todd is to be returned to the custody and care of Keith Todd. I stress that it is 'with immediate effect'. I have determined that is in the child's best interests."

She stands up. Everybody else stands. The Magistrate bows briefly and leaves the room.

The Court is silent. The pair of CSOs from the Department are gobsmacked.

Keith is elated.

He sees the CSOs discussing the situation with the foster carer. She was not required to give evidence after all. So, the issue of Eppie supposedly masturbating was not raised.

CHAPTER 14

Assault

Immediately after the Magistrate finishes reading out her decision, Keith's lawyer Paula Wellings passes him a copy of the Orders. He looks at it, folds it, and puts it in his shirt pocket. He tells her he is driving to Toowoomba. From Court proceedings, Keith already knows the foster care address.

Paula Wellings: "Okay. I'll phone the Department and tell them you're coming. When you arrive, there should be somebody from the Department there ready to hand her over. The foster carer is busy with these two CSOs for the moment. Then she'll do the school run picking up kids. So, she won't be there."

Keith: "Oh, thank you. Please tell them I'll be there in little over an hour."

She smiles and gives him the thumbs up.

About an hour and fifteen minutes later he is there. He parks his car up the driveway. He walks to the main house, knocks on the door, and waits. There is no answer. He walks around the house. Still, nobody. When he gets to the little 'donga', he hears a voice. It's a youthful male voice. He looks through a window. There are curtains but they are not fully drawn. He is shocked at what he sees. He can just make out Eppie lying on a bed. A young late teenage man is standing next to a bed. Looking behind the young man, he can see Eppie lying on the bed spreadeagled and naked from the waist down. The young man is leaning over her and his hands are at her throat. Her limbs are flailing about.

He quickly creeps around to the door. He tries the handle. It is not locked. He carefully opens it and steps inside. The air-conditioning is masking any faint noise he makes. He picks up a little kids folding camp chair, rushes at the young man, and starts vigorously hitting him with it.

The young man turns to face Keith and starts punching him. Keith continues hitting him with the chair. His head starts bleeding lots. He takes off out of the 'donga' to the main house.

Keith looks at Eppie. She is dazed and seemingly not fully conscious. He picks her up, sits on the bed, and cuddles her. She whimpers. He doesn't talk to her. That can happen later.

After a few minutes, he picks up her shorts and *broekies* from the bed and carries her to the car. As he drives out along the driveway, a car with 'QG' number plates pulls into the driveway.[221] There are two women in it. He realises they must be the Child Safety Officers sent to hand Eppie over to him. However, he is upset about what he has just seen happening to Eppie. He has Court Orders in his pocket. So, he decides not to stop and talk to them. Instead, he drives around the Child Safety car, across the grass, and on to the road. He heads straight for home.

She is still semi-naked and she whimpers every now and then. That's when he often holds and gently squeezes her hand. He notices, not only her bloodshot eyes, but bluish bruises around her neck. And, he can see her cheeks have been smacked. But, he doesn't ask her anything. She is still largely out of it. He is focussed on taking her home. As he drives, there is silence between them except for her whimpering.

At home, it is five p.m. He takes her to her bedroom, changes her into her nightie, and puts her in bed. He brings her a cup of Milo. He sits her up. As she drinks, he sits on a chair next to her but doesn't talk except to say: "The judge at the Court gave you back to me. So, I drove straight to that foster care place to collect you."

She smiles: "Love you Mumma."

He asks if she'd like to brush her teeth. Nodding, he lifts her up and takes her to the bathroom where she does her teeth and does a piddle. He puts her back to bed with a 'dark story'. It's an old favourite: *Goldilocks and the three bears*. She's heard it many times and loves it. It is very reassuring for her. She falls asleep as he sings an impromptu lullaby.

---

[221] Many cars belonging to the Queensland government have number plates beginning with 'QG'.

He has not questioned her about her ordeal. That can come later when she wants to talk. Looking at her peacefully asleep, he is full of admiration for her. He has to wipe his eyes.

Next morning after she has had restful night at home and breakfast of Weet-Bix and scrambled egg, she talks. They sit on the couch and discuss her ordeal, a sort of debriefing but in a kind supportive way. She initiated it. She wanted to tell Keith.

He asks about her escape because it was mentioned in Court. Slowly and with many halts, she explains to Keith what happened although she is quite lucid. The following is a partially paraphrased and partly verbatim version of what she says about her escape and

her sexual abuse.

"They locked me in that 'donga' by myself. You can't open the door from the inside. Somebody has to open it from the outside. No escape."

Keith: "That's like the doors on prison cells."

"I was very upset. They gave me pills. But, I threw them away. Two days locked in that 'donga'. Nothing to do or to read or anything. I was really pissed off. I decided I had to escape. When they took me to dinner in the big house and everyone was eating dinner, I said: 'Excuse me, I need to go to the toilet.' They saw me going into the toilet. I squeezed out of the small toilet window. I walked along the road to where the roads join."

Eppie walked in the dark along the Eton Vale - Cambooya Road for just over a kilometre. "When a car came, I hid in the grass."

At the New England Highway, she walked to the United Petroleum petrol station. She wanted to phone Keith. (*Google Maps.*)

"I walked to that petrol station. I wanted to ask if I could make a phone call to you. But, I was worried and scared. So, I waited between two parked cars. Then, along came this Toyota ute. It came from Toowoomba. I watched the lady who was driving. She was alone. I had an idea. It had yellow New South Wales number plates. So, I thought it must be going my way."

"When the lady went to pay, I just walked over to the ute.[222] I climbed into the back and lay down. When she came back, she didn't see me in the tray. She didn't know I was there. She hopped in and away we went. We were going in the right direction."

She noticed the Toyota Land Cruiser ute had yellow New South Wales number plates. When the woman went to the cashier to pay, Eppie walked over and climbed into the back.

"Not much to hold on to. Was very bumpy. See, I didn't hitch hike."

Keith held her hand: "Wow! Clever girl!"

She smiled.

"Oh, it was so cold in the back of the ute. The wind was rushing in and then it was raining. I got all wet, soaking wet. I was shivering cold."

"That ute driver, she went straight through Canning Town. We were still going the right way. She didn't stop. I was getting worried. She might go all the way to NSW before stopping. And, it was so cold with the wind blowing in. It was dark and bumpy. Couldn't jump out. I didn't know what to do. Then, we came to Graniteville. She didn't take the by-pass road. She drove into town and

A soaking wet Eppie.
(*iStockphoto*. Posed by model.)

---

[222] 'ute' : common Australian term for a small pick-up truck or "utility".

stopped at another petrol station. She didn't pull up at the petrol pumps. No. The lady went into the office for something. So, I leaped out of the ute and hid between two parked cars. I saw her come out with a cup of coffee. See, that's how I got to Graniteville. I was going to find a phone booth so I could phone you. It's free now."[223]

Keith squeezed her hand. "You amaze me! You are very clever and brave! But, tell me, how did the Police catch you?"

Eppie: "After that lady drove away, somebody saw me hiding between two cars. I was hiding there because I had to do a piddle. I was desperate."

She giggled a little.

Eppie: "A Police car came past. The man who saw me stopped it. I finished piddling and pulled up my *broekies*. I tried to run but a Policeman chased me. He caught me.

Eppie relieving herself between parked cars. (*Dreamstime*. Posed by model.)

There was another Policeman with him and they took me to the 'Cop Shop' there in Graniteville. So, I couldn't phone you. But, those Police saw I was cold and they put a rug around me and sat me in front of a heater in a comfy chair. It was nice to warm up because I was shivering so loud 'coz I was scared, too. They asked me what my name was. I didn't answer. They asked me where my mother was and where I lived. Still didn't answer. I saw them talking on the phone. Then, they took a photo of me.

I fell asleep in the chair. It was late. I saw the clock. It was about midnight.

Then, they carried me to a police car. They said: "We're taking you home."

I thought that was nice. I'm going home. As they drove off, I fell asleep again.

Oh Mumma, when I woke up, we were at the foster carer's house.

The foster care witch locked me in the 'donga'. I banged on the door and shouted. Can't be opened from the inside. I was so, so sad and upset. I cried and cried.

The following description is a mixture of paraphrase and Eppie's own speech.

---

[223] From August 2021 phone calls to destinations within Australia are free when made from a public phone booth. https://www.telstra.com.au/consumer-advice/payphones

When the boss foster carer witch brought me Weet-Bix and juice for breakfast she told me: "I'm going to Canning Town today. I'll be back in the afternoon to pick up school kids. So, I'm leaving Jason in charge. He'll bring you some lunch."

Warning: The following three pages are confronting.

Before lunch Jason brought me some cheese and Vegemite sandwiches and a pill. He was bossy. "Don't forget he pill!"[224]

(*FineArtAmerica*. Posed by model.)

He went away and locked the door behind him. I put the pill in my white shorts pocket..

Later, he came back in, still bossy. His iPhone was playing a song. He put it on the table. It played over and over.[225]

"Mum's away today and Dad's at work. So, I'm in charge."

He orders her: "Get off the chair! Lay on the bed!"

Suspicious, she tells him: "I don't want to! "

"Ya have to! I'm boss of you."

Eppie: "You're not boss of me."

"You're so up yourself.[226] Lay on the bed! Do it! Now!"

He smacks her face twice. She falls on to the floor.

She holds up her hand: "Please. No!"

He grabs her firmly and literally throws her onto the bed.

"Mumma, I was so scared. I was going frozen. Quick as a flash, he pulled my white shorts and my *broekies* together straight down and off. He was rough."

(*MediaStoreHouse*. Posed by model.)

Putting her shorts and *broekies* on the bed next to her, he sits on the edge of the bed.

He puts his hand at her throat.

---

[224] Giving her that pill was a deliberate ploy by Jason to render Eppie docile and compliant. One was supposed to be daily before dinner. That extra lunchtime *Chlorpromazine* tablet amounted to an overdose.

[225] Samuel, C. & Bruder, S. "Andrew Tate's theme song 'Tourner Dans Le Vide'". *The Sun*, London, 20 November 2023. https://www.thesun.co.uk/news/19517486/what-is-andrew-tates-theme-song-tourner-dans-le-vide/

[226] As we've seen, Eppie's accent sometimes causes her problems. She is seen as snooty.

"He started squeezing. Couldn't breathe properly. My arms and legs kicked out by themselves. Was going dizzy. Started seeing stars."

I heard him: "Do what I tell ya! Okay?"

An almost inaudible: "Yes."

"If ya don't, ginna slap, choke, an' fuck ya!"[227]

He lets go. She goes limp.[228]

"You're here 'coz ya garbage. Yeah, thrown away. Nobody want ya. But, ya lucky. Now ya belong to me. I own ya."

She is very scared, her throat is sore, and she is feeling dizzy.

"You're a girl an' girls only good for fuckin'. An' you're my girl. You get me?"[229]

A weak: "Yes."

"Cool!" He spreads her legs. No resistance.

Holding her outer labia apart, he has a close look.

"Looks like ya never been fucked before. Gotta break you in slow, like."

She is very scared and still feeling dizzy.

He puts a finger between her outer labia.[230]

---

[227] This is a noted Andrew Tate technique. See: Derbyshire, V., "Andrew Tate 'choked me until I passed out', UK woman claims." *BBC Newsnight*, London, 07 June 2023. https://www.bbc.com/news/uk-65822365 "He kept saying: 'I own you, you belong to me'," she says. On the BBC there are other interviews of him where he expresses his misogynist views.

[228] With that language, this eighteen-year-old has clearly been influenced by access to web sites of that "king of toxic misogyny" Andrew Tate. See: "Andrew Tate", *Wikipedia*. https://en.wikipedia.org/wiki/Andrew_Tate
He is using Tate's language of violent misogyny against a very small physically immature child.
Also: Armstrong, C., "Harmful voices dominate chat". *Courier Mail*, Brisbane, 14 June 2024. (Paywall). About Tate's influence on young men and boys in Australia.

[229] Classic toxic masculinity, something which is sometimes rife among school boys especially teenagers. Is it on the rise? This author doubts it. It is not new. The author can remember this culture of boys tormenting school girls in a sexual way from his primary school years in the 1950s.
Achenza, M. "Australian teachers expose disturbing trend of toxic masculinity in schools", *ABC News*, Sydney 04 April 2024. https://www.news.com.au/lifestyle/parenting/school-life/australian-teachers-expose-disturbing-trend-of-toxic-masculinity-in-schools/news-story/e258e309559c2f971c8ea70a1f93b169
Wescott, S. & Roberts, S. "Research exposes alarming impact of 'manfluencer' culture on Australian schools." 03 April 2024, Monash University, Melbourne. https://doi.org/10.1080/09540253.2023.2292622
In foster care, Eppie is extremely vulnerable to toxic masculinity especially if she becomes drugged.

[230] Defined under section 349 of the Queensland *Criminal Code Act* this is 'rape'. It has a maximum penalty of life imprisonment.

She squirms as it's sore. She tries to straighten her legs.

He slaps her twice again and touches her throat. "Keep them legs spread!"

Fearful of more choking, she co-operates instantly. She parts legs as much as she can and pushes her knees up towards the side of her chest.

I didn't like that choking. So, I did it for him. I wanted to please him. And, I did please him. He liked that.

He tells her: "Awesome!"

Later, she told Keith: "Don't know why but I sort of smiled at him. I was so scared. My throat was sore. I didn't want to be choked any more. Choking's just the pits. So I opened my legs a lot just for him."[231]

He started undoing the belt on his pants.

That made me freak out: "No! No! Please! Please! No! Please don't do it to me!"

She rolls over onto her side and curls up into a tight protective foetal position.

Before he drops his pants, he rolls her over onto her back. He grabs her knees and pushes them apart with force despite her resistance.

Standing next the bed and leaning over her, he slaps her face twice. She whimpers.

"Shut up! Bitch!"[232]

Grabbing her throat, he starts squeezing again.

Her arms and legs thrash about involuntarily. Stars flash across her vision. She is dizzy.

Gasping for air, she is losing consciousness.

Preoccupied with what he is doing and with the music, Jason has not noticed the door opening quietly as Keith stealthily steps inside.

---

[231] "The 5 Fs", *Rape crisis England & Wales.* https://rapecrisis.org.uk/get-help/tools-for-victims-and-survivors/understanding-your-response/fight-or-flight/ Accommodating their wishes or "befriending the person who is dangerous, for example by placating them, is not you giving your attacker consent. It is an instinctive survival mechanism." Little Eppie was in this situation.

[232] This is almost precisely the Andrew Tate recommendation: "That's how it goes, you go slap, slap, grab, choke, 'shut up bitch,' sex." Quoted in "Andrew Tate", *Wikipedia.* https://en.wikipedia.org/wiki/Andrew_Tate

He picks up the small child's folding camp chair near the door and starts hitting Jason with it hard across his back and head.

Although he is almost eighty, Keith has risen to the occasion and is in full primal attack mode. Nature has driven him to protect his child. Yet, but for the child's camping chair, it would have been be a unequal battle. Jason is less than a quarter of Keith's age and well-built.

Jason is taken completely by surprise and lets go of Eppie. He turns and sees the fury in elderly Keith's face. He is challenged by this old codger who has suddenly appeared. He faces Keith in strong defensive anger. He swings a punch at Keith. He gets Keith fair and square at his mouth. He hits Keith more, on his jaw and torso. His youthful eighteen-year-old superior strength is clear. Keith struggles on valiantly, hitting back repeatedly. Although stunned from being punched, he doesn't give in. As he receives more punches, he summons up reserves of strength and returns the blows. But, despite his instinctive drive to defend and protect his child, his blows are wilting and weakening. He is failing but he just has to keep on hitting at Jason. Many of his blows miss. But, he can't opt out. He is still driven to defend his child to the end, even at the cost of his own life.[233]

Then, Jason's scalp starts bleeding profusely. Blood pours out down his face and onto the bed cover. Jason realises that he pouring blood.[234] He backs off, pulls up his pants as

---

[233] Keith is driven to protect. There are many definitions of this fundamental aspect of mother love. Here is one: "The love of a mother is primal. When faced with grave danger she will stop at nothing – and spare no one – who threatens the lives of her children." Rachel Norman, (2023), *A Mother far from Home*. https://amotherfarfromhome.com/the-love-of-a-mother-what-does-it-do/

See this primal instinct in action where a mother bear protects her off-spring in an unequal battle between a sloth bear and a much larger tiger. "Mother Bear Fights Tiger to Save Her Cub", *National Geo Wild, YouTube*, https://www.youtube.com/watch?v=0ggJ627z4jU

Elderly Keith's battle with this 18-year-old man was unequal. But, his instinctive drive to defend his child prevailed because nothing could stop him in what was a battle which could have caused his death.

[234] Injuries to the scalp often result in prolific bleeding. "Why do head injuries bleed so much?" *University of Utah Health*, 17 November 2016. https://healthcare.utah.edu/healthfeed/postings/2016/11/head_injuries.php

Keith is still hitting at him, although much less vigorously. He bolts away out through the door and across to the main house.[235]

Jason realises he is bleeding profusely.
(*Depositphotos*. Posed by model.)

Mumma, he skedaddled out.

Eppie has finished her story.

When Keith arrived and had despatched Jason, Eppie was lying semi-naked, spreadeagled on the bed, and not quite conscious. Keith picked her up, sat on the bed, and cuddled her. She whimpered. He didn't say anything to her. Talking can happen later. He ignored the song still playing on the iPhone, though he could hear that it is in French.

Keith picked up her shorts and *broekies* and carried her out to the car. He drove straight home. He had the Court Orders in his pocket.

After he giving her dinner and putting her to bed with a favourite dark story, *Goldilocks and the three bears,* and cuddles, she crashed asleep.

In the morning, after breakfast they talk. She tells him about what Jason did. But, as she talks they notice that her voice is sort of gravely or husky. By the next day her voice has improved remarkably. (Her vocal cords had been strained by the choking.)[236]

"After the Court gave you back to me, I drove straight to the foster car house. I had a copy of the Court Orders in my pocket. Those Orders returned you to my care 'with immediate effect'."

He shows her the Orders. "I couldn't find anybody and walked around. Then, I found you and Jason in that 'donga'. I sneaked in quietly. He had a song playing on his iPhone which was on the table. He was busy choking you and didn't notice me until I hit him with

---

[235] What Keith did to Jason could legally be regarded as self-defence because he was defending a child from serious assault: "Self-defence information sheet", Queensland Law reform Commission. https://www. qlrc.qld.gov.au/data/assets/pdf_file/0003/783246/criminal-defences-review-information-sheet-on-self-defence-nov-23.pdf Also: Queensland *Criminal Code Act* section 272 and especially section 273 which provides for defence of another person.

[236] "Non-Fatal Strangulation", *Government of Western Australia*. https://www.kemh.health.wa.gov.au/~/media/HSPs/NMHS/Hospitals/WNHS/Documents/Patients-resources/SARC---Non-fatal-strangulation.pdf

that kid's camping chair. He shot through quick smart. He knew he was doing a terrible thing. Then I took you home."

"Thank you so much, Mumma. I do remember him hitting me and starting to choke me. I was so scared. I was going to let him fuck me. No escape. I was like the rainforest tree, trapped by the strangler fig.[237] Couldn't run away. No chance."

Keith hugs her.

Eppie: "When you came, I was not quite aware of everything. I saw your face. I remember you carrying me to the car. I was dizzy and my eyes had stars zooming across my view. I still have sort of tunnel vision with blackness at the sides but it's getting better."

Not wanting to be alarmist, he talks in a calm almost analytical way but at the same time he is very loving, holding her hand, and kissing her forehead frequently.[238]

"He could go to jail for putting his finger between your labia.[239]

She is quiet and listening.

Keith: "Anyway, as you know, little foster care kids are easy game. They are trapped and nobody to stand up for them. He knew you were upset at being taken into foster care. He knew you were likely very upset at having escaped, been captured, and the returned. You were alone and vulnerable like a trapped animal. He deliberately made you scared so he could dominate and control you. I reckon he must be an Andrew Tate follower, only he was using those techniques on a very young little girl."

Eppie: "Who is that Andrew?"

---

[237] See: *Ficus watkinsiana* in *Wikipedia*, https://en.wikipedia.org/wiki/Ficus_watkinsiana

[238] Judith Herman wrote in the latest afterword to her *Trauma and Recovery*: "Healing from the impact of human cruelty requires a relational context of human devotion and kindness." The therapist's role is to "affirm a position of solidarity with the victim." Orbey, E., "A trailblazer of trauma studies asks what victims really want". *New Yorker*, 02 May 2023. https://www.newyorker.com/books/page-turner/a-trailblazer-of-trauma-studies-asks-what-victims-really-want

[239] Placing his finger between her labia was rape at section 349(2)(b) of the Queensland *Criminal Code Act* even though her vagina was not penetrated. By hitting Eppie and threatening to penis rape her, he had already committed an offence at section 351(1). These offences would be aggravated or made worse because of Eppie's very young age.

He opens his computer and looks up Andrew Tate in *Wikipedia*. He reads parts to her.[240]

Eppie: "He must be a fan of that guy. He was so bossy. And then, with that choking and saying he owns me. Yes, he's like that Tate. That choking's horrible, horrible! I sort of froze and did what he wanted. Couldn't help it. Hated that choking. Awful! It's like strangling, isn't it?"

"Yes, the same. If he had actually penis raped you then and there, it would have been devastating. You would have needed serious hospital operations to repair you. You are just too small. But, I think he would have started with digital penetration, you know, putting his finger between your labia. Soon, when you were used to that, he would start penetrating you with his penis. Then it would be regular penis rape. It would always be painful for you because you re small. But, you'd have to let him do it."

Eppie: "He said he owned me. How can somebody own me? And, he said nobody wants me because I'm rubbish. A little thought flashed across my mind of how I was dumped like rubbish at Bolivia Hill."

Keith hugs her. "That was his strategy to humiliate you and make you give in to him."

They look at another website. It includes Tate's theme song.

Eppie exclaims: "That's the song he was playing on his iPhone! I recognise it. Yes! He's an Andrew Tate freak!"[241]

Keith continues: "Yes, he must be a Tate fan. But, you're not alone in having this sort of thing happen." He showed her a news item on his computer involving 11-year-old boys.[242]

---

[240] "Andrew Tate", *Wikipedia*. https://en.wikipedia.org/wiki/Andrew_Tate

[241] Andrew Tate's theme song sung in French: https://www.youtube.com/watch?v=zwyPNtiNL70 A male admirer said: "This song is the most masculine song ever. I play it non stop when I drive . Ppl look at me with both fear and respect. I emulate Tate, bare chested and smoking cigars. The females love me, they feel I am alpha!" Like admirer Jason.

[242] Fellows, T. "Girls strangled in care." *Courier Mail*, Brisbane, 12 July 2023, page 3. https://www.couriermail.com.au/subscribe/news/1/?qld-juvie-home-crisis-girl-allegedly-strangled-assaulted-by-11yo-boy (There is a paywall on this story.) Girls were strangled Andrew Tate style. A grandmother complained about the sexual assaults of girls in foster care by two 11-year-old boys but the Department of Child Safety did nothing.

"And, there was another little girl in Brisbane. A foster carers's teenage son started sexually abusing the newly arrived four-year-old little girl. Scared and alone, he trained her to have him for regular penis rapes by the time she was six-years-old." [243]

Eppie looks at the item: "Like a secret little girl sex slave. … That was going to be me."

Keith: "I think you're right. That was the start of your training."

Eppie: "Yes."

Keith: "So, although it was training by the foster carer's son, it could even have been training by a woman like in this *ABC News* item."[244] He shows it to her on his computer.

Eppie: "Gosh! So, a lady did it to a foster care girl."

Keith: "Yes. And, she was a Child Safety Officer."

Eppie is quiet.

Keith: "And, note how in the rest of the item some Child Safety Officers were upset by things they witnessed and had to do. You saw how one former Officer or CSO was asked: "Are Australia's children safe in the Department's care?" She answered straight away: "No."[245] Those are the sort of reasons why our friend Fiona resigned from the Department and became a teacher."

Eppie: "Now I understand."

---

[243] Houghton, D. "Horrors in foster care". *Courier Mail*, Brisbane, 31July 2018. "In a tragic Child safety blunder a four year-old girl who was removed from her loving grandmother and placed in a foster home was brutally raped repeatedly for 14 months by the foster carer's son." https://documents.parliament.qld. gov.au/com/HCDSDFVPC-48D8/RN956PC201-8B6E/tp-31Jul2018-08.pdf This news item was tabled in the Queensland Parliament. The little girl in foster care was raped regularly from ages four to six. As with Eppie's situation in foster care, the predator was the foster carer's teenage son. Isolated from family support, the girl was an easy and obedient target for him.

    With the secrecy provisions of the *Child Protection Act,* one would wonder how this story got out. And, how many other similar cases have never seen the light of day because of that secrecy.

[244] In this *ABC News* item, a foster care victim reveals sexual abuse by a female Child Safety Officer. It starts 2 minutes through. "The forgotten children removed from their parents and subjected to abuse in state care." *ABC News*, Brisbane, 19 June 2022. https://www.abc.net.au/news/2022-06-19/ the-forgotten-children-subjected-to-abuse-in-state/13936094

[245] This is what a former Child Safety Officer said at 5.10 minutes through the program: "The forgotten children removed from their parents and subjected to abuse in state care." *ABC News*, Brisbane, 19 June 2022. https://www.abc.net.au/news/2022-06-19/the-forgotten-children-subjected-to-abuse-in-state/13936094 The same program may also be found on *YouTube* at https://www.youtube.com/ watch?v=J6UeR56h4Go

Keith: "That's the foster care life you could have ended up in. So, I think Fiona was very good to give up being what you call 'a Child Safety witch'. She hated the job."

Eppie: "Yes. I like her. … You know with that Jason, I couldn't escape. They were all against me, everybody, even from when they took me from school. I was trapped. Scared. Nobody to turn to. So, when he started that choking, not only was it so awful, I had to give in to him."[246]

Keith: "Then you would have given in almost daily until it became routine, like that little girl in Brisbane."[247]

Keith holds her close as she cries a little.

Then she says: "Mumma, I escaped but they captured me … and they put me back in that 'donga'. I was locked up … just right for Jason. And, he always had a key. … he could do what he wanted whenever he wanted. Choking was so horrible. He knew how to force a kid to do what she didn't want to do. So, I did what he wanted and I opened my legs for him. … Yes, I did it for him. He liked that. … I had to do what he wanted. … But, I was pleased that he liked me doing it for him. I was sort of his to do what he wanted … sort of like I was inviting him. He said: 'Awesome' … and he smiled at me. That made me a little bit happier because I think I was hoping he would go easy on me.[248] … But then, he started choking me again."

Keith wipes her eyes with a tissue.

Eppie: "That's when you came and took me away."

---

[246] This scenario is not unusual. Girls (and boys) in foster care are often easy targets for sexual abuse. They are trapped, have no family protection and are extremely vulnerable. Eppie's situation has similarities to the sexual abuse a girl in foster care at the hands of boys living in the foster care home. Utting, A. "Woman who was allegedly sexually and physically abused in foster care sues Queensland government for almost $2 million". *ABC News*, Brisbane, 06 July 2023, https://www.abc.net.au/news/2023-07-06/qld-foster-child-sues-state-government-after-abuse/102562586?

Also: Asher, N., "Melbourne woman placed in abusive foster home receives record $2.6m payout". *ABC News*, Melbourne, 05 April 2023. https://www.abc.net.au/news/2023-04-05/foster-care-abuse-survivor-receives-record-court-payout/102174764

And so it goes on. Very little of this type of news about children sexually abused in foster care gets out because of secrecy provisions in child protection legislation in each state. So, what happened to Eppie in this story is not fantasy.

[247] Houghton, D. "Horrors in foster care". *Courier Mail*, Brisbane, 31 July 2018. https://documents.parliament.qld.gov.au/com/HCDSDFVPC-48D8/RN956PC201-8B6E/tp-31Jul2018-08.pdf

[248] "The 5 Fs: fight, flight, freeze, flop and friend." https://rapecrisis.org.uk/get-help/tools-for-victims-and-survivors/understanding-your-response/fight-or-flight/

CHAPTER 15

Quiet at Home.

Later that morning, they talk more.

Eppie : "You know, I've been thinking. I reckon it was Melanie's Mum who sent those Child Safety witches to get me. Well, I didn't like her."

Keith: "Maybe. It could have been her. But, don't worry about it. The first Court hearing had already given you to me. The Child Safety ladies tried by going to Court again but they didn't stand a chance. The Magistrate's decision about you staying with me had already been made weeks before. That's why the Magistrate kicked out their case. She knew. They didn't. It was news to them. They were embarrassed."

Eppie smiles.

Keith: "I've been thinking about Melanie's Mum, too. I agree with you. I reckon it was her who caused that trouble. Remember when you were last at their house she asked you if I was once a teacher in Townsville."

Eppie: "Yes, I didn't like her quizzing me."

Keith: "Well, I reckon she must have been curious about you and me. So, she went to the Department to dob me in as living alone with a little girl in the bush. The Child Safety people took on her notification about us, investigated a little, and found news reports from long ago about me raping a girl at the school in Townsville. So, they came to Kinross State School to protect you from me. That's where they went so wrong.[249] The Magistrate was actually angry with them and told them so. She didn't like the Child Safety Officers' removing you into foster care."

---

[249] Keith and Eppie's suspicions were correct. But, they never find out for certain that it was Belinda Shaw. Her name was not mentioned in court because the *Child Protection Act* forbids naming of people who 'notify' the Department about suspected child abuse or harm (section 186A: "Identity of notifier not to be disclosed").

"Mumma, you've never done sex things with me. And, remember Dr Morton looked in me and found a septate hymen there."

Keith: "Yes, that's one form of proof. Anyway, I think we'll talk to our lawyer about this so that the boy can be made accountable for what he did and make sure he does not sexually abuse more girls like you. The Department caused you harm by not protecting you which they are supposed to do. It's a classic case of the Department's acting on a 'false positive' going dreadfully wrong. The trouble is that it causes terrible trauma for the child. That is exactly what happened to you. It should never have happened. They caused you harm.[250] I think we should see Paula Wellings about it. She would know the best way to sort out that boy without you being involved."

Relaxing at home with two black eyes. (*MayaMalesa*. Posed by model.)

They decide that Keith should take photographs of her. He photographs her blood shot eyes, bruised eye sockets, and some of the bruises on her neck.

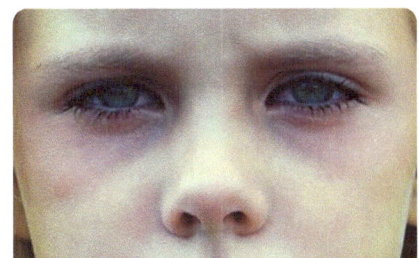

(*iStockphoto*. Posed by model.)

Then, she starts worrying about what the foster carer's son, Jason, did to her vulva with his finger. She is not sore but concerned. She asks Keith to have a look at her.

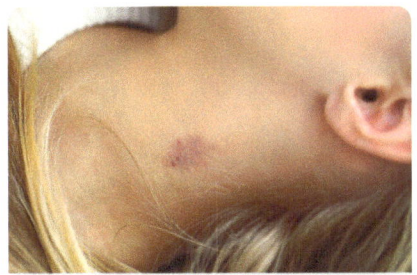

A bruise on Eppie's neck. (*iStockphoto*. Posed by model.)

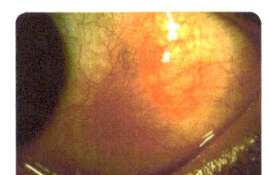

Bloodshot eye. (*Wikimedia*.)

250 Ainsworth, F. & Thorpe, R. (2013), *Child Protection in Queensland. The Carmody Inquiry.* James Cook University, Townsville. http://www.childprotectioninquiry.qld.gov.au/data/assets/pdf_file/0010/177427/James-Cook-University-Thorpe,-Prof-Rosamund-and-Ainsworth,-Dr-Frank-Response-to-Discussion-Paper.PDF "… too many 'false positives' i.e. child removal when the child should have remained in parental care".

Trivedi, S., "The Harm of Child Removal", *Review of Law & Social Change,* New York University, 523 (2019). Available at: https://scholarworks.law.ubalt.edu/all_fac/1085 "Research shows separating a child from her parent(s) has detrimental, long-term emotional and psychological consequences that may be worse than leaving the child at home. This is due to the trauma of removal itself, as well as the unstable nature of, and high rates of abuse in, foster care."

She takes him into her bedroom. She removes her *broekies*, sits on her bed, and parts her legs. He has a look. "I've looked at your vulva before. I can't see anything that looks wrong. There's no soreness?"

"It's not sore."

Next day, they drive to Toowoomba to see lawyer Paula Wellings. Keith thanks her for what she's done for them. He also pays her company's substantial bill..

Keith asks: "Should we pursue the Department for the sexual abuse?"

Paula: "I'll be frank with you. The Department would vigorously defend themselves. Crown Law barristers will make all sorts of allegations about you, Keith, and about Eppie making things up. Sorry to say this, I would caution you. May I suggest that you go on the internet and look up an item by a British journalist Carol Sarler.[251] It's called … ."

Keith interrupts: "We've already seen it and discussed it. Eppie, tell her what you think."

Eppie: "We talked about it after that foster carer's son had a go at me. I reckon we should go dark on this. I just don't want a lot of '*kak*' flying around.[252] I've had enough. Scares me."

Paula: "Is that still what you feel?"

Eppie: "Yes."

Keith: "It happened to Eppie, not me. So, I respect her feelings on this."

Paula turning to Eppie: "Do you know that 18-year-old who digitally raped you has been complained about before. I told your Dad while you were in 'care'. The Department did nothing. When faced with a complaint they always respond with a bland statement like: "We take allegations of sexual abuse by careers seriously and investigate fully."[253] Now, if I complain, would you accept being interviewed by the Police?"

Eppie: "No way. A Policeman grabbed me at Mrs McGregor's office and carried me to the Child Safety car. I struggled. He was rough and he whacked me. He held me down hard

---

[251] Carol Sarler, "Sex abuse DOESN'T have to scar you for life." *Daily Mail*, London, 22 June 2006. https://www.dailymail.co.uk/femail/article-391901/Sex-abuse-DOESNT-scar-life.html

[252] '*kak*' is crude Afrikaans for shit.

[253] Typical bland Departmental responses to allegations of sexual abuse by carers seen at 1:20 and at 2:35 minutes through: "The forgotten children removed from their parents and subjected to abuse in state care." *ABC News*, Brisbane, 19 June 2022. https://www.abc.net.au/news/2022-06-19/the-forgotten-children-subjected-to-abuse-in-state/13936094

into the seat while a witch did up the seatbelt. He said: 'Stay in there there little mongrel!' Sorry, I don't trust them."

Paula: "I understand."

Keith: "Because of what happened to me, I don't trust Judges. And, while Eppie doesn't know about Xan Fraser, I do and I don't want any hint of that happening to her. That Judge said she may have consented. How can a blind drunk twelve-year-old virgin consent to a gang rape?"[254]

Paula: "That was in 1981. Court procedures have changed since then but I take your point about the trauma and risks for her. So, I would make a complaint to the Police about him. I will say my client is too afraid to be involved. But, legally, Keith, you are now required to report an incident of child sexual abuse to the Police.[255] However, in the *Act* there is a reasonable excuse for you not reporting.[256] In this case, it is fear of litigation because you would be up against the Department of Child Safety and the extraordinary powers they have and your fear of how the child would be affected by it. And, Eppie, there is nothing in law that compels you as a child victim to report what happened. So, I will do it for both of you. I'll report and name him. That'll get Police to interview him. As your lawyer, I am not compelled to reveal my clients' identities. Okay?"

They both thank her.

Now changing the topic slightly, Keith gives Paula a pill they tried to force Eppie to take. Eppie tells her about what happened. "They wanted to make me into zombie." Paula: "Well done Eppie! I'll have it analysed."

---

[254] In 1981 at the age of twelve, Xan Fraser was plied with alcohol and lost consciousness before being gang raped and left for dead. The perpetrators' legal team blamed her for what happened. The Judge accepted that argument, did not send the perpetrators to prison and said: "she may have consented". Later, she told *ABCTV*: "The judge, I feel like, he raped me again.". The Xan Fraser case had troubled Keith for a long time. It was another reason why he didn't want Eppie ever to be cross-examined in Court even with a remote video link.
    Taylor, J. 'Raped, left for dead and seeking justice 30 years on'. *7:30 Report - ABCTV*, Sydney, 11 June 2012. https://www.youtube.com/watch?v=tTs5ukjdseA This is an *ABC News* interview with Xan Fraser.
    Taylor, J., "Xan Fraser's life on stage". *ABC News*, Brisbane. 03 November 2016. https://www.abc.net.au/news/2016-11-03/centre-stage-in-her-own-nightmare/7990388

[255] The *Criminal Code Act* at sections 229BB(b)(i) and 229BB(c): 'Failure to protect child from child sexual offence'.

[256] The *Criminal Code Act* at section 229BC(4)(d)(i): 'Failure to report child sexual abuse to Police .. if the adult reasonably believes disclosing the information to a police officer would endanger the safety of the adult or another person'. This allows for not reporting child sexual abuse.

A week later, she phones Keith about the pill. Eppie is listening as Keith has set his phone on speaker phone mode. She tells him: "That pill is a *Chlorpromazine* anti-psychotic tablet. It is only available on prescription. It must have been prescribed for Eppie to make her docile and compliant with the foster care regime she had been put into. At 100mg each tablet and taken once a day, it would have sedated her, possibly turning her into a docile dreamy kid. Easy to manage. With prolonged use, there would have been medical complications like rapid weight gain, low blood pressure, seizures, sedation, and movement problems. I believe the foster carer was excessively keen to have a potentially troublesome Eppie calmed."

Eppie adds: "And make me into zombie."

Paula nods seriously: "Yes, you'd be an easy target for a sex offender. Okay, I'm going to protest to the Department about those pills. It's a criminal offence for them to be prescribed for that purpose. And, that sexual abuse is the sort of thing that can result when a child is stupefied from those pills. Eppie, you were incredibly vulnerable."[257]

---

[257] Asher, N., "Melbourne woman placed in abusive foster home receives record $2.6m payout", *ABC News*, Melbourne, 05 April 2023. https://www.abc.net.au/news/2023-04-05/foster-care-abuse-survivor-receives-record-court-payout/102174764 Professor Bromfield: "In addition to adults preying on children both online and in the real world, more children are falling victim to physical and sexual violence perpetrated by other children in care."

Lohberger, L., "Azra Beach was sexually abused in her foster home and government workers did nothing". *ABC New*s, Hobart. 16 June 2022. https://www.abc.net.au/news/2022-06-16/commission-of-inquiry-hears-azra-beach-abused-in-foster-home/101157720 She was continually sexually abused as a toddler by the foster carer's children.

12-year-old Tiahleigh Palmer: sexually abused and raped by the foster carer's 19-year-old son. Stephens, K., "Was Tiahleigh Palmer pregnant when she died?" *News.com.au* 21 September 2016, https://www.news.com.au/national/queensland/crime/murdered-schoolgirl-tiahleigh-palmers-mother-says-car-seized-by-Police-belonged-to-foster-family/news-story/e9fb1d6b9a7cc316e23685294918b867 She was killed by the foster father to protect his son. The father was was convicted of murder and the son did time.

Utting, A., "Woman who was allegedly sexually and physically abused in foster care sues Queensland government for almost $2 million" *ABC News*, 06 July 2023. https://www.abc.net.au/news/2023-07-06/qld-foster-child-sues-state-government-after-abuse/102562586?

Uibu, K., "Bad parent". *ABC News*, Sydney, 25 May 2023. https://www.abc.net.au/news/2022-06-20/hundreds-of-people-speak-out-against-child-protection-system/101094220? Outlines several cases of sex abuse in foster care and problems faced by case workers when they try to protest and who were "performance managed" out of the Department.

A *Google* search will find a few similar cases in Australia of children sexually abused by other foster care children and children of foster carers. However, published cases are rare. Because of child protection legislation, it is unusual for these cases to appear in the press. Usually, cases which come to light are when the child leaves foster care at 18 and sues the Department. Thus, while a child is in 'care', the Department is protected by the law. And, as a consequence, so is the perpetrator.

Keith: "And, your vulnerability was not because you made a stupid mistake or because you were too trusting. It was not like you voluntarily getting in that man's car. No, this is different. You resisted all the way from the school principal's office onwards. The violence and rape you suffered was the direct result of malicious negligence on the part of the state. You stood up to that all by yourself. You even ran away. They still put you back in danger. They knew from a previous complaint what could happen to you. And, it did. My dear Eppie you were wonderful!"

Smiling, she steps over to Keith and hugs him.

Typically, the Department does not respond even to a letter from a lawyer. Without a response, there is less chance of press and media attention. A response usually only occurs when the Department ends up in Court. Generally, that is when the victim has turned eighteen.

However, the Police interview 18-year-old Jason. They keep a record. He now knows that he is on notice and he will always have a tainted Police record. He will never get a Blue Card. For that foster caring business to continue, he has to leave the foster carer's home because he is an adult with a Police record.[258] Later, Paula tells Keith that the Child Safety Department warned the foster carers that if Jason returns to the premises or even pays a visit, the foster caring business will be closed down.

After that good news, Eppie spent more time up at the cubby house. She was feeling so happy. When she came back down to the house, Keith was starting to make dinner. She saw it's a stew with mushrooms in it. "Mushrooms! *Lekker*!"[259]

She insists that she must help. As they prepare the dinner together, she tells him: "Up at the cubby house I was thinking about you and those Safety witches and that mean foster carer. You know, I must learn from you. You have stuck by me, that yukky little baby you found all covered in that vernix stuff. You loved me right from the start. Always loving,

---

[258] There is a sad item by noted Queensland journalist Madonna King which is worth reading. It tells the story of a little girl removed from her mother at the age of six and placed 'in care' with a family where she was sexually abused regularly by family members until she left foster care at 18. The Australian High Court allowed her to pursue the Department for damages. See: Madonna King, "High Court puts children first". *Courier Mail*, Brisbane, 20 May 2006.

[259] '*Lekker*' is Afrikaans for nice, delicious.

gentle, kind, and honest with me, never sneaky or bossy. You have been … well just the best! You know, I can't remember when I was a baby but I have always felt that deep down inside me I loved you, that old man who was my mother who brought me into the world from an old grocery bag. That's why you are my 'Mumma'."

They talk more about how their first contact at Bolivia Hill has affected their lives.

They also stray from the topic as they discuss things further.

Eppie: "When I grow up, I want to be like you, Mumma. I must stick to my gut feelings and see things through, you know, through thick and thin like you have wth me. Your gut feelings made you decide to look after and love that teensie weensie little baby. And, you did. You never stopped. Thank you, Mumma. And, I'm so very sorry for being bossy with you."

Keith stops what he is doing: "Oh, Eppie. You really are such a lovely thoughtful person. And, I love you so much for it." He wipes his hands and gives her a hug.

Eppie: "What happened at South Bank and with Jason shows something so important about you. You're nearly eighty but you're not past your use by date. No way!"

Keith: "Wow! Thank you! But it was just luck with the sand I threw at the South Bank and luck that I got there in time to stop Jason."

"When I grow up, I want to be like you." (iStockphoto, Posed by model.)

Eppie: "No, not luck. You sorted them out. And, you know, that Jason taught me a lesson that some people are just so, so horrible. Then, you came along and showed me that some people are so, so nice. Later, you said you felt bad about hitting him and making him bleed so much. But, he was bigger and stronger than you and he was hitting you badly. Still, you didn't give in. So, he had to shoot through and run back to his car. I saw all that."

Keith: "Okay, but at the time I had no choice. It was primal, you know, an instinctive love. I just had to do that. I had my child to protect."[260]

---

[260] There are many definitions of this fundamental aspect of mother love. Here is one:
    Rachel Norman, (2023), *A Mother far from Home.* https://amotherfarfromhome.com/the-love-of-a-mother-what-does-it-do/ "The love of a mother is primal. When faced with grave danger she will stop at nothing – and spare no one – who threatens the lives of her children."

"I know what you mean, Mumma. I've said this stuff before but I'll say it again. I know your love. What I'm saying is that you still did it. You put him out of action all by yourself and that saved me. There's no way you're past your use by date."

He smiles: "Maybe, but I don't think I could have done those protective things without that instinct. It's been in me right from when I found you at Bolivia Hill."

Looking back at him seriously: "Yes, it must be from Bolivia Hill. I love you, Mumma. But, there's something else. I've been wondering again. Why was I dumped at Bolivia Hill? Did that lady who gave birth to me not want me?"

Keith: "I wish we knew who she was and why she left you."

Eppie: "Yes. I wonder if my being so scared and giving in to the that Jason at foster care was because of something that happened to that lady who left me at Bolivia Hill. You know, was it something in me that I inherited from her?"

Keith: "Wow! Such profound thoughts."

He gets up and goes to a bookshelf and takes out a fairly thick book. "This book is about the idea that the way we are was set in place from the moment we were conceived. It says we are what our biological parents gave us. For example, if a woman had a stressful life, she would pass on that stress to her baby."[261]

She understands what he is on about. But, he realises the book is just too much for a little six-year-old. So, he doesn't even suggest she try reading it.

She loves their discussion. She fetches her iPad. "Would you please listen to this."

Keith recognises the music immediately. It is emotional. It is Elgar's *Nimrod* played by an orchestra and his eyes become watery. And, sitting next to him, she holds his hand.

When it is finished: "Mumma, this music is about you. You are my quiet rock to cling to. You have always been there for me, always, always. And, you always respect me. You are not like a teacher. We always talk one on one. *Nimrod* is you."[262]

Keith: "Wow! Thank you, thank you."

They hug each other.

---

[261] Sapolsky, R. (2023), *Determined: Life without Free Will*. The Bodley Head (Penguin), London.

[262] Edward Elgar's Enigma Variations, Op.36: IX. (Nimrod) https://www.youtube.com/watch?v=7iM5dymBBI4

Then, she passes him the chopped mushrooms. He tips them into the stew. He goes to a cupboard and takes out his classy 'Villaroy and Boch' dinner service. She knows why. Together, they set the dining table to celebrate her return with a special dinner with some alcohol free wine.

After dinner, they get out Keith's computer and look up 'maternal bonding'. *Wikipedia* is the first reference they go through. They find others but they now realise that those first few moments of contact between them at Bolivia Hill were fundamental in their relationship.

Eppie says something equally significant: "I reckon when the safety witches take a kid into foster care, it is really damaging for the kid. I felt it. I reckon I would have survived but for the rest of my life there would be a damaged part of me, like a black hole of emptiness."

(See the quotation of Weinberger in the next page.)

Keith: "That's so true. Too often, the trauma of separation eventually leads to problems in adult life like drug addiction, domestic violence, and inability to form lasting love relations."

Eppie: "I'll never forget my feelings of, well, I don't know how to say it … yes, I felt so, you know, whats the words … so shattered when they first took me to that foster care house. My whole world crashed. I just wanted to curl up and die."

As she talks to Keith, she has tears in her eyes. He leans over and gives her a long hug.

Eppie: "It was horrible for me. They just took me and dumped me into that foster care house with those other poor kids who I didn't know. And, with a bloody child rapist!"

Keith: "Hostile strangers just arrived at school and forcibly took you away. Heroically, you resisted. You even ran away."

Eppie: "That's because I didn't want to be taken away from you."

Keith: "That's because we are bonded, you know, from Bolivia Hill onwards. As I said, smashing that bond was potentially very harmful for you in later life like making you prone to drug addiction, crime, and having too many brief sexual partners. But, those Child Safety Officers or 'witches', well, you were just another kid to 'save' from an 'evil man'. Some have a thing about men. Some call it 'misandry'. They just wanted to take a child."

Eppie looked it up in her iPad dictionary and smiled.

Keith: "As a parent committed to your welfare, I simply could not have used you sexually. I am bonded to you. I can't undo that.[263] And, you know when you were less than a day old at Bolivia Hill, I made a promise to you that I would stick by you, protect you, and love you until you were old enough and ready to leave the nest and live on your own.[264] That's why I just had to do those things, you know, sorting out that Jason. You know Paula warned me that somebody in that foster care household had been sexually abusing little kids. So, at all costs I had to get you out of foster care. And, with Paula's help, I did it legally through the Court."

"Thank you Mumma."

The trauma of what happened to Eppie through foster care is not swept under the carpet. Keith is aware of what this kind of trauma does. See what Prof. Daniel Weinberger of John Hopkins University, Baltimore, USA says:

> The real danger of separating children from parents is not the psychological stress – it's the biological time bomb. The screaming and crying, the anguish and desolation is gut-wrenching. But the fallout pales in comparison to the less visible long-term effects that are more sinister and dangerous. [265]

Eppie experienced that extreme stress when she was taken into foster care. Then, again during the rape in the 'donga'. Fortunately, she has resilience partly acquired through the independent sometimes wild bush life she has lived with Keith which has 'steeled' her to respond to the trauma of foster care by stubbornly resisting and then running away.[266] However, he feels most of that resilience came from her unknown biological parents. He tends to downplay his own rôle.

He sees that kind of stress and trauma as just another reason why removal of children into foster care is so often harmful for them. So, he deliberately sets out to try and normalise

---

[263] This is the "Westermarck effect", *Wikipedia*. https://en.wikipedia.org/wiki/Westermarck_effect
[264] Towards the end of Chapter 5.
[265] Weinberger, D.R., "Extreme stress in childhood is toxic to your DNA." *The Conversation*, Melbourne, 28 June 2018. https://theconversation.com/extreme-stress-in-childhood-is-toxic-to-your-dna-99009
[266] This term 'steeled' is used in Rutter, M., (2012), "Resilience as a dynamic concept", *Development and Psychopathology*, 24(2), page 337, Cambridge University Press. For an abstract, see: https://pubmed.ncbi.nlm.nih.gov/22559117/.

the home environment. He thinks about calming Eppie's life, if he can. But, she has always been a stubborn often feisty little girl with an independent outlook on life, something he had encouraged. In the next chapter we see what she does when faced with a bully at school.

Anyway, this evening she loves the way they are talking and interacting. She is calm, happy, and feeling secure, which is what he wants for her.

She talks more: "I've been thinking. You know how I was alone in that plastic grocery bag, crying all night long. Well, of course, I can't remember it. I was too young. But, I think I was crying out for somebody. I was alone and abandoned. Yes, I was crying for help and for love. None came. I was all alone for hours and all night. I was probably scared because nobody came, not even the woman who gave birth to me. I can't prove this but I really believe that was what was going through my newborn baby's mind. I was alone and scared. Incredibly, then you came along. I clung to you. I believe that was the same scared aloneness I had when that foster carer's son took my *broekies* down it was that same scared aloneness. Then, you came along."

Keith: "What incredible insight! I think that's a wonderful interpretation."

Eppie: "That's why after each of those alonenesses, I have needed to sleep in your bed with you. You are my rock. And, you have been since Bolivia Hill. Anyway, that's how I see it."

Keith has to wipe his eyes. He then gives her another massive long hug.

That night she sleeps with him in his bed. It was like that for the next two weeks.[267]

Four days after her return, Eppie raises a serious issue with Keith: "Mumma, why do men and boys want to rape me? That man who enticed me into his car wanted to and then that foster carer's boy. You don't."

"Oh Eppie, I think I'll have to be honest with you. That man who picked you up at the roadside and that teenage boy at the foster care house, well, they saw you as vulnerable or unprotected. You were an easy target. You see, men, women, and teenagers are driven to want to have sex. So, when men and boys come across a girl unprotected and vulnerable, some want to have sex with her. They are opportunists. But, not all men and boys are

---

[267] The Child Safety Department would have reacted with peremptory vigour if they had known this.

predatory opportunists like that, you know, seeing an opportunity and acting on it. If I see a house with a window open, should I climb in and steal things? Most people wouldn't."

"Yes, you told me about opportunists."

"Not many men want to have sex with little girls. Most prefer mature females. That man who picked you up was one of those paedophile men who fancy sex with little girls. He saw a golden opportunity and took it. But, I'm sure not even all paedophiles would take the opportunity if they saw a vulnerable little girl. Jason probably fancied a little girl and he took the opportunity."

Eppie: "Yes, but why me?"

Keith: "Tell me, was that other girl in foster care pretty?"

Eppie: "Yes, sort of. She was thirteen, I think. And, she liked to wear short skirts."

Keith: "And, she was given pills to calm her down?"

Eppie: "I think so. Kids used to call her 'Dopey'. I heard some kids talking at dinner. They reckon her Mum and Dad are in jail for drugs. Boys laughed and called her 'the bike'."

Keith: "That means one or more used to use her for sex, you know, ride her like a bike."

Eppie: "That's what I thought."

Keith: "Well, you are pretty, in fact gorgeous. For some boys mature enough and for some grown men, you're a turn on. Then, if you are exposed and vulnerable, some opportunists will be driven to have sex with you and if you don't want it, it'll be rape. Somebody once said to me that for a girl to be pretty is a health hazard. But, I just couldn't. I treasure you and could not violate you. I value you. You are a worthwhile person. And, I believe it is because of that bond. You know, what happened to both of us at Bolivia Hill."

"So, if there was another girl and you had an opportunity … ?"

"I still couldn't. Why should I cause harm to another person even if she is gorgeous? You see, sex must be consensual so that both can enjoy it and each other. I've been married before and I know that about sex and when it can be really good for both."

Eppie is silent. Then: "But, I don't want sex."

Keith: "That's because you are not yet grown-up. When you've developed boobs and started periods, you will. That's the way our bodies work. But, even while you are a little girl you can still feel sexy because you are developing. That's good for you but, as you know, actual sex and little girls can kill them. So, you have to be developed enough. So, please, when you are old enough and developed enough, please always make sure it is consensual. That means you must both want it. Then, it will become wonderful. But, don't have anything to do with a bloke who is pushy, you know trying to pressure you to take your *broekies* down or sneakily puts his hand inside them or even tries to force you. That Jason was forcing you. He didn't think of you. You were just a little girl to fuck. He was driven to have sex with you regardless of what you wanted. He was selfish in the extreme."

Eppie: "I so hate them!"

Keith: "Okay. But, don't forget, not all men and boys are like that. You just have to be careful and not let yourself get into a situation where some can make use of the opportunity you give them. The man who put you into his car made use of the opportunity. Remember, he stopped, thought, and then reversed back to you. Standing at the roadside, you had allowed yourself to be vulnerable or available to his opportunism. And, I suppose I was responsible, too, for not keeping an eye on you."

"No, Mumma. I made life really difficult for you. I was so stupid. You warned me not to walk at the roadside but I ignored you. I was being spiteful. With me being like that towards you, you still tracked me down and saved me."

Keith: "Maybe. But, look, taken into foster care, the situation was different. You didn't put yourself in danger. And, I was not negligent. You were put in a horrible situation with almost no escape, put there by the Department. By law they are supposed to protect you. They let you down badly. Terribly! There was a previous complaint about Jason. So, they knew. That boy knew you were a little girl taken from her family and dumped into foster care. He saw you as very vulnerable with nobody to protect and look after you. He also thought you would become dopey from taking those pills. Sensibly, you didn't take them. You were excellent in trying to protect yourself even in that no escape situation which the Department forced you into."

"No, you are too kind to me. It was your chasing after me in that man's car that saved the day. It wasn't my cleverness. The problem was that I was stupid. It's like Daniel Morcombe accepted a lift."

Keith: "Nobody rescued him. He was alone. And, the same thing happened to that French boy Luc Taron. Remember?"

"Yes, I was alone, too. And, they were stupid like me."

Keith: "No, not stupid. Too trusting."

Eppie: "Okay, too trusting. And, I was on an adventure and I was grumpy with you.."

"But, you're six. Daniel was thirteen. Luc was eleven. Both much older than you. No disrespect intended towards Daniel and Luc, but a six-year-old should be easier to trick than a thirteen-year-old or an eleven year old."

Back at home two days later, early in the morning Keith receives a text message from the Australia Post. It tells him a parcel is to be delivered. Later, before lunch the parcel arrives by courier. To their surprise, it is from the Child Safety Department. In it are Eppie's school uniform dress, her *broekies*, and her shoes and socks. They seem the be washed and the dress ironed. They are all neatly folded and wrapped. There is no note or card.

Eppie insists that she washes them again.

One morning Eppie walks into the living room with her iPad. She's in tears. Sitting next to Keith she shows him an item she has seen on *YouTube*.[268] It is a compilation about animals being eaten alive by predators. She shows Keith a small clip towards the end where a mother Wildebeest his just given birth and her baby is struggling to stand up for the first time. However, some Jackals rush in and start attacking and eating the baby calf while it is still alive. The mother is helpless to intervene and has to walk away from her baby.

"Mumma, please cuddle me. She left her baby to be eaten alive by Jackals."

He cuddles her.

---

[268] "16 Moments of Animals Being Eaten Alive". *YouTube*. https://www.youtube.com/watch?v=tW1u6INNN0c This happens towards the end at 14:30 minutes through the video item. The baby wildebeest is eaten alive by the Jackals.

She says: "That could have been me, abandoned by my mother at Bolivia Hill. Then, possibly eaten alive by a dingo, just like like Azaria at Uluru."

She is very upset. "Thank you so, so much, Mumma."

She hugs him.

He can't say anything. It is a horrible raw truth about the world and something most likely to have happened to baby Azaria Chamberlain at Ayers Rock/Uluru.[269]

---

[269] "Death of Azaria Chamberlain" *Wikipedia*. https://en.wikipedia.org/wiki/Death_of_Azaria_Chamberlain. In 1980, 9-week-old baby Azaria Chamberlain was dragged from the family's tent by a dingo at the Ayers Rock-Uluru camping ground, taken away, and eaten by the dingo or dingoes.

CHAPTER 16

Eppie's return to School

On the Wednesday after the Court's decision to release Eppie from foster care, Keith takes her in to the Canning Town Telstra shop and buys her an iPhone 16 mobile phone. She is ecstatic and loves it. Of course, Keith is showered with hugs and kisses. But, he cautions her: "Please, never upload photos of yourself for all and sundry to see." He shows her a recent news item about a girl whose face was Photoshopped onto a pornographic image and then distributed among kids at her school.[270] She accepts his caution: "Yes, was so easy to do. And, it was a horrible outcome for that girl and her Mum."

He adds: "Putting photos of yourself on the internet, like on *Facebook* or establishing your own channel on *YouTube* might lead to some men doing a screen save of your image. Some might look at that photo and imagine they are raping you as they masturbate. I'm serious. You are very attractive and would turn on many men just like that man who picked you up at the roadside."

"Oh, I so hate men!"

He holds her hand and she gently squeezes it.

He adds: "And, be careful what you download especially where there's any hint of nudity. Others might see or know what you downloaded and report you. *Facebook* might. Also, Police in Australia and America may be watching and may pounce. They use artificial intelligence to screen the internet for naked or near naked children. You'd be off to foster care again."

She is impressed.

---

[270] King, M., "Time to get real on fighting children's online abuse". *The New Daily,* 13 June 2024. https://www.thenewdaily.com.au/life/education/2024/06/13/madonna-king-childrens-online-abuse?

He also sees this powerful mobile phone as a means of Eppie learning about dangers even immediate ones. They talk about traps like being conned into sending them photos of her in the nude, blackmailing her into meeting them, scams to get her to part with money, and so on. "Like the baby bird who falls out of the nest, there are opportunist predators like ants, cats, or goannas just waiting for a tasty morsel. So, please, please talk to me always. I love you like anything and I admire your ability with computers. Please keep me in your loop."

With her experience of child sex abusers, he knows she takes his cautions seriously. "Yes Mumma, you're my rock and I need you."

He tells her: "I'm not spoiling you. You are switched on with computers and the internet. And, you're especially switched on about sex predators. I've bought this for you for your protection. Please use your iPad and iPhone to keep an eye on what is happening. Knowledge is your best early protection."

"I know exactly what you mean, Mumma. Thank you, thank you."

Keith: "It's not for fun. It's for safety."

Then, with her approval, he drafts an email to the Principal of Kinross State School. He gets Eppie to read it. She likes it.

Dear Mrs McGregor,

As you are Eppie's school principal, I can tell you that Eppie was very upset about being placed in foster care. So, during the Thursday night after the Department took her into 'care' she absconded. While trying to get home, brave Eppie made it all the way to Graniteville where Police caught her and took her back to the foster carer's house near Toowoomba. She was extremely distraught that her efforts had come to naught.

Next day, the day she was returned to foster care by the Police, Eppie was digitally raped by an 18-year-old youth at the foster care premises.

However, during that same Friday afternoon, the Children's Court in Canning Town returned her custody, care, and guardianship to me "with immediate effect". The Magistrate then took the Department to task for their unwarranted interference in our lives. With those Court Orders, I drove straight to the foster carer's house and collected Eppie. Understandably, she was overjoyed to see me and to be taken back home. But, having just been raped she was quite distraught.

We have spent the last few days relaxing at home in peace.

Eppie now wishes to return to school and, with your approval, we feel that next Friday morning would be a good time for her return. We have all her school exercise books and other materials which you gave me.

I believe Department of Child Safety officers misinformed you. It seems from Friday's Court hearing they did not know the full story and acted peremptorily:

1. Yes, I was convicted of raping a 14-year-old girl. But, after nearly two years, the Supreme Court overturned the conviction and I was released from prison.
2. The girl who accused me of raping her made it all up, confessed, was convicted of perjury, and sentenced by the District Court in Brisbane.
3. Two years after my conviction was quashed and I was released, the state government made two substantial *ex-gratia* payments to me as compensation for wrongful arrest and wrongful imprisonment.
4. On 16 November 2018 I found an abandoned baby in the bush some 37km south of Tenterfield at Bolivia Hill. I mistakenly thought it was dead. Because I was in a mobile phone 'no service' area, I was about to drive up the hill to phone the Police when I saw a dingo sitting in the grass watching. I photographed it and my camera recorded the time and place. That's when I discovered the dead baby was actually alive. If I had not taken that baby into my car and sorted it out, it would have become a dingo's breakfast. The Court in Canning Town knows this and so does Eppie.

Please note that I am NOT a convicted child rapist which you alleged when you ordered me off the school grounds last week. Instead, I have every right to be on the school premises in support of the child who I have legal responsibility for.

Therefore, I would like you to verify this information with the Registrar at The Canning Town Court House and then facilitate the smooth return of Eppie to her class on Friday. This will mean that you will have to inform her class teacher of Eppie's and my situation.

By law I am not allowed to make public comment about what the Department did by removing Eppie into 'out of home care'. So, I will not speak publicly to others about it. However, Eppie is only six-years-old and there is nothing to stop her talking to others about what happened. She feels upset and wronged about it all and, with her forceful personality, I know she will probably do so and without my coaching. I think you need to be aware of this. Legally, she cannot be stopped.

When we arrive at school on Friday morning we will go to your office. An allegation of child sexual abuse is one of the most pernicious and devastating things a person can face. So, I hope you will then be in a position to apologise to both of us for what happened and then be able to correct any misunderstandings which her teacher and other staff may have regarding my past and Eppie's situation. I would like her to be welcomed back to school.

Kind regards,
Keith Todd.

Eppie: "I love it, Mumma! … You should be a lawyer!"

Keith smiles: "Yes, they make lots of money."

Eppie: "Please send it to her." He does.

During the afternoon Keith received a phone call from Mrs McGregor. She apologised profusely. She had spoken to the Court Registrar in Canning Town. She also asked for more time to discuss the situation with staff and Eppie's teacher in particular. She suggested that Eppie return to school on the Monday morning when she could also be formally welcomed back to school during the weekly school assembly.

Keith: "Eppie has been listening on speaker phone. I'll ask her if a return on Monday morning is okay. … She's given me the thumbs up."

Mrs McGregor: "Wonderful. Please come to my office at 8:30 and we'll walk together to the 9:00 a.m. Monday assembly."

After that assembly, Eppie walks off with her class mates. She is bouncy and happy.

Everything goes well for Eppie. Much of this was due to the now supportive attitude of school principal Mrs McGregor.

As Keith predicted, Eppie tells other kids how mean Child Safety 'witches' took her, how she escaped and was captured, and how a Judge gave her back to "my Mumma". She is a bit of a hero among kids for a while. Teachers don't really know how to handle this headstrong frank-speaking little girl. A few days later, a teacher on playground duty at big lunch break tackled her and told her she should not speak like that about Child Safety officers. Her response was: "I can speak the truth! They are mean witches and that's why a Judge told them they were wrong!"

The teacher tried to caution her: "They do a wonderful job protecting children from people who want to harm them."

Eppie: "They took me from my loving and caring parent by force and for no good reason. A policeman even smacked me. That's not protecting! And, I was raped in foster care. I am allowed to speak about it because I'm a child. What they say is all Blah Blah Blah!" (Having seen Greta Thunberg on *YouTube*, she is inspired by Greta's taking down of pompous politicians mouthing platitudes.[271])

The bell rings and the teacher discreetly leaves.

After a month, Mrs McGregor came to meet Keith at the school gate in the morning just after he had dropped Eppie off. After some pleasantries, she says: "Can I have a word. I don't know how you have parented Eppie but she is a no-nonsense outspoken little girl."

Keith: "Well, I think I warned you that she can be quite 'bolshy' at times.[272] Ever since she was toddler we've watched the evening TV news together and we talk about what has happened. And, she has access to he internet. I've never treated her as child. Well yes, I have but what I mean is that I've always been open and frank with her in an adult way. So, I think she doesn't tolerate spin or what she sees as untruths. She may grow to be a new Greta Thunberg!"

Mrs McGregor smiles: "Yes. Some staff find her a bit of a handful."

Keith: "She's going to go a long way in life … and disappointments will not faze her."

Mrs McGregor: "She's an impressive little child. May I ask, how have you turned out such a character. What I mean is, how has your parenting made her this way?"

Keith: "Not sure. I think there's a biological factor in this. I believe her personality and innate intelligence were fundamentally the product of her biological parents, who ever they were. I don't think she's a genius, just very bright. You know, as a baby she often had a mind of her own. She could be quite stubborn. So, bright and iron-willed."[273]

Mrs McGregor: "Don't you think you are a factor?"

---

[271] Greta Thunberg giving her "blah blah blah" speech at a Climate Conference. *BBC News*, London, 28 September 2021. https://www.youtube.com/watch?v=ZwD1kG4PI0w

[272] 'bolshy' is an old fashioned derivation of 'Bolshevik' from the 1917 Russian Revolution.

[273] See: Sapolsky, R. (2023), *Determined: Life without Free Will*. The Bodley Head (Penguin), London. Keith is convinced that Eppie is the product of her unknown parents and this has determined her personality. He believes his parenting and love have modified her personality only to a relatively small degree.

Keith: "Yes, I do. I've probably modified her personality but to what degree I don't know. Quite apart from the way we interact in an almost adult/adult way, she has experienced things many kids can't imagine. We always discuss events in her life."

Mrs McGregor: "She certainly is very worldly wise for her age."

Keith: "Since I found her, our fear was always been that if her origin became known, the Child Safety Department would step in and remove her into foster care on the grounds that basically I'm a man and too old to parent her. And, she knows about the murder of Tiahleigh Palmer and other kids abused in foster care. She uses the internet a lot and we listen to the news. As you know, the Department tried to take her. Well, they did. But, we had a good lawyer, a good psychologist's report, and a magistrate who knew our full story which they didn't. That fear has now passed. And, the fact that she is a foundling is no longer an issue."

Mrs McGregor: "That brings me to why I've come to meet you at the gate. Yesterday our school celebrated 'Pyjama Day', you know, in support of children in foster care."[274]

Keith: "Yes, you sent out a circular. She refused to wear pyjamas to school. I let her decide what to do. She has first hand experience of foster care. So, I wasn't going to influence her in any way."

Mrs McGregor: "Well, she caused a bit of a sensation in her class. I was there. All the other kids were in pyjamas. She was the only one in her uniform. Anyway, she walked up to the front and interrupted her teacher, Mrs Selkirk. She did say: 'Excuse me, please.' She told the class that Pyjama Day is all 'Blah Blah Blah!' She told the kids she had been in foster care and it's the one of the worst things that can happen a kid. She told us a teenage boy held her down and removed her underpants. She said she was 'shit scared'. The big boy molested her and said he was going to 'fuck' her. That's when my Mumma arrived. He ran away and left me."

Keith: "That's what happened. 'Molested' is putting it mildly. It was digital rape."

Mrs McGregor: "Oh. Well, she told the class 'Kids should not be put in foster care. It's dangerous and rotten for them. Instead, the government should help parents to be better

---

[274] The Pyjama Foundation and National Pyjama Day: https://thepyjamafoundation.com

parents. Pyjama Day just helps the government keep kids in foster care.' Or words to that effect. She then walked back to her seat fuming. I must confess, we didn't quite know how to handle her. The class was silent."

Keith: "Eppie has told the truth about foster care. That is what happened to her. She doesn't tell furphies. The youth who digitally raped her is eighteen, not a boy but a man. She was saved when I sneaked into the room while she was being choked Andrew Tate style. He shot through and left her. She was dazed and not fully with it. He had already digitally raped her and had been strangling her. Gasping for air, her eyes were bloodshot, and she had bruises on her neck."

Mrs McGregor: "Oh my gosh. Have you complained to the Department?"

Keith: "No point. I've photographed her bloodshot eyes and bruises on he neck. But, they are far too powerful and secretive. It would be Eppie's word against arguments put forward by Crown Law barristers. If you complain, they investigate themselves and always whitewash the Department's activities.[275] And, they would find a way to blame me. It would be a financially ruinous court case. I wouldn't want to traumatise Eppie more with Departmental and Police interviews. Removed into foster care was bad enough. But, our lawyer has formally complained to the Police."

Mrs McGregor facetiously: "Well, it's clear she didn't find it fun."

Keith smiled: "However, I must say she's stronger for the experience. The pity is that, from what she has told me, I'm sure she is not the first foster care kid that boy has assaulted. She has told me of another girl who used to be regularly used by that teenage boy. And, I'm also sure that kind of assault has occurred and will continue to occur in other foster care environments across the country. That's human life and she has learned. It has made her

---

[275] Although the following example is about the NSW Department, the same applies to child protection departments across Australia. "NSW forcibly removes more children than any other state and any other western nation per head of population. NSW has a proven record of failure, is not held accountable, and too many innocent lives are being destroyed. Forced adoption is now the first priority for children in care in NSW for arguably economic reasons as they have taken more children than the system can cope with while only spending 10% of funds on family support and preservation and are constantly reducing support services." *Change Org*, 22 May 2015. https://www.change.org/p/the-premier-of-nsw-and-all-nsw-members-of-parliament-a-royal-commission-into-the-failures-of-family-and-community-services-nsw-facs?

stronger as a person. You know, because she was stroppy in foster care, the Department got a doctor to prescribe anti-psychotic tablets to be taken one every evening before dinner. The foster carer wanted Eppie made docile and compliant. Eppie knew about tablets used to make foster care kids, as she put it, 'make them into zombies'. So, she always pretended to swallow but tucked the tablet to the side of her mouth and then spat it out as soon as she could."

Mrs McGregor: "I'm shocked."

Keith: "That short time in foster care has affected her deeply. And, perversely, I think for the better. She's now steeled and much more worldly wise."

Mrs McGregor: "That's sad but she's tough."

Keith: "That's what I mean by steeled. She's tough but not hard. She's a lovely soft kid inside. She and I love it when we cuddle."

Mrs McGregor: "Anyway, she was really quiet the rest of yesterday. But, her protest has made me realise that it takes a child like her to show us that what we as a society see as a given should at least be open to question. Has your parenting made her so independent?"

Keith: "When I found a tiny little abandoned newborn baby in the bush, I undid my shirt and held that grubby naked little baby close to my chest and cuddled her. Her tiny little hands clung to my chest hairs. It was a magic moment. I cannot undo the bond that came about. She can't either."

Mrs McGregor touched him on his shoulder: "Now I know why when the Child Safety Officers took her away she made such a mess of my office. She struggled like anything and screamed, calling out: 'Mumma! Mumma!'. She hid under my desk. The Policeman who came with Child Safety Officers had to capture her and carry her to the car. Papers, files, books, and pens went everywhere. My desk was almost toppled. For such a small child, her resistance was incredible. They had great difficulty. She struggled and screamed all the way to the government car and continued resisting as they forcibly did up her seat belt. As the car drove away, I heard her screams. Anyway, I'm glad I've been able to discuss her with you this morning."

Keith is upset to hear how his little girl had resisted so strongly.

Mrs McGregor can see the tears in his eyes. As he wipes his eyes with his handkerchief, he tells her: "I didn't know about her struggle. What you've told me upsets me. It was state perpetrated violence against a very little child. As you now know, it was illegal, totally unjustified, and so, so wrong. And yet, nobody stood up for her! Just nobody! She was a tiny child on her own, utterly alone."

Feeling a pang of guilt, Mrs McGregor is silent.

Keith: "And, she was sent to a place where she was raped! … And, strangled!"

He walks away in tears.

She follows after him: "Mr Todd, I'm so sorry."

One afternoon when Keith was waiting at the school gate to take Eppie home, he was chatting to another waiting mother. She said: "I've heard that Eppie was found as a newborn abandoned in the bush. Is that so?"

Keith: "Yes, I found her in an plastic bag in the bush."

The mother: "Have they found the mother?"

Keith: "No. Police have searched. We haven't a clue who the birth mother was and we don't know why she was abandoned in the bush. So, I've cared for her alone since she was born."

The mother: "Oh, the poor motherless child."[276]

This is an example of a real case of a five-year-old little girl desperately screaming and struggling as she resists being removed from a parent's care. It was Court ordered and a Policeman is removing her from behind a couch where she was hiding. The full video is no longer available but short excerpts can still be seen at: https://newsroom.co.nz/2017/08/07/taken-by-the-state/ The circumstances of this case were totally different to Eppie's and it occurred in New Zealand. Yet, what is shown is typical of the resistance little children can sometimes put up and the violence inflicted upon them by the state during removal. At the end of the clip a policewoman threatens the grandfather. (*Newsroom*, New Zealand, 07 August 2017.)

---

[276] As a single male parent, the author once received a similar hurtful comment while outside a school gate when his daughter was five. (Though, of course, she was not a foundling.)

He didn't like the comment and felt it was sexist.

At that moment, Eppie has just arrived. She can see that he is chatting to a mother and, not wanting to interrupt adult conversation, she stops at the gate. She heard the woman's comment and got the gist of what it was about. So, she comes out through the gate and gives Keith a big hug. He kneels down and she kisses him on his mouth.

He asks her: "What is your name for me? You know, what do you call me?"

Astute Eppie says: "I call you 'Mumma'. That's 'coz you're my mother."

Keith wonders if the woman sees Eppie's love for him as a 'mother' is wrong, even obscene.

A month later, Eppie found *Silas Marner* on a bookshelf in the living room.

She told him: "Now I know why you called me Eppie. I like it. It's me. Although I've almost finished it, listen to this. It's what Eppie says about Silas:

'He's took care of me and loved me from the first, and I'll cleave to him as long as he lives, and nobody shall ever come between him and me.' [277]

She leans over and hugs him.

Keith: "Thank you, thank you for that."

She adds: "This book is hard to read."

Keith: "That's because it's in the English of more than 150 years ago. Our language has changed over time. But, as you know, babies are still abandoned these days."

She smiles: "And, as you know, there are still Silas Marners around these days."

---

[277] George Eliot (1861), *Silas Marner: The Weaver of Raveloe*, William Blackwood: London., page 299. (George Eliot is the pseudonym for Mary Ann Evans. Her novel is set in early nineteenth century rural England.)

CHAPTER 17

Eppie in trouble.

A few months later Eppie is seven and in trouble. Some kids at Kinross State School are not impressed with her reading, her way with sophisticated words, her knowledge about the world, and her outspoken opinions. Her accent which she has inherited from Keith is seen as arrogant. An eleven-year-old boy in year 6, Trent Matson, starts teasing her. "You're so up yourself!"

Moreover, because she had resisted so strongly and loudly when she was taken by the Department form the school and placed into foster care, Trent Matson had heard his parents and others discussing what happened to Eppie. So, parents know. Some parents have discussed the situation on Facebook. Speculation on the local grapevine is rife. Some parents researched Keith's background and found press reports of his being convicted and jailed for raping a 14-year-old girl. Of course, because of confidentiality provisions of the *Child Protection Act*, there are no press reports of the girl's later conviction for perjury and Keith's conviction being quashed.

So, in front of other kids, Trent accosts Eppie during big lunch break: "Does Daddy fuck ya when you get home? He puts his dick inside your cunt, hey? You ask him to fuck you?"

Trent is a lot bigger and twice Eppie's age.

Other Year 6 kids laugh. A girl sniggers: "Your Dad's a kiddie fucker!"

Much laughter. Eppie is silent.

Trent gives her a teasing push and adds: "Yeah, he's a 'peedfile'!"

This is the last straw for Eppie. She explodes into a bundle of lightning. She slaps him left and right and then immediately rains a barrage of rapid punches to his nose and mouth.

Eppie starts boiling.
(*iStockphoto*. Posed by model. The same model used in most previous photos of Eppie.)

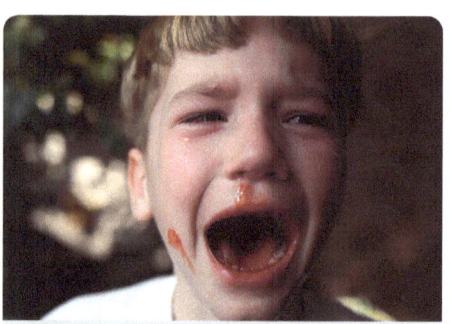

Trent Matson howling with shock and a little pain but more from embarrassment.
(*Alamy*. Posed by model.)

The boy backs off and retreats to a bench, crying loudly. Other kids grab hold of Eppie and restrain her. She shouts at him: "Voetsak!"[278]

The playground duty teacher marches both Eppie and Trent to the Principal's office where another teacher treats the boy's bleeding lips and nose. Eppie is made to sit quietly outside the office.

When she is questioned, she tells Mrs McGregor that Trent Matson teased her. "He's a loud-mouth. He said my Dad's a 'peedfile'. He can't even say it right. And, he said my Dad fucks me every afternoon when I get home. They all laughed at me. And then, he pushed me. Well, that was it! So, I sorted him out. And, you know, when that doctor gave me a check-up for the Court, she saw I have a hymen in my vagina and its 'septate'. And so, it partly blocks the entrance to my vagina. Yes, she wrote it in her report for the Court. And, it's still there. So, I just can't handle that kind of stuff from anyone, especially from a big full of himself woos like Trent."

Mrs McGregor is momentarily stunned both by Eppie's choice of words about Trent and her frank candid revelation about herself. Nevertheless, knowing about Keith's conviction and then later exoneration, she is sympathetic but tries not to let it show. "I think I'll phone your Dad and ask him to take you home for a day or two while this problem settles down."

She phones Keith who arrives quickly. He sees Eppie and a boy sitting at opposite sides of the door to the school office. He is whimpering and holding a damp cloth over his mouth and nose.

---

[278] "Voetsak" is the Afrikaans word for 'go away' in an offensive way. Often used insultingly especially towards a dog.

In front of both kids, Mrs McGregor explains the fight as best she can. She tells Keith how Eppie attacked the boy. Keith accepts her decision that as today is a Wednesday, Eppie and should return to school only on Monday. Keith asks that it be explained to the boy's parents what the true relation ship between Eppie and him is. Mrs McGregor says she'll talk to his parents about that. She also suggests that on Monday the boy should apologise to Eppie for what was said and that Eppie should apologise to him for hitting him. "They can do that in the privacy of this office. In the meantime, I'm also sending Trent home for two days. In effect, both kids are officially suspended until Monday."

At home, Eppie is still bristling and doesn't accept that she should apologise to Trent. "He got from me what he deserved. He's a bullshit artist and up himself. And, I've seen him scared of the climbing frame in the playground. He's a big 'woos'![279] I told him to "Voetsak!"

Keith smiles at her word choice and then praises her. "You stood up for yourself. Just like you did in foster care by escaping. In my eyes you're a hero."

She surprises him: "This time, I didn't stand up for myself. No, I stood up for you. I didn't like Trent's garbage about you. He said you're a paedophile. You are my hero. You've saved my life two times! No, three times! You saved me when I was a teensie-weensie newborn baby left in the bush for a dingo. You saved me from being murdered when I hitch-hiked. And, you saved me from foster care when a big boy wanted to fuck me. You always give me true caring love even when I've been horrible to you. So, I can't handle anyone saying that sort of bullshit about you!"

Keith: "Thank you, dear. Thank you. That's really sweet of you." He then asks: "And, where did you learn about that way of hitting somebody?"

"I saw it on TV at the Oscars, remember. You know, when Will Smith slapped Chris Rock for saying things about his wife.[280] I know you don't like violence but I just felt like it. So, I smacked the shit out of him. And, I didn't just do it once like Will Smith. No, I let him have it. I was so ropable about what he said about you. It made me boil. So, I just had to do it."

---

[279] Australian slang for somebody who is a soft timid sissy. *Wiktionary:* noun, Australian colloquial: a coward.

[280] See it at: https://www.youtube.com/watch?v=myjEoDypUD8 Eppie even uses some of Chris Rock's words.

Keith, smiling: "Thank you, thank you. I really love you. ... Anyway, I think he's learned a lesson." He hugs her.

On Monday the kids apologise. Eppie even grabs Trent's hand and shakes hands with him.

Keith is pleased that his petite and frail-looking little girl with matchstick legs is not only tough and resilient but also values honour and fair-mindedness.

Later that day, Keith tells her that because she is still only six, what she did to Trent is ignored by Police. "If you were ten years old, the Police would arrest you and charge you with assault. You would have to appear at the Childrens Court and could be sent to a children's prison. So, please, please be careful. Ten is the age of criminal responsibility.[281] Juvenile detention centres or prisons are not nice places. They have separate ones for girls. Bigger girls bash smaller girls and some get sexually abused by bigger girls." She takes note.

Reminiscing to himself after Eppie's altercation with Trent Matson at school, Keith wonders about the foster carer's son's assault of her. He wondered whether she would again give in to future violence. Now, he is pleased that she attacked Trent Matson with such vigour. There was no tendency to give in. Even though he is a Quaker and non-violent, he is secretly pleased that she was violent. She did not give in. He wonders if she could develop *Karate* skills, she would be a formidable opponent for any attacker. So, he is not averse to defensive violence.

Then, he asks her something: "Would you like to have *Karate* lessons, you know, so that you can learn ways of defending yourself? There are classes starting in Graniteville in three weeks. I could drive you there each time."

"I've not thought of that. I'd love it. Would there be other girls there?"

Keith: "I'm sure. It's a defensive martial art. Possibly very useful for you."

That's what they do. Twice a week after school he drives her to Graniteville.[282]

---

[281] Davis, C. "The minimum age of criminal responsibility in Australia: a quick guide", *Parliament of Australia*, 17 June 2022. https://www.aph.gov.au/About_Parliament/Parliamentary_Departments/Parliamentary_Library/pubs/rp/rp2122/Quick_Guides/MinimumAgeCriminalResponsibility

[282] https://dojodirectory.net/queensland/stanthorpe-martial-arts-school/

A year later, he is watching her Karate class. He is amazed when he sees her topple a boy who is bigger than her. What he particularly notices is the expression of both anger and delight on her face as she throws the hapless boy. He is pleased for her.

(*iStockphoto.* Posed by models.)

Months later, they are talking about the school. She tells him: "I always feel like an outsider. I don't talk like other kids do. They're not interested in reading, politics, and stuff like that. They don't know about those Child Safety witches. It's just footy, pop singer stars and Minecraft[283]. And, of course sport. I do like Taylor Swift but I just can't handle team sports. I'm a loner. Their world is different. I'm the strange girl from Bolivia Hill."

Keith: "Does that make you feel sad?"

"No, 'coz I like the me that I am."

Keith holds her hand. "I'm pleased about that. And, I'm proud of you."

"And, you're a strange man from Africa. You and me, we're strangers together."

She continues: "But Mumma, I really hate boys and men. All they want is little girl's vulvas and vaginas. I've had a gut full of them. They're all ratbags."

He lets her continue: "That Jason was going to fuck me. He was a grown man and I'm only little. He told me I'm a girl and only good for fucking. Then, there's that stupid Trent. Well, I sorted him out. Yes Mumma, I really, really hate men and boys."

Keith is silent as he thinks about what his little girl has told him about hating. Finally, he tells her: "But, I'm a man."

"No you're not! You're my Mumma who I love so much.. I couldn't love a man. You're better than any lady could be. The news is full of men who have been horrible to women, you know that domestic violence stuff and men being sent to prison for raping girls. Men and boys are just the pits. There is so much of it, you know, what they call 'toxic masculinity'. But, not you. You're not a toxic man. You're my mother, always have been." She is fuming.

---

[283] Minecraft is a kids computer game popular in the 2020s.

This is when he opens his computer at an Australian Bureau of Statistics website. He shows her and agrees with her: "The number of women killed in domestic or family violence is shocking. The press and media remind us of this continually. You'r right. It's so often in the news. If we look at the latest Australian Bureau of Statistics figures on what they call 'Homicide Victims of Family and Domestic Violence', you know killing, the figures are very reliable and quite shocking. See here. It shows that most of FDV related homicide victims were female (53% or 71 victims). Yes, 53% victims were female, more than half!!!! But, what about the other 47%? Just under half. We don't read or hear much about all those male FDV homicide victims. The newspapers and TV news don't tell us. So, women also kill men."[284]

"I think I've noticed that, Mumma. The news is all a little skew. That's why so many don't like you being a mother to a little girl. The news wants a lady to be a mother. And, those Child Safety witches wanted to punish you for being so nice to a little baby girl from the bush."

"I think you're right. I'm a man so they think I just must be bad or probably a paedophile."

"That's right. And, we showed them."

They hug.

He adds: "Of course, that shooter at the South Bank was woman."

Eppie: "Yes. And, she killed a heap of people. Lots were men. Like I said, I reckon she had a big problem with men. Things may have happened to her." Then she adds: "I know what you're saying. She was a lady and she killed. But, Mumma, I still really hate men and boys. They give me the shits. I can't change that. It's in me. Maybe that lady who gave birth to me a Bolivia Hill had big problems with men. Yes, that could be it. And, it's been passed on to me."

Nevertheless, Eppie has an enquiring mind and doesn't let matters rest. She does some of her own research about raped little girls being murdered. Next day, using her new iPhone she shows Keith two cases she has found of women who have raped and murdered little

[284] Australian Bureau of Statistics 2023. "Victims of family and domestic violence related offences: Homicide and related offences". https://www.abs.gov.au/statistics/people/crime-and-justice/recorded-crime-victims/latest-release#victims-of-family-and-domestic-violence-related-offences

girls: "Sandra Cantu"[285] and "Lily"[286]. And, there's other cases of women who raped little girls but didn't murder the like a lady called Christina Regusters. That little girl was only five and she had to wear a colostomy bag for six months because she was wrecked inside. I looked up 'Colostomy Bag'. I was lucky I didn't have to have that bag because that foster carer's Jason didn't get a chance."[287]

He is stunned at her research and congratulates her.

She then tells him: "So, you're right. Ladies do it too. I think you've got a balanced view, you know even handed. But you know, I still hate boys and men. I really do."

Keith is impressed by her choice of words: "Do you think that's because of what has happened to you? Has foster care has done it."

"Maybe. Well, I see it's like this. I love you so much, Mumma. That's because you're not a man. I can't love a man but I really love my Mumma. I think it's more than what boys and men have done to me. I think it's in me to hate them. I've been thinking a lot about this. Perhaps, I've inherited it from the lady who was pregnant with me. I reckon she had a big problem with men and I think it was while she was pregnant with me. So, it's in me.[288] Then, you came along at Bolivia Hill and straight away started giving me love. But, you're not a woman. That has upset things."

"Wow! What insight you have!"

---

[285] "Murder of Sandra Cantu", *Wikipedia*. https://en.wikipedia.org/wiki/Murder_of_Sandra_Cantu

[286] Quigley, R., "Stepmother murdered and sexually assaulted toddler", *Daily Mail*, London, 29 February 2012, http://www.dailymail.co.uk/news/article-2107704/Renee-King-guilty-murdering-raping-stepdaughter-soiled-pants.html. She got life without parole for the murder and fifty years for the sexual assault. For a collection of news reports on the case: http://murderpedia.org/female.K/k/king-renee.htm. The sexual assault with an object occurred before the fatal twenty blows to Lily's head. For an emotional view of this sad story, see *Lily's Story* at https://www.youtube.com/watch?v=_2yZPXzZ3fY.

[287] Christina Regusters abducted and raped a five-year-old girl with a broken broom handle. The girl survived but had to wear a colostomy bag for six months. Glover, S., "Christina Regusters found guilty", *NBC Philadelphia, USA*, 12 September 2014, http://www.nbcphiladelphia.com/news/local/Verdict-Reached-in-Christina-Regusters-Child-Abduction-Rape-Trial-Guilty-Not-Guilty-274772501.html.

[288] See: Sapolsky, R. (2023), *Determined: Life without Free Will*. The Bodley Head (Penguin), London. What Eppie is saying is in line with what Sapolsky says about our behaviour: it has genetic underpinnings shaped probably even at our conception. Keith tends to agree and believes he has only modified her behaviour. An epilogue to this novel reveals the life of the woman who gave birth to Eppie and it reveals why Eppie loathes men and boys.

"So, I hate boys and men. I can't change that. I also can't change the love I have for the person who has always been my mother. … Please cuddle me, Mumma."

He lifts her up and sits her on his lap. He puts his arms around her. She snuggles in to him.

For her next Christmas, Keith gives her a microscope set rather than some stereotype girl present. She loves it. It opens yet another new world for her. This is typical of the way he enhances her academic growth and knowledge which began when he taught her to read. It grew from there as she got more advanced computers and internet access. Again, he has been deliberately opening the world to her.

(*Shutterstock.* Posed by model.)

Academically, she manages well at school and socially is very independent.

During June, the school's annual cross country races are held. Because of small numbers, Year 1 and 2 boys and girls are grouped together to run around the outer perimeter of the school grounds. When they start off, skinny and petite little new girl Eppie bolts ahead of the other 14 kids, all bigger than her. She doesn't let up and comes in ahead of the rest. Keith is amazed at her performance and congratulates her with hugs and kisses. She is beaming and bouncy with her victory, especially when she has to go and receive a certificate from the principal. The whole school and parents clap. "See, I beat all those boys!"

One Saturday morning, they are returning from grocery shopping in Graniteville. They are listening to the 'Science Show' on ABC *Radio National*. There is discussion about quantum computers. "Mumma, I've read about those quantum computers. Can I use your phone?"

He stops and passes it to her. She immediately Googles 'quantum computers' and starts reading a recent article.[289] She is quickly engrossed in it.

---

[289] Woodford, C., "Quantum computing". *Explain that stuff.* 23 August 2023. https://www.explainthatstuff. com/quantum-computing.html The author of this website explains that it is intended mainly for families and children who are 10+.

As they get home and turn into their driveway, she tells Keith. "That's what I want to do when I'm grown up. I want to work with quantum computers. But, I suppose when I'm grown up quantum computers will be yesterday's fad."

Keith smiles at her cynicism: "I wouldn't have a clue what you're talking about. You're way ahead of me. But, I think you are wonderful! You're going to go a long way. Would kids in your class have any idea of what you are talking about, you know, quantum computers?"

She smiles at him: "No way! But, that's why I like living here away from people. I'm isolated and I can let my mind think and use my computer."

Keith: "I understand. Sometimes, when you've been in the bush among the rocks, I've seen you rushing back to the house and going straight to your computer. I assume that's because you've thought of something and need to find out more."

Eppie: "That's right. Computers and the internet are just wonderful like that. But, there's more about life that you have taught me and still are teaching me. It's all because of you. You know Bolivia Hill, the South Bank, foster care, and even every day. If you see what I mean. There's a difference between learning from a computer and learning from you. A big difference."

As they carry their groceries inside, she sings part of a Taylor Swift song which is her current favourite: *Willow*.

"*Life was a willow and it bent right to your wind but it come back stronger … .*" [290]

She is a very happy little girl.

She has learned from the near abduction, the near death at the South Bank, and the awful intimidating digital rape in foster care. They have affected her profoundly, especially in her relationship with her Mumma. The first event reversed their souring relationship. The second one reinforced that reversal dramatically. The third one was more reinforcement. And, she has become a more stubborn intelligent girl who puts up with no nonsense. At school, she is not feared but respected. Her reaction to Trent teasing her and her cross-country race victory sealed that. Now, *Karate* has given her much more confidence.

---

[290] Taylor Swift: "Willow". https://www.youtube.com/watch?v=RsEZmictANA

She has been growing up valuing Keith's persistence in ignoring societal perceptions about single male parenting and about old age. Her frequent discussions with him about society and injustices have added to her almost strident independence. On her seventh birthday she told him: "I'm boss of myself. But, I know I've still got to be careful, like not putting myself in danger. That means being careful about people who want to do me harm like AK47 ladies, randy boys, and Child Safety witches. It also means you're a rock for me to cling to."

Yet, in his modest way, he now knows that should he fall off his perch tomorrow, through his parenting he has been at least partially instrumental in moulding a child who can stand up for herself and survive well. She is the opposite of a 'woos'. He feels very proud not only of his parenting but of her as a brilliant foundling he found.

On her eighth birthday, they are returning from their annual Bolivia Hill visit. It is quite a cool blustery day. They stop in Tenterfield for lunch at a café in the main street, Rouse Street.

Eppie (facing the camera) and Keith (his back to the camera) at a café in Rouse Street, Tenterfield.

He is quite stunned by what she says to him: "I've been thinking. You know when you found a baby at Bolivia Hill and you picked it up and cuddled it against your bare chest even though it was all yukkie. Well, that was the real moment of my birth. Suddenly, I wasn't breakfast for a dingo anymore. I found somebody. I wasn't alone and scared anymore. But, you were not saving me from a dingo. If you were, you would have done the proper thing and handed me in at the Tenterfield Hospital. But, you couldn't hand me in. You couldn't because you were giving me love, real love. That was the moment, the beginning of my life when you held me against your chest. That's why you'll always be my 'Mumma', nobody else can be."

Keith: "Wow! Thank you!"

During the last few years, Eppie sometimes wondered wistfully about her origins. Now, as a contented ten-year-old, her origins don't matter any more. She has fully accepted herself as 83-year-old Keith's foundling from the bush and is proud of him as he is of her. She is a beautiful, happy, independent-minded, and confident child. She is also a loner who stands up for herself.

And, this foundling's loyalty to and love for her Mumma is unbreakable.

(iStockphoto.
Posed by model.)